University of
Hertfordshire

College Lane, Hatfield, Herts. AL10 9AB

Learning and Information Services

For renewal of Standard and One Week Loans,
please visit the web site **http://www.voyager.herts.ac.uk**

This item must be returned or the loan renewed by the due date.
The University reserves the right to recall items from loan at any time.
A fine will be charged for the late return of items.

D1438469

DIANA HOLMES and ROBERT INGRAM *series editors*
DUDLEY ANDREW *series consultant*

FRENCH FILM DIRECTORS

Claude Chabrol

GUY AUSTIN

Manchester University Press
MANCHESTER AND NEW YORK

Published by Manchester University Press
Oxford Road, Manchester M13 9NR, UK
and Room 400, 175 Fifth Avenue, New York, NY 10010, USA
www.manchesteruniversitypress.co.uk

Distributed exclusively in the USA by
Palgrave, 175 Fifth Avenue, New York NY 10010, USA

Distributed exclusively in Canada by
UBC Press, University of British Columbia, 2029 West Mall,
Vancouver, BC, Canada V6T 1Z2

British Library Cataloguing-in-Publication Data
A catalogue record for this book is available from the British Library

Library of Congress Cataloging-in-Publication Data
A catalog record for this book is available from the Library of Congress

ISBN 0 7190 5272 6 paperback

First edition published 1999 by Manchester University Press

First digital, on-demand edition produced by Lightning Source 2006

Contents

List of plates

All courtesy of BFI Stills, Posters and Designs except for 8, courtesy of Tartan Video

Series editors' foreword

To an anglophone audience, the combination of the words 'French' and 'cinema' evokes a particular kind of film: elegant and wordy, sexy but serious – an image as dependent on national stereotypes as is that of the crudely commercial Hollywood blockbuster, which is not to say that either image is without foundation. Over the past two decades, this generalised sense of a significant relationship between French identity and film has been explored in scholarly books and articles, and has entered the curriculum at university level and, in Britain, at A-level. The study of film as an art-form and (to a lesser extent) as industry, has become a popular and widespread element of French Studies, and French cinema has acquired an important place within Film Studies. Meanwhile, the growth in multi-screen and 'art-house' cinemas, together with the development of the video industry, has led to the greater avail-ability of foreign-language films to an English-speaking audience. Responding to these developments, this series is designed for students and teachers seeking information and accessible but rigorous critical study of French cinema, and for the enthusiastic filmgoer who wants to know more.

The adoption of a director-based approach raises questions about *auteurism*. A series that categorises films not according to period or to genre (for example), but to the person who directed them, runs the risk of espousing a romantic view of film as the product of solitary inspiration. On this model, the critic's role might seem to be that of discovering continuities, revealing a necessary

coherent set of themes and motifs which correspond to the particular genius of the individual. This is not our aim: the *auteur*
perspective on film, itself most clearly articulated in France in the
early 1950s, will be interrogated in certain volumes of the series,
and, throughout, the director will be treated as one highly
significant element in a complex process of film production and
reception which includes socio-economic and political determin-
ants, the work of a large and highly skilled team of artists and
technicians, the mechanisms of production and distribution, and
the complex and multiply determined responses of spectators.

The work of some of the directors in the series is already
known outside France, that of others is less so – the aim is both to
provide informative and original English-language studies of
established figures, and to extend the range of French directors
known to anglophone students of cinema. We intend the series to
contribute to the promotion of the informal and formal study of
French films, and to the pleasure of those who watch them.

DIANA HOLMES
ROBERT INGRAM

Acknowledgements

Thank you to Joanne Austin, Thomas Austin, Ben Clift, Màire Cross, Di Holmes, Dave Platten, David Walker, Julie René and Laure Boissou at the Cinémathèque française, Paul Morrissey at Tartan, and the staff at the British Film Institute stills department. This book is dedicated to Thomas and Patrick.

1

Chabrol and friends

In the autumn of 1997, at the age of 67, Claude Chabrol released *Rien ne va plus*, his fiftieth film. The leading French film magazine, *Cahiers du cinéma*, marked the occasion with a special issue devoted entirely to his work. The editorial described him as 'le cinéaste français le plus productif, et peut-être le plus "rentable", des quatre dernières décennies'[1] (Toubiana 1997: 4). (His achievement is all the more remarkable when one notes that in recent years several previously successful French film directors have been more or less obliged to abandon the cinema, including Léos Carax, Jean-Jacques Beineix and Bertrand Blier.) Chabrol's forty-year career is in some ways a history of recent French cinema and society: neorealism, the new wave, the trauma of the Algerian War, the political legacy of 1968, the rise of the consumer society and the 'pompidolien' bourgeoisie,[2] the perennial popularity of the thriller, the tension between television and cinema, the decline of Marxism. Chabrol has known periods of great success (the launching of the new wave in 1958, the superb Hélène cycle of the late 1960s – including his most famous film *Le Boucher* – his return to form in the 1990s), and also periods of inactivity and failure (a year in the early 1960s without shooting a single scene, a general loss of direction in the late 1970s). Twice he has relaunched

1 'the most prolific and perhaps the most "profitable" French film-maker of the last four decades'
2 That is to say, the bourgeoisie of 1969–74, the period of Georges Pompidou's presidency.

his career, with the comeback films *Les Biches* in 1967 and *Poulet au vinaigre* in 1985. Through it all, Chabrol has seen his artistic reputation questioned because of the sheer volume and perceived inconsistency of his output.

Until recently, Chabrol suffered from a paradoxical reputation as simultaneously lazy and prolific: lazy in his uncritical acceptance of any project that came along, prolific in the number of such projects that made it to the screen. His own belief was that 'la première qualité d'un musicien, c'est de composer, d'un écrivain, d'écrire, d'un peintre de peindre, d'un cinéaste de filmer'[3] (Chabrol 1976: 353). But his willingness to accept commissions and to be a director for hire flew in the face of the new wave conception of the film director as an *auteur*, a sacred, isolated artistic figure. In contrast with this Romantic conception of cinema as art rather than commerce, and as solitary rather than collective, Chabrol has always acknowledged and enjoyed the fact that cinema is most often a collective, commercial enterprise. This has implications for his filming methods and his choice of popular genres, as we shall see. However, it has also resulted in neglect or condescension from the critics. For twenty years, between 1962 and 1982, *Cahiers du cinéma* (for which he himself once wrote in the 1950s) did not interview Chabrol once. In 1976 he could say without fear of contradiction that 'je suis plus respecté hors de nos frontières qu'en France'[4] (Chabrol 1976: 231). Five years later, *Cahiers* was still ranking him in French cinema's second division.[5] But the last ten years or so have seen a gradual reassessment of his work. On the release of *La Cérémonie* in 1995, *Cahiers* asked if Chabrol was not in fact 'le plus grand cinéaste français'.[6] Two years later, with the publication of the *Cahiers* special issue, Chabrol's belated critical rehabilitation was complete. (Their previous neglect of Chabrol is further illustrated

---

3 'a musician must compose, a writer must write, a painter must paint, and a film-maker must film'

4 'I am more respected abroad than in France'

5 In the first divison were the usual (new wave) suspects, Godard, Truffaut, Rohmer and Rivette. See Blanchet 1989: 120.

6 'the greatest French film-maker'. See the editorial of *Cahiers du cinéma* 494, p. 22.

by the fact that *Cahiers* had long since devoted special issues not just to his contemporaries such as Godard and Duras but also to the newcomer Léos Carax and, ironically, to one of Chabrol's favourite actresses, Isabelle Huppert. Most tellingly, Carax merited a special issue for his third film – Chabrol only for his fiftieth!)

Chabrol's films break down the dubious critical barrier between art cinema and popular cinema. Commercial as well as artistic considerations are crucial to his film-making, and he remains disdainful of those directors (like Godard) whose films are élitist rather than populist. Chabrol sees no shame in considering himself a craftsman and takes pride in bringing his films in on or under budget. For *L'Œil du malin* in 1961, he even agreed to shoot the film at half the originally agreed cost. His pragmatic and practical approach to cinema dates from the early 1960s, when a series of box-office disasters (including, ironically, *L'Œil du malin*) left him unable to find financial support for any more personal projects. In order to keep filming, he decided to accept various comedy-thrillers and spy movies considered (by his colleagues in the new wave) artistically beneath him. In the terms of the *politique des auteurs*, he had become a *metteur en scène* rather than a *cinéaste*.[7] But it was this commercial and auto-didactic period which made Chabrol. It allowed him to hone his technical skills and to come to terms with popular genres, thus paving the way for his mature style of the late 1960s and 1970s. Since that period, he has been happy to take on projects suggested by others as well as those he has long nurtured himself. He has also shot films – such as *Le Cri du hibou* in 1987 – against the advice of his regular producer (in this case, Marin Karmitz, who refused to be involved in the project). For Chabrol, cinema has to be learned by filming (not by writing about it, hence his dismissal of film criticism, including his own for *Cahiers* in the 1950s). And one must never be afraid to get one's hands dirty on a supposedly inferior or unworthy project: 'il ne faut pas avoir peur de tremper les mains dans la merde s'il le faut pour tirer des choses'[8] (Biette *et al.* 1982: 6).

7 In other words, according to the new wave conception of the film-maker, he had become a director for hire rather than a true artist.

8 'you mustn't be afraid to put your hands in the shit to get something out'

The result is a filmography which contains turkeys (*Folies bour-geoises, Quiet Days in Clichy*) as well as masterpieces (the Hélène cycle, *Betty*, *La Cérémonie*), but which is finally being recognised as a landmark in French cinema.

Typically, Chabrol's autobiography is published not in an *auteurist* cinema collection but in the series 'Un homme et son métier'.[9] For him, directing is a job which can be demystified from the *auteurist*/Romantic idea of it. His concept of cinema privileges the spectator as well as the creator – hence the importance of genre in his work, since it is often via the expectations aroused by popular genres that a spectator approaches a given film. Rejecting the avant-garde and the experimental, Chabrol chooses (even when he doesn't have to, financially speaking) to work within the confines of established genres. In 1979 he declared that 'I've always tried to hold on to the cinema of genre because I think it's the only way to make films. These days in France, but not only there, one veers mostly towards an overly intellectual vision of things, and I think the only solution is to make some good *policiers*, some good soap-operas and comedies' (Yakir 1979: 2). Chabrol has in fact filmed farce (*Folies bourgeoises*), melodrama (*La Rupture*), fantasy (*Alice ou la dernière fugue*), war films (*La Ligne de démarcation, Une affaire de femmes*), spy films (the *Tigre* series and *La Route de Corinthe*) and glossy literary adaptations (*Quiet Days in Clichy, Madame Bovary*). But the crime thriller is his usual choice of genre, because it allows him to engage the spectator via the plot, and then explore the complexities of character, morality, society and politics within an accessible and satisfying framework. Or as he puts it, 'c'est le genre qui emmerde le moins le public'[10] (Sorg 1998: 35). He has often been described as specialising in the psychological thriller, but this is slightly misleading. Although he is greatly interested in character and situation, Chabrol does not concern himself with psychology as an area of knowledge. Human motivations remain obscure rather than transparent. Actions (particularly crimes) and

---

9 'One man and his job', published by Robert Laffont. Includes accounts by a private detective, an agronomist, a king, and, despite the series title, by a businesswoman and a (female) singer.
10 'it's the least boring genre for the audience'

their consequences are shown in uncompromising – and often blackly comic – detail, but no comforting explanations are given. As Chabrol says, 'mon grand plaisir, c'est de révéler l'opacité'[11] (Guérin and Jousse 1995: 30). This is particularly true of his female characters. How much do we learn about the enigmatic and ultimately disembodied[12] female protagonists of films such as *Le Boucher*, *Les Innocents aux mains sales*, *Violette Nozière*, *Betty* and *La Cérémonie*? Even the male characters – whose psychology is often less obscure – tend to maintain an ambivalence which thwarts simple definitions of good and evil. From *Le Beau Serge* and *Les Cousins*, via *Que la bête meure* and *Le Boucher*, to *Masques* and *Le Cri du hibou*, they are simultaneously victims and perpetrators. Moral relativism is the recurrent theme of Chabrol's work: 'my "great testament," my "definitive message" is ... Don't judge!' (Yakir 1979: 5).

Although there is a personal (moral) imperative underlying Chabrol's films, their means of production is collective. This is of course true of almost all films, but with Chabrol there is great emphasis on the contribution of the film crew. From his very first films, Chabrol built up a trusted team which has continued to work with him more or less throughout his career. The heart of the crew has been as follows: Jean Rabier (cinematography), Guy Chichignoud (sound), Pierre Jansen (music), Jacques Gaillard/Monique Fardoulis (editing). There have also been favourite actors at various periods of Chabrol's career, including Jean-Claude Brialy, Michel Bouquet, Jean Yanne, Stéphane Audran and Isabelle Huppert. Audran and Huppert have been especially important, incarnating the enigmatic and ultimately unknowable heroines of some of Chabrol's most famous work. Audran was Chabrol's second wife, and has appeared in over twenty of his films, from *Les Cousins* in 1958 to *Betty* in 1992. Above all, she starred in the Hélène cycle of 1968–71, in which she embodied the bourgeoisie of the period and facilitated Chabrol's ambivalent attitude towards it: 'Elle en représente une idéalisation ... L'idée était que les films devenaient

11 'my great pleasure is to reveal opacity'
12 Many of these films end with a close-up of the protagonist's face, apparently floating in space.

doubles: à la fois une satire de la bourgeoisie et un aboutissement, une sorte de modèle'[13] (Jousse and Toubiana 1997: 8). In 1978, Isabelle Huppert took the lead in *Violette Nozière* while Audran played her mother. The torch was in a sense being passed from one to the other, with Huppert going on to work regularly with Chabrol over the next two decades.

Always a metaphorical family, Chabrol's film crew has recently become something of a literal family too. His third wife Aurore is still the 'script-girl' (as she has been since the 1970s) and his step-daughter Cécile Maistre is now the first assistant. One of his sons, Matthieu, composes the score (replacing Pierre Jansen in 1982), while another, Thomas, has appeared in *Une affaire de femmes*, *Madame Bovary*, *Betty* and *L'Enfer*. Chabrol has always been renowned for his good humour on the set, and for the affection generated within his film crews, actors included: 'La création se fait mieux dans la joie. Pourquoi ne pas vivre en bons compagnons, être doux les uns avec les autres, de temps en temps faire la fête, en tout cas se marrer le plus souvent possible, bien bouffer?'[14] (Chabrol 1976: 186). It may well be that the relaxed atmosphere of his shoots and his well-known love of good food and drink added to his long-standing reputation as a casual film-maker. It is certainly true that he filmed *Ten Days' Wonder* in Alsace solely in order to enjoy the local cuisine, and that he was drunk for most of the shoot on *La Ligne de démarcation*. But his attitude remains unchanged. As he recently told *Télérama* on the set of his fifty-first film, *Au cœur du mensonge*, 'On ne sait jamais si un film sera réussi ni s'il aura du succès. ... Par contre, on peut toujours réussir le tournage, et en faire un succès'[15] (Sorg 1998: 35).

Although Chabrol wrote some of his most famous films alone (including *La Femme infidèle* and *Le Boucher*), he collaborated with

13 'She represents an idealisation of it ... The idea was that the films became double-edged: at the same time a satire on the bourgeoisie and its culmination, a kind of model'
14 'Creativity is aided by happiness. Why not be good friends, why not be nice to each other, live it up now and then, in any case have a laugh as often as possible and eat well?'
15 'You never know if a film will work, nor if it will be a success. On the other hand, you can always make the filming work, and make it a success'

his friend Paul Gégauff on many screenplays over the first twenty years of his career. Perhaps the most productive influence within Chabrol's crew, Gégauff was also the most destructive personality. Chabrol first met him in 1950 at Le Celtic film club in the Latin Quarter of Paris. Chabrol was in the audience as Gégauff, dressed as a Nazi officer, interrupted the screening of a British war film to complain that it was in bad taste. This anecdote encapsulates Gégauff's dangerous appeal: a dandy and a joker, a Germanophile, a scourge of good taste, of bourgeois manners and morals. He was also, in the early 1950s, a successful novelist and something of a playboy. He became an influence on several of the young new wave directors, including Eric Rohmer and Jean-Luc Godard. To Chabrol, he became a close friend and a fascinating model of cynicism and amorality. Gégauff's apparent racism and right-wing views, like his drinking and womanising, made a tantalising contrast with Chabrol's own left-wing humanism, and his status as a Catholic family man.[16] The attraction and contrast between Chabrol and Gégauff was to be represented time and again in two character types, Charles and Paul. (Usually they are male rivals for Hélène, a female character based to a degree on Stéphane Audran.) Charles is an ironic version of the young Chabrol: innocent, reserved, repressed. Paul is Gégauff: cynical, charismatic, provocative. Established in 1958 with *Les Cousins*, Chabrol's second film and the first on which Gégauff collaborated, the pairing was to reappear, with slight variations (and changes of name) in *Les Godelureaux* (Arthur and Ronald), *Les Biches* (Paul), *La Femme infidèle* (Charles and Victor), *Que la bête meure* (Charles and Paul), *Le Boucher* (Charles and Popaul), *La Rupture* (Charles and Paul), *Juste avant la nuit* (Charles), and *Docteur Popaul* (Popaul). The series culminated in 1974 with *Une partie de plaisir*, after which Gégauff's dandies tend to disappear from Chabrol's work. (The final film collaboration between the two was *Les Magiciens* a year later, featuring a dandy called Édouard. It was a commercial

16 Although Chabrol has always maintained that Gégauff's racism was simply a ploy to wind up left-wingers like himself, Antoine de Baecque, in an excellent essay, has accused Gégauff of genuine anti-Semitism. I have made use of this essay (de Baecque 1997) for my account of Gégauff's life and death.

disaster, and Chabrol reckons it is one of his very worst films.)

Une partie de plaisir dramatises – and hence exorcises – the power of Gégauff's personality. That power is described by Chabrol as follows: 'Il fascinait par son côté jusqu'auboutiste dans l'auto-destruction, un goût du paradoxe extraordinaire et une élégance vraie. Mais il m'a montré également jusqu'où cette direction pouvait aller dans l'autodestruction'[17] (de Baecque 1997: 90). Based on an autobiographical screenplay by Gégauff, *Une partie de plaisir* details the break-up of an apparently happy family. Raw and traumatic in its realism (brought home by Chabrol's decision to have Gégauff, his ex-wife, and their little daughter all play their fictional selves – in their own house!), the film is also telling in its symbolism: a working-through of Chabrol's fears about Gégauff's destructive potential. Although at times fascinating and impress-ive – entertaining his guests, discoursing on art and philosophy, arguing brilliantly with hippies[18] – the fictional Gégauff is also repulsive (he is equated at one point with a spider attacking its prey). Like an intimate version of the right-wing patriarchs from certain Chabrol films, Gégauff's character is autocratic and mani-pulative: he uses his daughter and patronises, humiliates and assaults his wife, finally appearing to kill her. It is in fact Chabrol's own ideal – the family – that is threatened by Gégauff (fictional and real). (Chabrol tends to make a distinction between the bour-geois family – which he considers a valid target for Gégauff and his alter egos – and the 'real' non-bourgeois, family – which he idealises.) On screen, Gégauff ends up in prison. Off screen, he began to drink more and more heavily, and gradually ceased to work with Chabrol. His last scenario for the latter was a television adaptation of Edgar Allan Poe in 1981. In late 1983, Gégauff rang Chabrol to say that after spending Christmas in Norway, he hoped to collaborate on a film project once more. On Christmas Eve, his young Norwegian wife stabbed him to death.

17 'He fascinated me by pushing at the limits of self-destruction, by his taste for extraordinary paradoxes and his real elegance. But he also showed me just how far this could take him into self-destruction'

18 Compare the attacks on pseudo-intellectualism and Eastern religions that Chabrol makes in *Les Biches, Que la bête meure* and *Le Boucher*.

Chabrol's frequenting of film clubs in his youth opened him up to a less controversial but equally crucial influence: the cinema of Fritz Lang and Alfred Hitchcock. It was Lang's *The Testament of Dr Mabuse*, made in 1933 and seen by Chabrol in Paris after the war, that inspired him to become a film-maker. Lang has remained one of Chabrol's heroes, and in 1976 he dedicated *Alice ou la dernière fugue* to the dying German director. What Chabrol learned from Lang's cinema was the use of dispassionate, objective camerawork to evoke the theme of fate, and the importance of expressionist *mise en scène* – in other words, the manipulation of décor and objects to convey atmosphere and meaning. As Chabrol explains, in Lang's expressionism 'On devrait comprendre de quoi il s'agit, même s'il y avait une chaise à la place de l'acteur'[19] (Chabrol 1976:120). In contrast with Lang, Hitchcock uses the subjective camera (the point-of-view shot) to realise the more intimate themes of voyeurism, guilt and innocence, and to generate a complicity between the spectator and the narrative: 'Par principe, par définition, il n'y a chez Lang aucune subjectivité, alors que chez Hitchcock, dès les premiers films réalisés en Amérique, presque tous les plans sont faits du point de vue d'un personnage, tantôt l'un, tantôt l'autre, puis intervient l'objectivité, c'est-à-dire la subjectivité du spectateur'[20] (*ibid.*: 133–4). Like Lang, however, Hitchcock has been a recurrent influence on Chabrol's thinking about cinema, from the book on Hitchcock that he co-wrote with Eric Rohmer in 1957 to the use of subjective camera and voyeurism in his own work. The influences of Lang and Hitchcock are especially recognisable in certain films and in certain periods of Chabrol's career. Hence the Langian style of *Les Biches*, *Que la bête meure* and the films of the 1970s, and also of *Dr M* in 1989 (in some ways a remake of Lang's *Mabuse* series). While the 1960s thrillers *L'Œil du malin* and *La Femme infidèle*

19 'You should be able to understand what it's all about even if the actor was replaced by a chair'
20 'On principle, by definition, there is no subjectivity in Lang, while in Hitchcock, from his first American films onwards, almost every shot is filmed from the point of view of one character or another. Then objectivity – that's to say, the spectator's subjectivity – intervenes'

both owe a clear debt to Hitchcock, Chabrol's main Hitchcockian period dates from 1986 and *Masques*, a film littered with seventeen references to the 'Master of Suspense'.[21] By 1995 and *La Cérémonie*, Chabrol could declare:'A un moment j'étais très langien ... Je crois qu'avec l'âge on devient hitchcockien'[22] (Guérin and Jousse 1995: 30). However, Chabrol's understanding of Lang and Hitchcock most frequently results in a productive tension between their two legacies – between expressionism and voyeurism, objective camera and subjective camera, fate and personal responsibility.

Probably the most important lesson that Chabrol learned from the example of Lang and Hitchcock was that a film-maker's personal vision need not be incompatible with the demands of genre cinema. Lang and Hitchcock worked throughout their careers in popular genres, predominantly the thriller, but also the western and the fantasy film (Lang), the comedy and the melodrama (Hitchcock). Ironically, and cruelly for Chabrol, while in the 1950s the critics on *Cahiers du cinéma* (himself included) were able to reassess Lang and Hitchock's artistic status by observing that a great *auteur* could work within genre cinema, in the 1960s this point seemed to be forgotten in the widespread condemnation (led by *Cahiers*) of Chabrol's fall from artistic grace into the spy film and the popular thriller. This irony is also symptomatic of Chabrol's general relationship with the new wave – a movement which he helped to create, and which was quick to reject him – as we shall see in the next chapter.

References

de Baecque, A. (1997), Gégauff, le premier des Paul, *Cahiers du cinéma*, Numéro spécial Claude Chabrol (October), 88–91.

Biette, J.-C., Daney, S., Toubiana, S. (1982), Entretien avec Claude Chabrol, *Cahiers du cinéma*, 339 (September), 5–14.

Blanchet, C. (1989), *Claude Chabrol*, Paris, Rivages.

21   These include references to *North by North-West* (the first glimpse of Townsend/Legagneur's house), and *Psycho* (the body in the car boot).

22   'At a certain point, I was very Langian. I believe that one becomes Hitchcockian with age'

Chabrol, C. (1976), *Et pourtant je tourne ...* , Paris, Robert Laffont.

Guérin, M.-A., and Jousse, T. (1995), Entretien avec Claude Chabrol, *Cahiers du cinéma*, 494 (September), 27–32.

Jousse, T., and Toubiana, S. (1997), Claude Chabrol de A à Z, *Cahiers du cinéma*, Numéro spécial Claude Chabrol (October), 7–31.

Sorg, C. (1998), Chabrol fait le Malouin, *Télérama*, 2527 (17 June), 32–6.

Toubiana, S. (1997), L'Œil du malin, *Cahiers du cinéma*, Numéro spécial Claude Chabrol (October), 4.

Yakir, D. (1979), The Magical Mystery World of Claude Chabrol: An Interview, *Film Quarterly*, (spring), 2–14.

2

The new wave

Chabrol has excellent new-wave credentials and is in some ways a representative figure for this innovative movement in French cinema. A film fan from an early age, he ran a film club in the village of Sardent (to which he had been evacuated from Paris during the Second World War). On his return to the capital, he frequented student film clubs where he met the future new-wave directors François Truffaut, Jean-Luc Godard, Eric Rohmer and Jacques Rivette. Like them, he venerated Hollywood cinema, wrote film criticism for *Cahiers du cinéma* in the 1950s, and shot his first films at the end of the decade. He collaborated with Rohmer on a study of Hitchcock, and with Truffaut and Godard on the latter's film *À bout de souffle* (1959). But there are also several ways in which Chabrol contradicts the new-wave model. His account of *À bout de souffle* suggests that Godard took over the project because Chabrol and Truffaut were at odds with each other (Chabrol 1976: 137). Unlike the others, Chabrol had some experience of the film industry from within, having worked as press officer for the American studio Fox. Whereas his colleagues tended to work for other directors or to experiment with short films before trying their first feature, Chabrol's first venture in filmmaking was the feature-length (and commercially successful) *Le Beau Serge*. The film was financed by Chabrol himself, using his first wife's family inheritance. His company, AJYM, produced several early new-wave films, including *Le Beau Serge* and *Les Cousins* (both 1958), but also Jacques Rivette's *Le Coup du berger*

(1956), Eric Rohmer's *Le Signe du lion* (1958) and Jacques Gaillard's *La Ligne droite* (1961). Despite the financial support he gave his colleagues, Chabrol has stated that the supposed solidarity and coherence of the group was just a myth – as in the case of *À bout de souffle* – and that the new wave was never an artistic movement like, say, surrealism. In fact, the marketing of the new wave in the late 1950s struck him as cynical and manipulative: 'Entre 1958 et 1959, les copains des *Cahiers* et moi, passés à la réalisation, avons été promus comme une marque de savonnette. Nous étions la "nouvelle vague". ... si la grande presse a tant parlé de nous, c'est qu'on voulait imposer l'équation: de Gaulle égale Renouveau. Dans le cinéma comme ailleurs. Le général arrive, la République change, la France renaît'[1] (*ibid.*: 135). None the less, Chabrol's first half a dozen films can be defined as his new wave period, featuring as they do several characteristics of *nouvelle vague* cinema: the filming of one's own scripts, a preference for shooting on location rather than in the studio, a degree of formal experimentation, an interest in neorealism, and some reliance on popular genres such as the melodrama and the thriller.

Le Beau Serge

To make his first film, Chabrol returned to the scene of his wartime childhood, the village of Sardent in central France. The reason for this was mainly financial: he had intended to shoot *Les Cousins* first, but that story was set in Paris and would have been twice as expensive to film. For the small budget of 32 million old francs, he was able to shoot *Le Beau Serge* (1958) over nine weeks in the winter of 1957/8, and to film it in what was essentially his home village (several generations of Chabrol's family had come

1 'Between 1958 and 1959, me and my friends on *Cahiers*, once we'd gone into film directing, were promoted like a brand of soap. We were the "new wave". If the daily papers talked about us so much, it was only because they wanted to establish the idea that de Gaulle equals Renewal. In the cinema as elsewhere. The General arrives, the Republic changes, France is reborn.' (In 1958, General Charles de Gaulle was elected president of France and inaugurated the Fifth Republic.)

from Sardent). The village is a crucial backdrop to the narrative and also provides extras and minor characters, such as the baker Michel Creuse. *Le Beau Serge* is most notable for its realistic setting and for the autobiographical elements within it. The latter include a religious message (Chabrol was at this time a practising Catholic), the death of a baby (which he and his wife had experienced), and above all the central theme of a Parisian student returning to his provincial roots. The clash of personalities between François (Jean-Claude Brialy), the convalescent student returning from Paris, and his old friend Serge (Gérard Blain), a local boy who has stayed in the village, stuck in the rut of poverty and alcoholism, also heralds the power struggles between the Charles and Paul characters that were to appear in *Les Cousins* and again in the Hélène cycle.

Originally, the finished film ran to two hours and thirty-five minutes, before Chabrol cut many of the scenes of village life, reducing it to the standard hour and a half. He later regretted losing this quasi-documentary footage, but even so, many critics saw – and praised – *Le Beau Serge* as a neorealist work. Established in postwar Italy, and extremely influential on the cinema of the new wave, neorealism has been defined according to the following principles: 'Un message, actualité du scénario, sens du détail, sens des foules, réalisme, vérité de l'acteur, vérité des décors, vérité des éclairages, photographie de style reportage, caméra très libre'[2] (Martin 1975: 34). Neorealist films tend to be characterised by 'location shooting, lengthy takes, unobtrusive editing, natural lighting, a predominance of medium and long shots, respect for the continuity of time and space, use of contemporary, true-to-life subjects, an uncontrived, open-ended plot, working-class protagonists, a nonprofessional cast, dialogue in the vernacular, active viewer involvement, and implied social criticism' (Marcus 1986: 22). Although Chabrol's later work was to deviate far from this model (particularly via the use of sophisticated editing, formal construction, stylised colour and expressionist *mise en scène*), *Le Beau Serge* sticks to it pretty closely. Where it differs most clearly is

2 'A message, a contemporary screenplay, a grasp of detail, a grasp of the masses, realism, truth in the acting, the décor and the lighting, reportage-style photography, and very free camerawork'

in its middle-class protagonist, François, and in its (his) contrived plot to bring about Serge's salvation. Any social criticism implied by the film is in this way submitted to a religious message, and the result is moralistic rather than political. However, as we shall see shortly, the ending of Chabrol's film is perhaps more open-ended and ambivalent than first appears.

Despite the vivacity of the camerawork and the occasional lyricism of the setting, *Le Beau Serge* is rather a schematic film. This is because of Chabrol's religious convictions, which permeate not just the characterisation, but also the composition of individual shots and the themes of Émile Delpierre's score. In his positive review of the film for *Arts* magazine, Truffaut called it 'une partie de dames jouée par deux jeunes hommes, Gérard Blain le pion noir, et Jean-Claude Brialy le pion blanc. Au moment précis où les deux se rencontrent, ils changent de couleur et gagnent *ex-aequo*'[3] (Truffaut 1958: 54). Truffaut's perceptive first comment is certainly borne out by the characterisation of 'bad' Serge (associated with black) and 'good' François (associated with white). But his conclusion seems a little generous and is not shared by Chabrol. He speaks instead of a heavy-handed symbolism (Braucourt 1971: 112), which is evident from the very start of the film, and which reaches its pitch at the end. In the opening scene, François arrives by bus in the village square. As the camera (mounted on top of the bus) pans to one side to reveal Serge and his father-in-law Glomaud, both drunk, a sudden burst of music emphasises the threat posed by these characters to the innocent newcomer. Throughout the film, distinct musical themes are used to characterise François (bright, lyrical strings and flutes) and Serge (ominous, rumbling brass and drums). When François runs round the village like a child, it is to the sound of flutes;[4] when Serge, like a drunken ogre, chases the schoolchildren from the square, it is to the sound of drums. On their second meeting,

---

3 'a game of draughts played out by two young men, Gérard Blain as black and Jean-Claude Brialy as white. At the precise moment when they meet, they change colour and both win'

4 The flutes are also associated with the schoolchildren, whose innocence and goodness François apparently shares.

when the two friends embrace, their musical motifs are mingled before the lyrical, optimistic theme wins out (a microcosm of the narrative itself). The categorisation of 'good' François and 'bad' Serge is mirrored by that of the female characters, the long-suffering Yvonne (Serge's wife) and her promiscuous younger sister Marie. As Truffaut suggests, colour is used symbolically in the film, for the women as well as the men. This results in a *mise en scène* which, although not always formulaic, does at times seem heavily allegorical. For instance, when François visits Serge's house for breakfast, the 'bad' pair (Serge and Yvonne) are grouped on the left of the frame and the 'good' pair (François and Marie) on the right. Both sisters are standing, both men sitting at the table. Dressed in white, Marie holds a bottle of milk (signifying her maternal role and also François's childlike innocence), while Yvonne, dressed in a dark dress, hands a dark bottle of wine to the alcoholic Serge. While Marie pours milk into François's coffee bowl, Serge pours wine into his.[5]

The tension between good and evil, the clashing of opposite personalities, and the over-dramatic score all lend *Le Beau Serge* an air of melodrama which it shares with several of Chabrol's films,[6] and which is also present in some Italian neorealism. But a degree of ambivalence also becomes apparent as the struggle between François and Serge develops. Serge may be equated with the stagnant village pond (which, he says, should be cleaned out, emptied, and started again), but François's mission to cleanse his old friend is not always presented as an unequivocally good thing. Marie tells him 'Tu as l'air de nous regarder comme si on était des insectes – tu n'aimes personne'.[7] The emphasis placed on François's voyeurism (we often see him looking at other characters, sometimes from the elevated safety of his hotel-room window) associates him with many of Chabrol's later anti-heroes, including Albin in *L'Œil du malin* and Forestier in *Le Cri du hibou*. (It also positions him as a kind of alter ego for Chabrol, an outsider in his

---

5 One should note, however, that the colour symbolism is not absolutely categorical: Serge is wearing white in this scene, and François black.

6 Including *Le Boucher* (1969) and, in particular, *La Rupture* (1971). See Chapter 3.

7 'You seem to look at us as if we're insects. You don't like anyone'

own village, an intellectual returning to Sardent to let his camera record village life with a documentarist's curiosity.) Like Albin and Forestier, François is in many ways an interloper, an intruder who disturbs the natural order, spreading discord wherever he goes. This is most evident when he tells Glomaud what the whole village knows but has never admitted: that Marie is not his daughter. When Glomaud proceeds to rape her, François, rather than blame himself, dismisses the villagers as 'animals' beyond redemption. His plan to save Serge, meanwhile, involves breaking up his marriage with Yvonne (despite the fact that she is pregnant), and soon alienates all those around him. He is told by Yvonne that Serge has become even more unhappy since his arrival. (The original reason for Serge's despairing alcoholism is the death of his handicapped baby son.) Eventually all the villagers, including the maternal landlady, tell him to leave. And yet the film ends with an apparently triumphant portrayal of François's efforts to save the village, to give them a Christ-like example, and to redeem the principal sinner, Serge, by dragging him through the snow to witness the birth of his (healthy) child.

It is this moralising conclusion, complete with symbols of crosses and the martyrdom of François, which Chabrol now disowns, and which sets *Le Beau Serge* apart from the rest of his work, where there are few value judgements and where the endings are resolutely ambivalent. The key is provided by Chabrol's Catholic faith at the time he made the film, and by his subsequent loss of faith. As he explains, *Le Beau Serge* 'm'a complètement déchristianisé. J'avais surchargé ce film de tout un symbolique imbécile. Il fallait le faire pour que j'en sois débarrassé. Maintenant, c'est fini'[8] (Braucourt 1971: 112–13). Chabrol remains vague as to exactly when his crisis of faith took place: 'J'étais chrétien dans le temps, j'ai cessé de l'être entre 1957 et 1959'[9] (*ibid.*). This begs the question, when exactly did Chabrol lose his religion? Was it actually during the making of *Le Beau Serge* (winter 1957/8)? And if not, was the crisis not at least signalled (unconsciously) in the

---

8 'it completely de-christianised me. I had loaded the film with stupid symbolism. I had to, in order to rid myself of it all. Now, that's all over with'

9 'I used to be a Christian, in the past. I stopped being one between 1957 and 1959'

final section of the film? One thinks of Chabrol's assessment of Balzac as a novelist whose work has a meaning completely opposed to his conscious intentions: 'Il a dit qu'il écrivait à la lumière de deux flambeaux, l'Église et la Royauté. De conviction, il est vrai qu'il était monarchiste et catholique. En même temps, ce qu'il écrit clame le contraire'¹⁰ (Chabrol 1976: 346). The same could be said of Chabrol and *Le Beau Serge* – the film in fact deconstructs and lays bare (as a comforting illusion) the moralising Catholicism it ostensibly celebrates.

If this is so, the canonical reading of the film (which Chabrol shares) is undermined by a second interpretation. The first might be said to be the conscious reading, the second the 'dream reading'.¹¹ According to the dream reading, the final twenty minutes or so of *Le Beau Serge* would be François's subjective fantasy.¹² The main clue to this possibility is the dreamlike *mise en scène* of the conclusion, and in particular the fairytale atmosphere evoked by the falling snow. After he is beaten up by Serge at the village dance, and rejected by the entire village, François is confronted with the image of a cross (in fact the frame of a window), the first of many in the closing scenes. He returns to his hotel room, where the landlady appears and advises him to leave Sardent once and for all. In response he leans his battered face against the door of his room and mumbles 'Non'. The beautiful image that follows suggests that we are passing from bleak neorealism into comforting fantasy: while François's face remains in close-up (providing the anchor for the subjective scenes to come), Chabrol superimposes onto it a shot of swirling snowflakes. The effect is as if François has entered a dreamland, a childhood of the mind where he becomes the Christian saviour he has longed to be, and where, like an affronted child, he finally gets to 'show' everyone who doubted or rejected him. In the next shot, the village is covered in

10 'He said that he wrote by the light of two flames, the Church and the monarchy. It is true that, by conviction, he was a monarchist and a Catholic. But at the same time, what he wrote proclaims the opposite'

11 The term 'dream reading' is taken from Chris Marker's superb reinterpretation of Hitchcock's *Vertigo*, according to which 'the entire second part would be nothing but a fantasy' (Marker 1995: 126).

12 Two critics have suggested as much (Magny 1987: 83-5, Blanchet 1989: 17).

snow and young children are going to school. Gentle music is heard as we are given François's view of the village from his window. Whether he has really woken or is dreaming, whether he in fact leaves his bed or remains in it, fantasising as he lies dying, all that follows conforms to his wish for martyrdom. Telling the priest that the villagers need his help, François goes out for the first time in a fortnight. He is reconciled with Yvonne. Then, in the night, he is told that she is in labour. Disregarding his own weak health, he runs through the snow, first to find the doctor and then to look for Serge. Like Father Logan in Hitchcock's *I Confess* (1953), he embarks on a physical journey which parallels the stations of the cross.[13] At each stage of his journey, François is met by crosses: the window frame at Glomaud's house (where he finds the doctor), the fence by the hen-coop (where he eventually finds Serge, in an alcoholic stupor) the door and window frames of Yvonne's house (where he drags Serge in time for the birth). As he searches for Serge in the snow, the light from his torch throws a halo around him. And when he finally collapses, having engineered Serge's redemption, his final words are 'J'ai cru'.[14] Everything seems to have been resolved through his powers of faith – or, if one chooses the dream reading, through his powers of fantasy.[15]

Les Cousins

At the last minute, *Le Beau Serge* was pulled as the official French entry for the 1958 Cannes film festival. Even so, Chabrol showed the film outside the competition, where it was well received, and he managed to sell it to one or two foreign distributors. He was now in a position to shoot *Les Cousins* (1958) in Paris as he had wanted (at a cost of 62 million old francs). The film tells how

13 See Rohmer's interpretation of *I Confess* in the book he co-wrote with Chabrol (Rohmer and Chabrol 1957: 117). Hitchcock's film is a probable influence on *Le Beau Serge*.

14 'I believed'

15 The ominous music, Serge's mad laughter, and the blurred close-up on his hysterical face (which suggests a skull) do go some way to qualifying this 'feel-good' ending.

Charles, a provincial law student (Gérard Blain), stays with his Parisian cousin Paul (Jean-Claude Brialy). Cynical and charismatic, Paul parties hard, cheats at his law exams, and seduces Florence, with whom his cousin had fallen in love. Under the strain, the 'good' Charles (who works hard but fails) is tempted to murder his cousin, but cannot even manage that. The next morning, Paul kills Charles accidentally with the loaded gun intended for him. Where *Le Beau Serge* attracted seventy thousand spectators in Paris, *Les Cousins* was seen by over two hundred and fifty thousand (Braucourt 1971: 177). The new wave was taking off, and Chabrol was in the vanguard. The reception of *Les Cousins* was, however, in one way problematic – and was a sign of things to come for Chabrol.

Les Cousins deviates from neorealism in ways that *Le Beau Serge* does not. For instance, contrary to neorealism's long takes and unobtrusive editing, *Les Cousins* features a bravura sequence of fast editing, a new-wave celebration of Parisian landmarks seen from a speeding car (comparable to a similar sequence in Godard's *À bout de souffle*). None the less, Chabrol's second film does also have a realistic setting: the Latin Quarter, and in particular the so-called 'capo de droit' run by Parisian law students. But while critics had been quick to praise Chabrol's portrayal of Sardent as completely naturalistic, there was a certain reluctance to acknowledge the accuracy of his view of student Paris. *Les Cousins* was in fact based on Chabrol's own experiences at the 'capo de droit' between 1947 and 1949. One of the very few left-wingers to be welcomed by the group (apparently because of his sense of humour), Chabrol witnessed their flirtations with Fascist ideology, and the charismatic presence of their leader, a certain Jean-Marie Le Pen.[16] The rationale for the film was therefore, among other things, to show the dangerous appeal of Fascism. (One could also say that it dramatises the dangerous appeal of Chabrol's friend and the film's co-writer, Paul Gégauff.) As Chabrol discovered, although *Les Cousins* was a great commercial success, it was the first of his films to be totally misunderstood by some critics: 'Les gens, à l'époque, ne croyaient pas qu'il y avait des fascistes en France. C'est aussi bête que cela. Ils ont donc cru que c'était moi le

16 Later to become leader of the French National Front.

fasciste, puisqu'ils ne voulaient pas croire que c'était ceux qu'ils voyaient sur l'écran'[17] (Collet and Tavernier 1962: 7). Although Chabrol's point was proved by events of the early 1960s (such as the *putsch* of 1961 and the activities of the OAS – Organisation de l'armée secrète – terrorists), the 'Fascist' tag unfortunately stuck long enough to dominate the critical reception of *Les Bonnes Femmes* in 1960 (see p. 28).

The narrative of *Les Cousins* reworks the fable of the town mouse and the country mouse. But it is also derived from the novels of Balzac, especially the rites of passage faced by Rastignac in *Le Père Goriot*. Like Charles, Rastignac is a provincial law student, devoted to his mother, eager to make his way in Paris, and in many ways repulsed by the cynical society he finds there. But where Charles turns inwards and destroys himself, Rastignac adapts to the unpleasant realities of his new environment. A similar story is told in *Les Illusions perdues*, the Balzac novel which Charles is given by the bookseller and which he refuses to read (he has lost his own illusions by himself at the end of the film). The parallel with Balzac is not just limited to the narrative, however. *Les Cousins*, co-written by Gégauff, sees the introduction of the Charles and Paul characters (and, in Florence, a prototype Hélène) which were to recur in the Hélène cycle of the late 1960s and early 1970s. Balzac himself had, in the early 1830s, toyed with the idea of using the same initials or first names for characters in different works. From 1832 onwards, he went further, and certain characters appeared and reappeared in various novels. The intention behind this – to create a huge, coherent whole out of numerous smaller works – is echoed by Chabrol's films from *Les Cousins* onwards (and, in microcosm, by the Hélène cycle). In his autobiography Chabrol describes Balzac's *Comédie humaine* as a giant mosaic, where the whole is more important than any constituent part, before adding: 'En toute modestie, c'est ma démarche ... Il n'est pas indispensable que chacun de mes films soit considéré comme parfait. Il se peut que j'aie seulement voulu illustrer une

17 'At the time, people didn't believe that there were Fascists in France. It was as stupid as that. So they thought that I was a Fascist, because they didn't want to think that the characters on the screen were'

idée qui était apparue dans un film et que je reprendrai. Ce que je cherche c'est que l'ensemble de mes réalisations donne une idée très précise d'une vision des choses'[18] (Chabrol 1976: 347).

Where *Les Cousins* suggest the Chabrolian vision much more clearly than *Le Beau Serge* is in the ambivalence of the characterisation and in the detailed exploration of power relations (usually expressed spatially). The 'good' and 'bad' roles from the first film are resurrected in the second only to be more strongly challenged. In this case, Charles is not only innocent, diligent and well-meaning, he is also naïve, over-idealistic and puritanical. On several occasions he actually rejects Florence so that he can keep studying for his exams. Paul, meanwhile, although manipulative, egocentric and cynical, is also a fun-loving pragmatist (in this he actually ressembles Chabrol as well as Gégauff). As Florence's choice suggests, Paul is sexually more magnetic than the inhibited and rather adolescent Charles. And, in the final analysis, while Charles tries to murder Paul, the latter is quite possibly in love with the former, and is certainly grief-stricken by his death (see below, p. 24). The interrelations between the two cousins (and Florence) are expressed spatially, but without any of the religious or moral symbolism that weighed down *Le Beau Serge*. In *Les Cousins*, spatial compositions express power rather than morality.[19] Unsurprisingly, the power tends to belong to Paul. This is best revealed in two sequences showing Charles entering Paul's apartment in Neuilly. On his first arrival, he finds his cousin on top of a ladder looking through a telescope. Naturally enough, Paul looks down at Charles, who has to look up to him. The construction is realistic, but also symbolic – a lesson learned from Lang's expressionism. The second example is even more explicit, since Chabrol shows two levels of the apartment in a single shot, to emphasise the

18 'In all modesty, that's also my approach. It's not vital for each of my films to be considered perfect. I might only have wanted to illustrate an idea that had appeared in a previous film, and that I'll take up again later. What I'm after is that my films as a whole give a very precise idea of a personal vision.' (This is probably Chabrol's most *auteurist* statement to date.)

19 The power relations in *Juste avant la nuit* (1971), *Les Innocents aux mains sales* (1975) and *La Cérémonie* (1995) are similarly expressed by open-plan decors and spatial compositions. See Chapters 3, 4 , and 7 respectively.

characters' respective positions. Having failed to meet Florence at the university, Charles returns to Neuilly, where he finds her together with Paul. The new couple are on the first floor, while Charles is framed on the ground floor, beneath them. A similarly expressive composition a little later – once Florence has moved in with Paul – shows her sunbathing topless in the bay of a window, with Charles standing, again, beneath her. Her idealised, unattainable status in his eyes is expressed not just by the spatial relation between them, but by the railings which literally bar his view of her body. In the closing stages of the film, Charles's inability to mentally shut out Paul and Florence is reflected visually by their ubiquitous presence behind the frosted glass doors of his study (either partying in the living-room or showering together in the bathroom). In short, the apartment becomes an expression of Charles's state of mind. And while Paul and Florence (and their numerous friends) use the open living-room, Charles himself remains closed off, isolated, unable actually to live (hence unable to enter the living-space).

Similarly, the *mise en scène* expresses Paul's embryonic Fascism. The décor of the apartment – the ranks of toy soldiers seen in the first shot, the trophies and guns on the wall – suggests a fascination with military power and with stylised violence. Emphasis is placed on the pistol which Paul, Charles and the Italian count all play with, and which is ultimately loaded by Charles with fatal consequences. (There is a similar emphasis on the décor of Frédérique's villa, with the dagger on the wall, in *Les Biches* (1967), *Les Cousins*'s sister film). Since German culture is actually used in *Les Cousins* as a shorthand for Paul's leanings towards Fascism, it is no surprise to see candlelight and huge shadows – associated with German expressionism – in the sequence where Paul, wearing a Nazi officer's cap, wanders through the party reading Goethe in German to the strains of Wagner's *Gotterdammerung*.[20] The precise piece of music used here is worth noting. Paul puts on the

---

20 Compare Chabrol's first meeting with Gégauff (see Chapter 1, p. 72). It should perhaps be noted that it was Chabrol and not Gégauff who devised the scene where the Jewish student is awoken by Paul shouting that the Gestapo are coming (see Collet and Tavernier 1962: 7).

'Death of Siegfried', an apparently apt choice for the recital of a poem about the death of a soldier. But the music has other connotations within the narrative, as the end of the scene reveals. As the music reaches its poignant close, Paul repeats the last line of the poem – 'love is born' – while staring despondently at Charles and Florence, who have just begun to kiss. There is a suggestion here (via the music and the poem) that Paul is mourning the birth of Charles's love for Florence, and hence the death of a possible love between the two cousins. This implicit theme – Paul's love for Charles – is reiterated by the film's brilliant ending, which first sees the complete destruction of Charles's identity (his failure at the exams, his virtual suicide when he throws his student card and notes into the Seine, his half-hearted attempt to kill Paul by a kind of Russian roulette) and then his accidental shooting by Paul. Again, Wagner's music evokes the death of love, this time literally (the piece is the *Liebestod* from *Tristan und Isolde*).[21] As the music reaches its crescendo, Charles falls dead at Paul's feet. The closing cadences drift away as Paul sits, stunned, by his cousin's body and realises what has happened. The *Liebestod* expresses his own mourning for Charles's death as much as Isolde's for Tristan's. Someone rings at the door, and while the music fades to silence and Paul goes to confront the future, a slow camera movement reveals the record-player. The stylus lifts up, the record stops, the film ends. Game over.

Les Bonnes Femmes

During the making of *Les Cousins*, Chabrol met Stéphane Audran (she plays the part of Françoise, one of Paul's friends). His relationship with his first wife, Agnès, was in disarray. They eventually divorced, and Chabrol married Audran in 1964. AJYM Films, the production company Chabrol had set up with Agnès's inheritance, was wound up in the early 1960s. The commercial pressures associated with making films for producers other than

21 *Liebestod* means 'love's death'. In the opera, Tristan dies from a wound only Isolde can heal. On hearing of his death, she dies of a broken heart.

himself were about to become a determining factor in the development of Chabrol's career. At first, there were no problems. The Hakim brothers financed his third film, allowing him not only to shoot the flashbacks he wanted, but also to film in colour – the other producers he approached had granted him one or the other but not both! The first of Chabrol's many adaptations of crime novels, *A double tour* (1959) was carefully constructed so that 'c'était le récit lui-même qui faisait un double tour. En outre, j'avais tourné avec beaucoup de mouvements circulaires. Le film devait représenter un cercle qui se dédouble sur lui-même'[22] (Chabrol 1976: 152). A double flashback was used, so that 'Le premier raconte ce qui s'est passé un peu plus tôt, le second raconte ce qui s'est passé pendant le premier'[23] (Collet and Tavernier 1962: 8). This attention to structure was only partly successful – 'C'était très construit, mais les gens ont cru que ça allait dans tous les sens'[24] (*ibid.*) – and was to be even more involved and even less understood in Chabrol's controversial fourth film, *Les Bonnes Femmes* (1960).

Despite the relative failure of *A double tour* at the box office (it cost twice as much as *Les Cousins*, but attracted only half the number of spectators), the Hakim brothers were prepared to finance Chabrol's next film – probably, he explains, because they thought from the title that *Les Bonnes Femmes* would be some kind of sex comedy (Chabrol 1976: 152). To the disappointment of almost everybody, it was nothing of the sort. Instead, the film painted a bleak picture of the boredom and alienation of four shop assistants, each of whom struggles to break out of her environment but fails, and one of whom is ultimately murdered. With a subtlety he had not shown before, Chabrol mixed together two distinct elements in an unsettling synthesis: neorealism and thriller, tedium and suspense, banality and menace. These strands are reflected by Pierre Jansen's score: by turns wistful and lyrical,

22 'it was the story itself which went round twice. What's more, I included lots of circular camera movements. The film was meant to represent a circle which doubled back on itself'

23 'The first one shows what happened a little earlier, and the second one shows what happened during the first one'

24 'It was very structured, but people thought it was all over the place'

in neorealist style (evoking the girls' frustrated dreams), and suspenseful and dark, as in a thriller (for the appearances of the mysterious motorcyclist). Chabrol and Gégauff also gave the film an intricate structure, made up of different episodes to reflect the comings and goings of the characters. The result was, according to Chabrol, a heptahedron (*ibid.*: 195). In other words, the film comprises seven sections,[25] identifiable as follows:

1 Jane (Bernadette Laffont) goes to a nightclub with Albert and Marcel and then back to their flat for sex;[26]
2 Rita (Lucile Saint-Simon) goes with the others to a restaurant, where she meets her fiancé Henri;
3 the four girls go to the zoo together;
4 Ginette (Stéphane Audran) is discovered by the others singing at a music-hall;
5 they all go to the swimming-pool, where Albert and Marcel reappear;
6 Jacqueline (Clotilde Joano) finally goes on a date with André, the motorcyclist, and is murdered by him in the woods;
7 in a cryptic coda, a fifth, unnamed *bonne femme* is introduced, dancing at a nightclub with a man whose face we do not see.

Each of the four young women (and by implication, the fifth) thus seeks a different route out of their situation: sex and a good time, marriage into the bourgeoisie, a theatrical career, romance. The only one who escapes is Jacqueline, and she does so not through romance but through death.

The neorealist depiction of Paris in the film – the scenes in the metro, the swimming-pool, the music-hall, and above all the nightclub, where the camera-work is so free and shaky as to suggest hastily snatched documentary footage – is complemented by the pacing of the narrative. There are long sequences where screen time and real time are one, and where nothing happens, slowly. The evocation of *durée* (the duration of time) is a trait of

---

25 Discounting the two 'empty' periods of time when all four girls are shown working in the shop.
26 Jacqueline is also present for the first half of the episode. The sex is implied but not actually shown.

neorealist cinema – 'substituant aux temps "dramatiques" du cinéma traditionnel des temps faibles ou des temps morts'[27] (Martin 1975: 35) – but it can also imply suspense in a thriller context. The thriller element is provided here by the repeated appearances of André spying on the girls, by the equation between him and the dangerous tiger made during the zoo sequence, and by Madame Louise's revelation to Jacqueline of her 'fetish' (not the romantic lucky charm one expects, but a handkerchief soaked in the blood of the guillotined serial killer Weidmann).[28] Consequently, in *Les Bonnes Femmes* time is both undramatic and dramatic, monotonous but (increasingly) suspenseful. The banality, the repetition, the waiting (especially in the shop sequences, where the girls wait for it to be time to go home) all beg the question, when is something *filmic* going to happen? By feeling this, the spectator is implicated in Jacqueline's murder, either as perpetrator (by wanting something to happen to one of the girls) or in the Hitchockian sense, as victim (identifying with her, feeling suspense and fear that something will happen to her). When Jacqueline's murder finally takes place, it is like a parody of romance. The long-awaited date with André is heavy with romantic expectation (both on the part of Jacqueline and, in all probability, the spectator). A drive in the countryside, lunch in a restaurant, and then a quiet walk in the woods ... But André is not the romantic hero he appears to be in the swimming-pool scene (where he rescues Jacqueline from Albert and Marcel). He is closer to the macabre Madame Louise. There are hints at his real motive when he praises Jacqueline's long and slender neck, but the possibilities – romance or death – are balanced against each other until the murder has been committed. Thus there are repeated facial close-ups (associated with the filmic representation of sex), and we see the two lying down together in the bushes. It is only when André climbs off Jacqueline's inert body that it becomes

27 'which replaces the "dramatic" time of traditional cinema with uneventful or empty time'
28 Weidmann was a sadistic killer of women (hence the suggestion that Jacqueline will end up being murdered). He was executed at Versailles in 1939 and some women in the crowd dipped their handkerchiefs in his blood (see Collet and Tavernier 1962: 12).

clear that we have been watching a strangulation rather than a sex scene.

Both the formal brilliance and the stark realism of *Les Bonnes Femmes* tended to leave spectators and critics cold. What attracted attention instead was Chabrol and Gégauff's supposedly cynical treatment of their inadequate central characters. Infuriatingly for Chabrol, the tenderness he felt for the four shop assistants and their attempts to break out of a restricted environment was completely ignored. The humour in the film was considered to be cruelty at their expense, although it is mostly directed at the men: Albert and Marcel the louche pick-up artists; Rita's ludicrous fiancé Henri, who coaches her furiously on culture while she waits to meet his parents; and the shop owner Monsieur Belin, who marks Jacqueline's first day at work by giving her a flower and serenading her, before explaining that all breakages will be deducted from her wages. There were accusations, particularly from left-wing commentators, that *Les Bonnes Femmes* was full of contempt for its working-class characters, that it was neorealism emptied of compassion, and even that it was a Fascist film. When asked in 1962 why the film had been considered Fascistic, Chabrol replied: 'd'une part, ça vient sans doute des *Cousins*, d'autre part, comme les gens sont eux-mêmes méprisants, ils croient que moi, aussi, je méprise'[29] (Collet and Tavernier 1962: 12). In fact, as Chabrol explained, *Les Bonnes Femmes* was an attempt to portray the alienating social conditions of the uneducated working class, and as such could claim to be 'un film profondément marxiste'[30] (*ibid.*: 10). This is never more clear than in the zoo sequence, where the girls are shot through barred grilles as they look at the animals: they too, are living their lives out in a cage.

Les Bonnes Femmes is perhaps above all a film which explores spectatorship. For all its (neo)realism, it is aware of itself as a spectacle, and frequently challenges the audience's expectations and desires. This gives it a certain new-wave self-consciousness

29 'on the one hand, that's because of [the 'fascist' interpretation of] *Les Cousins*. And also because, since people are themselves contemptuous [of the characters], they think they think that I also feel contempt for them'
30 'A deeply Marxist film'

which is not present in Chabrol's later work. The three central examples are the stage appearances of Dolly Bell and Ginette, and the closing scene of the film (the coda). Each scene could be said to address a different aspect of spectatorship: desire, identification and judgement. In the nightclub sequence, Chabrol considers the desire of the audience (both in the club and in the cinema itself) to see the stripper Dolly Bell. This is heightened by the *mise en scène* (the music announcing her imminent appearance, the curtains veiling the stage), but is denied – at least for the film audience – by the camera-work, so that when she finally appears, Chabrol cuts to a reverse-shot, revealing not the stripper but the nightclub audience, seen from her point of view. The filming of Ginette's performance at the music-hall (wearing a black wig, and transformed into the supposedly Italian singer 'Angela Torrini') refers back to the Dolly Bell sequence. But now (because of the narrative, which has introduced us to Ginette's singing ambitions, and which implies that she will be mortified if her friends find out), when we see the music-hall audience from the performer's point of view, we identify with Ginette and share her perspective (and her fears of discovery). Finally, after Jacqueline's murder – in which the spectator is, as we have seen, at least partly implicated – Chabrol closes the film with his enigmatic coda. The final shot is of the unknown young woman staring directly at the camera over the shoulder of her dancing partner. This look (and the apparent lack of connection between the coda and the rest of the film) asks us to conclude on what we have seen. What is our judgement on the lives of the *bonnes femmes*? Can we identify with them? The lack of point-of-view shot here implies that we might not. Can we at least empathise? Faced with the banal and sad realism of the film (and by the gaze of the fifth *bonne femme*), we are challenged to make a judgement. As the critical response to the film showed, the challenge was far too disquieting and difficult for some.

L'Œil du malin

After *Les Bonnes Femmes* – only 84,000 tickets sold in Paris – Chabrol could hardly afford another failure at the box office. In commercial terms, his career was in free-fall. The situation worsened with the release of the black comedy *Les Godelureaux* (1960). According to Chabrol, this was a useless film about uselessness (*ibid.*: 13). The public obviously agreed: a mere 23,000 watched it. However, the film's producer, Georges de Beauregard – who went on to finance *Landru* in 1962 and *La Ligne de démarcation* in 1966 – was not disheartened. He supported Chabrol's next project, *L'Œil du malin* (1961), although the film eventually had to be shot for half the original (rather modest) budget, because of problems with the German co-producer. Accepting the challenge, Chabrol shot the film frugally, mainly in and around Munich. Luckily, his scenario (written without Gégauff this time) called for a small cast, very few group shots, and a limited number of locations. The film was shot quicker and cheaper than any of Chabrol's work since *Le Beau Serge*. This may have been of some consolation when it proved another commercial disaster.

L'Œil du malin is narrated throughout by Albin Mercier (Jacques Charrier). A young French journalist, he is sent on assignment to a village in Bavaria. There he meets a French woman, Hélène Hartmann (Stéphane Audran in the first of her 'Hélène' roles), and her husband Andreas (Walter Reyer), a successful German writer. Andreas is everything that Albin is not but wants to be: famous, wealthy, physically and intellectually strong, and married to the beautiful Hélène. Albin is an outsider in this world, not only unable to speak German but also placed outside the apparently idyllic bourgeois lifestyle of the Hartmanns: he is frequently shown lingering by their wall or gate, looking in at what he imagines to be 'un univers rond, parfait, où tout est harmonieux'.[31] Gradually he befriends the couple and enters ever deeper into their house and their lives. Discovering that Hélène is having an affair behind Andreas's back, Albin first tries to blackmail her into leaving her husband. When she refuses, he shows Andreas

31   'a perfect, rounded universe, where everything is in harmony'

the photos he has taken of the lovers, with the result that Andreas murders his wife. Albin is again alone, outside the gates, as Andreas is taken away by the police. He has destroyed the very harmony that he envied.

In many ways, *L'Œil du malin* is the one film from Chabrol's new-wave period which best prefigures his later work. Two staple themes of his mature cinema are presented here: first, the disruption of an apparently perfect couple to reveal hidden truths and tensions behind the façade of bourgeois harmony (this recurs in *La Femme infidèle, Le Cri du hibou, L'Enfer,* and *La Cérémonie*). This theme is qualified by the second, since the revealer of unwanted truths, the outsider/avenger figure, is not unequivocally heroic: he is in many ways destructive, a voyeur whose gaze brings death, a coward and a manipulator who is afraid to engage fully with life (hence hiding his real identity and real motives behind masks and pseudonyms). Thus André Mercier (alias Albin) ressembles Charles Thénier (alias Marc Andrieux) in *Que la bête meure,* as well as Wolf in *Masques* and Forestier in *Le Cri du hibou.* He may see through appearances – 'Ainsi, ce bonheur, cette harmonie que j'enviais, tout n'était que mensonge et tromperie'[32] – but he also engineers their brutal destruction.

The central motif in the film is of penetration and entry: specifically, Albin's entry into the Hartmanns' private space (a metaphor for his sexual desire for Hélène and an expression of his wish to belong). This is reiterated verbally by his commentary – 'j'allais pénétrer chez eux'; 'mon but était de pénétrer dans l'univers de cet couple'; 'je voulais pénétrer en fraude'[33] – and visually by his gradual exploration of the Hartmanns' home: first the wall and gate, then the garden, the ground floor of the house (when invited to dinner), and finally (by a ruse) the first floor, where the more intimate space of bedroom and bathroom is found. While Andreas is away on business, Albin assumes his place in the house: taking a bath, wearing his bathrobe, sitting in

---

32 'So, the happiness and harmony that I had envied was nothing more than lies and deceit'

33 'I was going to enter their house'; 'my goal was to enter the universe of this couple'; 'I wanted to sneak in secretly'

his chair and drinking his brandy. The sequence ends with his triumphant comment (in voice-over), 'J'étais devenu leur intime'.[34] But rather than enable him to replace Andreas permanently, as he perhaps hopes, Albin's blackmail plan only leaves him alone on the outside again. The *mise en scène* of Hélène's murder is worth dwelling upon. Like the opening sequence of *Le Cri du hibou* (1987), the murder scene recalls the action of watching a film in a darkened cinema. Albin (like Forestier in *Le Cri du hibou*) hides in a dark garden looking up at the well-lit windows of a house. In this case, Hélène staggers out of the house on to the first-floor veranda, stares into space (towards Albin and the audience) and then collapses, her throat cut. The equation between Albin and ourselves (suggested by the composition but also by Hélène's gaze, which addresses both) emphasises that he – like us – has always been outside looking in, a tolerated voyeur rather than a true 'intime'.[35]

The first of Chabrol's films to owe a clear debt to Hitchcock, *L'Œil du malin* reprises the sequence from *Vertigo* (1958) where James Stewart, a detective, follows mysterious *femme fatale* Kim Novak.[36] Here, Albin follows Hélène to the secret rendez-vous with her lover. (The camera Albin uses to photograph the two together recalls another Hitchcockian voyeur, the photographer – again played by James Stewart – in *Rear Window* (1954).) As in *Les Bonnes Femmes*, during Albin's trailing of Hélène the thriller element is combined with neorealism: on the streets of Munich and at the *beerfest*, real crowds jostle the lead characters and Chabrol's hand-held camera jolts and sways. There is no sound-track music, only the ambient noise of the festival itself. But the rest of the film is much more stylised than *Les Bonnes Femmes*. This comes from the fact that *L'Œil du malin* represents Albin's romanticised account of events rather than an objective, realistic record. In Chabrol's words, 'L'histoire était vue par un minable, et

---

34 'I had become intimate with them'
35 'close friend'
36 *Vertigo* is also alluded to when Albin finds Hélène in the woods. *L'Enfer* (1994) also refers to *Vertigo* – see Chapter 5.

le film était forcément, en un sens minable'³⁷ (*ibid*.: 14). *L'Œil du malin* is a pathetic film because it is a subjective one. And Albin is pathetic throughout: in his attempts to enter the Hartmanns' world and in his petulant revenge on that world when he is excluded from it (the blackmail plot, but also his desire to avenge his embarrassment when the Hartmanns discover that he cannot swim). It is not just the voice-over that indicates Albin's control over the narrative, and that gives certain events a revised meaning (exaggerating the Hartmanns' affection for him, insisting on the duplicity of Hélène's affair when the images of it remain light, natural, almost innocent). At times it is the images too. Hence the repeated shot of him walking home in the evening from the Hartmanns' house: 'Lorsqu'Albin Mercier descend la pente en contre-jour, c'est que, lui, il se voit ainsi. C'est sûrement le type qui ne peut pas descendre une pente sans se voir auréolé d'un magnifique contre-jour'³⁸ (*ibid*.: 15). One might even ask whether the penultimate scene, in which Albin begs Andreas's forgiveness, is not simply a fantasy, in which Albin says what he should have said and so absolves himself of the sense of guilt he feels. As the conclusion suggests, the guilt remains, alongside a newfound self-awareness. Albin's final voice-over declares, 'Je ne peux pas m'empêcher de raconter cette histoire, et les gens me demandent pourqui un garçon aussi sympathique que moi prend plaisir à se salir les mains'.³⁹ As he has finally realised, and as we have learned during the telling of the tale, Albin is very far from being 'un garçon sympathique'.⁴⁰

---

37 'The story was seen through the eyes of a pathetic loser, and the film was therefore, in one sense, pathetic'

38 'When Albin Mercier is back-lit as he walks down the hill, it's because he sees himself like that. He is exactly the sort of person who can't walk down a hill without seeing himself basking in the glow of a magnificent light behind him.' Compare the romantic images of François (lit by haloes) in the closing section of *Le Beau Serge* and of Charles (picked out by melancholy tracking-shots) in the central section of *Que la bête meure*.

39 'I can't stop myself from telling this story, and people ask me why a nice young man like me is so keen to wallow in the dirt'

40 There is an added irony here at the expense of Jacques Charrier's star image: his usual roles were in fact 'garçons sympathiques' (see Chabrol 1976: 159).

Was *L'Œil du malin* another example – after *A double tour* and *Les Bonnes Femmes* – of Chabrol being too clever for his audience? It was certainly another nail in his coffin as a successful new-wave director. He has said of the film that it ran up against 'une terrible chose: le fait que le cinéma est obligatoirement un art de masse'[41] (*ibid.*: 16). This was to be drummed home with the failure of *Ophélia* (1962), which became Chabrol's fourth consecutive commercial disaster since *A double tour*. The figures for the Paris box office reveal a steady and apparently terminal decline: 130,000 for *A double tour*, 84,000 for *Les Bonnes Femmes*, 23,000 for *Les Godelureaux*, 14,000 for *L'Œil du malin* and 12,000 for *Ophélia* (Braucourt 1971: 177).[42] The lesson Chabrol was to take out of the new-wave period was that a director – whether he considered himself an *auteur* or not – could not disregard the tastes of the mass audience and continue to make popular films. The choice seemed to be between popular cinema (meaning genre cinema) and the artistic ghetto. It was a dilemma faced by the other new-wave directors too, and which saw Godard, Rivette and Rohmer remain in the ghetto with only Truffaut successfully managing to combine art and commerce. Unlike Truffaut, Chabrol was not yet in this position, but he was to get there by spending the five years after *Ophélia* making genre films: the (admittedly macabre) period drama *Landru* (1963), the spy films *Le Tigre aime la chair fraîche* (1964) and *Le Tigre se parfume à la dynamite* (1965), the war film *La Ligne de démarcation* (1966) and so on. In these wilderness years, he was rejected by *Cahiers du cinéma* and generally held to be the disgrace of the new wave. Although new-wave idols like Hitchcock and Lang, Nicholas Ray and Howard Hawks had worked entirely in popular genres, when Chabrol began to do so he ceased to be regarded as an *auteur*.

Although he was in this way the first to leave the new wave, Chabrol had made a major contribution to it, first as a critic and then, more significantly, as both director and producer. There are

41 'a terrible thing: the fact that cinema is by definition an art for mass consumption'

42 The figures for *L'Œil du malin* and *Les Godelureaux* are in fact estimates, since the number of entries was not high enough to be computed exactly!

competing views as to which film launched the *nouvelle vague* – Agnès Varda's *La Pointe courte* in 1954, Godard's *À bout de souffle* in 1959, Truffaut's *Les 400 coups* winning at Cannes the same year – but *Le Beau Serge*, shown on the fringes at Cannes in 1958 and hailed by Truffaut that summer as a turning-point in French cinema, probably has the best claim. In the films that followed, Chabrol experimented with film form, neorealism, editing and camerawork, genre and spectatorship in a manner which exemplifies new-wave cinema. Ironically, in late 1962 when his new-wave pedigree was threatened, and in his last *Cahiers* interview for twenty years, Chabrol defended the films of Truffaut and Godard and called for the *nouvelle vague* to regroup and work together again (Collet and Tavernier 1962: 19). The subsequent year did, in fact, see him working with Godard, each contributing a sketch to *Les plus belles escroqueries du monde* (1963). But by this time his career was in serious jeopardy. Apart from this 18-minute sketch, Chabrol shot nothing at all between July 1962 and April 1964. When he did return to film-making, it was no longer as a new-wave *auteur*, but as a commercial director of genre films. His way back into the industry was to be the spy movie *Le Tigre aime la chair fraîche*.

The final fling of the new wave was the portmanteau film *Paris vu par ...* (1964). It featured six sketches, by directors such as Eric Rohmer, Jean-Luc Godard and Jean Rouch. Chabrol contributed what is acknowledged as the best episode of the six, *La Muette*. This last, isolated example of Chabrol's new-wave cinema is sandwiched in his filmography between the commercial spy films *Le Tigre aime la chair fraîche* and *Marie-Chantal contre Dr Kha* (1965). He was now making films for producers who – in shocking contrast with the new-wave ideal of the self-sufficient *auteur*, an ideal he himself had once epitomised – considered him as their servant (Biette *et al.* 1982: 9). But Chabrol did not regard this as a defeat. Rather, he tried to learn from the workings of popular cinema, and began to question the cult of the self-penned screenplay: 'il y a des types qui se sentent absolument honteux d'avoir à tourner le scénario d'un autre. Pourqui pas? Ça peut être intéressant, on n'est pas le seul à pouvoir écrire un scénario'[43] (*ibid.*: 10). Four of the seven films that Chabrol was to make in the aftermath of the new wave – the two *Tigres*, *Le Scandale* (1966) and *La Route de Corinthe* (1967) – were shot without any contribution to the screenplay from Chabrol or his usual scriptwriter, Paul Gégauff. But Chabrol deliberately kept his film crew together during this time, and when he emerged from his period in artistic exile it was to shoot what are probably the greatest films of his career, the superb Hélène cycle.

References

Biette, J.-C., Daney, S., Toubiana, S. (1982), Entretien avec Claude Chabrol, *Cahiers du cinéma*, 339 (September), 5–14.

Blanchet, C. (1989), *Claude Chabrol*, Paris, Rivages.

Braucourt, G. (1971), *Claude Chabrol*, Paris, Seghers: Cinéma d'aujourd'hui.

Chabrol, C. (1976), *Et pourtant je tourne ...*, Paris, Robert Laffont.

Chevrie, M., and Toubiana, S. (1986), Attention les yeux! Entretien avec Claude Chabrol, *Cahiers du cinéma*, 381 (March), 9–13.

Collet, J., and Tavernier, B. (1962), Claude Chabrol [interview], *Cahiers du cinéma*, 138 (December), 2–19.

Magny, J. (1987), *Claude Chabrol*, Paris, Cahiers du cinéma, Collection 'Auteurs'.

Marcus, M. (1986), *Italian Film in the Light of Neorealism*, Princeton, Princeton University Press.

Marker, C. (1995), A free replay (notes on *Vertigo*), *Projections* 4 1/2, London, Faber & Faber, 120–30.

Martin, M. (1975), Le Néoréalisme vu par la critique française, *Écran*, 37, 28–36.

Rohmer, R., and Chabrol, C. (1957), *Hitchcock*, translated by S. Hochman as *Hitchcock: The First Forty-Four Films*, New York, Continuum, 1988.

Truffaut, F. (1958), Si des modifications radicales n'interviennent pas, le prochain festival est condamné, *Arts*, 21 May 1958, reprinted in *Cahiers du cinéma*, Numéro spécial: Histoires de Cannes, (April 1997), 53–4.

Yakir, D. (1979), The Magical Mystery World of Claude Chabrol: An Interview, *Film Quarterly* (spring), 2–14.

43 'there are some people who feel it's absolutely shameful to have to shoot someone else's screenplay. But why not? It can be interesting. You're not the only one who can write a screenplay'

1 Dreaming of an escape into martyrdom: Jean-Claude Brialy as François in *Le Beau Serge* (1958)

2 Filming should be a laugh: Chabrol and Stéphane Audran on the set of *Juste avant la nuit* (1971)

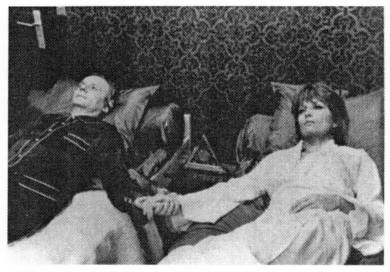

3 Which one is just – before the night? Michel Bouquet as Charles and Stéphane Audran as Hélène in *Juste avant la nuit* (1971)

4 Investigating the family: Donald Sutherland as detective Steve Carella, playing father in *Blood Relatives* (1978)

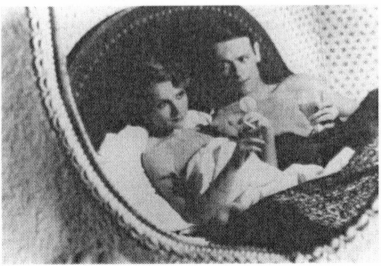

5 Violette through the looking-glass: Isabelle Huppert as Violette and Jean-François Garreaud as Jean in *Violette Nozière* (1978)

6 The gaze of the patriarch and its female object: Alan Bates as Marsfeldt and Jennifer Beales as Sonia in *Dr M* (1990)

7 Chabrol filming *Dr M* (1990) on the site of Fritz Lang's studio in Berlin

8 The servants are rising: Isabelle Huppert as Jeanne and Sandrine Bonnaire as Sophie, ascending the stairs to power in *La Cérémonie* (1995)

3

The Hélène cycle

By the mid-1960s Chabrol had, by his own admission, become the black sheep of the new wave: 'j'étais la honte, la honte de la famille'[1] (Biette *et al.* 1982: 6). His contribution to the movement, both as producer and director, was eclipsed by the apparently tawdry spectacle of the commercial films that he made after *Ophélia*. The professionalism and expertise that he lavished on spy films and outrageous thrillers between 1964 and 1967 seemed merely to confirm that he was no *auteur* but simply a director for hire. Yet his period in the wilderness served to develop his technical skill and his grasp of genres, and led directly to his mature style in the Hélène cycle of 1968–71. None the less, the intellectual press in France, and in particular *Cahiers du cinéma*, treated even this flowering of Chabrol's talent with almost as much disdain as they had shown for the espionage films a few years earlier. The dominance of Marxist, Maoist and structuralist concerns at *Cahiers du cinéma* during the late 1960s is largely to blame. Chabrol's tendency towards classical cinema – in contrast with the fashionable and more explicitly ideological experimentation of Resnais, Rivette or Godard – was considered too close to the *tradition de qualité* (the old-fashioned cinema of quality) that *Cahiers* and the new wave had always fought against. As a consequence, films as important as *Les Biches* (1967) and *La Femme infidèle* (1968) were granted barely a page and a half together, while *Cahiers* did

1 'I was the shame, the shame of the family'

not interview Chabrol once between 1962 and 1982.[2] More surprising was the widespread misreading of Chabrol's use of bourgeois settings and characters. *L'Express, Le Nouvel Observateur* and *Cahiers du cinéma* all remained blind to the sly critique of the bourgeoisie in films such as *Les Biches* and *La Femme infidèle,* choosing instead to detect in Chabrol's work a celebration of the middle classes. In a review of *Que la bête meure* (1969) for *Le Nouvel Observateur* entitled 'La bouffe et la bagnole',[3] Michel Mardore chastised Chabrol for having lost any critical distance on the bourgeoisie that he once had, and for becoming an apologist for the status quo. This represents both a breath-takingly wrong-headed interpretation of *Que la bête meure* – where, as we shall see, the ritual of 'la bouffe' is characterised as a torturous experience while 'la bagnole' is an instrument of death – and a misrepresentation of Chabrol's politics. Similarly oblivious to the ways in which Chabrol's brand of popular, classical cinema was able to undermine 'the system' from within, Pascal Kané asked in *Cahiers*: 'Beaucoup plus victime du "système" qu'il ne semble le croire, Chabrol prendra-t-il un jour ses distances?'[4] (Kané 1969: 55). The political subtext of *Les Biches* – a film which concerns the possibility of revolution against the status quo – was either too pessimistic to be greeted with approval, or was simply ignored. So too was Chabrol's contribution to the revolutionary spirit of May 1968, including Project 4, his radical proposal that cinema entry be free, uncensored, and paid for by taxation.

Chabrol's apparent willingness in the mid-1960s to compromise the supposed artistic purity and personal vision of the *auteur* became evident not just in his pursuit of commercial projects, but in his acceptance of the constraints of popular genres (spy film, thriller, melodrama) and in his continuing emphasis on the

---

2 In marked contrast, the British press, and above all *Sight and Sound,* featured long interviews and favourable reviews for Chabrol's work during the same period.

3 'Nosh and motors'

4 'One day, will Chabrol – much more a victim of "the system" than he seems to think – actually distance himself from it?'. The answer has proved to be a resounding 'no'.

collective nature of film-making. He was chastised in *Cahiers* for his reliance on generic models, seen as precluding any 'évocation d'un univers personnel'[5] (*ibid.*: 55). But Chabrol's fascination with genre remained, as did his loyalty to his film crew. The team that he had gathered around him early in his career was kept together for film after film, year after year, no matter what the project might be. Jean Rabier's photography, Pierre Jansen's music, and Jacques Gaillard's editing were thus perfected during the wilderness years in the same way that Chabrol's own directorial style was. To these were added the continued collaboration with Paul Gégauff on screenplays, and the increasing importance of Stéphane Audran, alongside actors such as Michel Bouquet, Jean Yanne, Michel Duchaussoy, Mario David, Henri Attal and Dominique Zardi. The Hélène cycle – strictly speaking, comprising *La Femme infidèle*, *Que la bête meure*, *Le Boucher*, *La Rupture* and *Juste avant la nuit* – sees Audran cast repeatedly in the central role as the often inscrutable Hélène.[6] The principal male roles, mostly incarnated by Bouquet and Yanne, repeat the contrasting figures of *Les Cousins*: the evil but charismatic Paul and the angelic, timid Charles (parodies of Gégauff and Chabrol respectively). Within the triangular relationships that result, Chabrol explores questions of identity, guilt, and class tension, with a degree of precision and craftsmanship at that point unprecedented in his career.

Les Biches

Chabrol has said that he never felt bitter about his difficulties in the 1960s, since 'J'ai d'ailleurs toujours pensé que ma véritable carrière commencerait avec la quarantaine'[7] (Braucourt 1971: 134). In 1967, at the age of 37, he found that his prediction was becoming true. Thanks to the support of the young producer André

---

5 'evocation of a personal world-view'
6 The exception here is *Que la bête meure*, in which Audran does not star. Contrary to some accounts, however, there is a Hélène in the film, played by Caroline Cellier. *Les Noces rouges*, in which Audran plays the mother of a girl called Hélène, is in some ways a coda to the cycle, as explained in Chapter 4.
7 'I've always thought that my real career would start round about the age of forty'

Génovès – who went on to finance Chabrol's next eleven films – he was able to shoot *Les Biches*, 'the first film which I made exactly as I wished' (Nogueira and Zalaffi 1971: 3). Co-written by Chabrol and Gégauff, starring Stéphane Audran in the lead role, and showing the influence of Fritz Lang (in the expressionist décor and the theme of revenge), *Les Biches* is the first film of Chabrol's mature style, and heralds the superb film-making of the Hélène cycle. It concerns the rich and manipulative Frédérique (Audran), who picks up a young pavement artist called Why (Jacqueline Sassard) in Paris and takes her home to St Tropez. A lesbian affair develops, but is complicated by the presence of Paul (Jean-Louis Trintignant), with whom both women fall in love. The uneasy *ménage à trois* is brutally put to an end when Frédérique and Paul leave for Paris. Why follows, murders Frédérique, assumes her identity, and awaits the arrival of Paul. The film has often been compared to *Les Cousins* (1958), since they both explore the power relations between two friends who are rivals in love. But there are three crucial differences. In *Les Cousins*, the rivals are male and the object of desire female – these gender roles are reversed in *Les Biches*. This allows a portrayal of female sexuality as predatory and active in the latter film, while it is passive and victimised in the former. Secondly, and as a result, where *Les Cousins* is a variant on the myth of the town mouse and the country mouse, *Les Biches* is a variant on the myth of the lesbian vampire. The third distinction is in the realm of politics: for all the explicit references to Fascism, *Les Cousins* does not lend itself to a clear political reading; *Les Biches*, on the other hand, can be justly described as a political film. As Chabrol has said, the subject 'isn't really a power struggle. It's a revolution: the replacement of one class by another' (Yakir 1979: 9).

The first motif to be introduced in *Les Biches* is the archetype of the lesbian vampire. Andréa Weiss has noted that 'the typical lesbian vampire film ... has certain fairly consistent characteristics: Gothic themes and images, large empty castles and dark, romantic landscapes, and the arrival, early in the film, of a mysterious, aristocratic figure' (Weiss 1992: 85). While the Gothic themes and settings have undergone a modernisation in Chabrol's film, they remain, in modified form: the drama of desire, possession and murder is played out in Frédérique's villa, a contemporary castle complete with obsequious servants and an array of weapons (including the poisoned dagger which Why uses at the end of the film). More explicitly generic is the characterisation of Frédérique. She is presented from the first sequence as the typically 'mysterious, aristocratic' vampire of convention. Chabrol's *mise en scène* here is unequivocal. Dressed in black boots, a long black coat and a black hat, Frédérique wanders on to the Pont des Arts, her world-weary air heightened by her pale make-up and the black kohl round her eyes. She is looking for a victim. The misty, sepia tones of the photography here and Pierre Jansen's eerie music unmistakably recall the melancholy vampire films of German expressionism. More naturalistic colour soon intervenes, but the point has been made. Even when the film leaves the horror genre (after the prologue), the relationship between Frédérique and Why is clearly vampiric, centring as it does on the theme of possession, and the appropriation of one woman by the other. At first it is Frédérique who appropriates Why – she literally buys her body. But as the narrative develops, Why gradually begins to appropriate Frédérique's clothing, jewellery, voice, sexual pleasure (the bedroom scene) and, ultimately, her identity. When she kills Frédérique (and puts on the black coat from the first sequence), the vampirisation is complete. To this extent, *Les Biches* is reminiscent of other European films of the period, such as Bergman's *Persona* (1965) or Fassbinder's *The Bitter Tears of Petra von Kant* (1972), wherein 'vampirism is suggested through the erotic relationship between two women, in which one woman takes over the personality or soul of the other' (*ibid.*). Chabrol's repeated use of mirrored compositions, and his close attention to costume in the film, underlines this exchange of personalities: as Frédérique changes from lesbian vampire to heterosexual woman, she dresses no longer in black but in white; Why makes the opposite change, from sexual innocent (in white) to lesbian vampire (in black). The *mise en scène* here would seem to suggest a demonising of lesbianism, in line with generic conventions: 'The lesbian vampire provokes anxieties in the heterosexual male spectator, only for the film to quell these anxieties and reaffirm his maleness through the vampire's violent destruction' (*ibid.*: 90). It would therefore seem that the threat of the lesbian vampire is destroyed with the murder of Frédérique. But despite first appearances, the ending of *Les Biches* goes against the grain. The film ends with continuation, not closure; the threat of the lesbian vampire is not contained but in fact renewed, since although the original (Frédérique) is killed, she is in fact no longer a lesbian (or a vampire). She has already been vampirised and replaced by the copy (Why). Frédérique is thus punished not as a judgement on her lesbianism, but because she has 'gone straight' and betrayed Why in order to fulfill her (heterosexual) love of Paul. And, as the final image of the film suggests, far from enjoying the vampire's 'violent destruction', Paul himself looks set to become her next victim.

In the 'bisexual triangle' of the archetypal lesbian vampire film, the vampire's female victim 'is usually a "nice, sweet girl" … who is merely a receptacle to assume the values' of the predatory lesbian and/or the male suitor (*ibid.*: 92). In *Les Biches*, Why certainly assumes this position. But Chabrol maps on to this archetype the question of political (rather than just sexual and moral) values. The film thus becomes a political vampire narrative about the appropriation of Frédérique's bourgeois values by the innocent and impoverished 'receptacle' that is Why. The brilliance of *Les Biches* lies in this portrayal of the *embourgeoisement* of the working classes through the metaphor of a vampire breeding new vampires. The vampirising in the film is thus doubled by class and power as well as by sex. When Frédérique first meets Why, the sexual and economic power relations between them are expressed spatially: Why kneels at Frédérique's feet, drawing does on the pavement. Leaning on the bridge, Frédérique tosses a bank note on to the ground: the vampire has bought her next victim. In this brief opening sequence, Chabrol combines the mythical power of the vampire with the economic power of money (and class: the vampire is of course an 'aristocratic figure', her victim penniless and possibly homeless). The twin themes of vampirism and *embourgeoisement* are succinctly expressed in the motif of replication which runs through *Les Biches*. In the prologue, after

Frédérique has picked up Why, they stop by the Seine to look at some prints. When Frédérique asks why two identical prints are priced differently, she is informed that the expensive one is the original and the cheap one is a copy. Crucially, Frédérique is however unable to tell them apart. The implications for the narrative are clear: in terms of politics and vampirism, the expensive original (Frédérique) will be replaced by the cheap copy (Why), without anyone (not even Paul?) being able to tell the difference.

If the episode with the print-seller functions as a clue to the development of the narrative, so too – in more explicitly political terms – does the first scene set in St Tropez. It is characteristic of Chabrol, particularly in the carefully crafted Hélène cycle, to include in his films miniature versions of the main narrative. These are often texts which operate as clues to the meaning of the film, and also as idealised models against which the behaviour of the characters is implicitly compared. The compromised revenge narrative of *Que la bête meure*, for example, is measured against Homer's *Iliad*, an idealised account of heroism and vengeance. In *Le Boucher*, Hélène's desire for romance is expressed in the form of the Balzac dictation that she gives her class, and against which Popaul can only be found wanting.[8] The idealised text in *Les Biches* is the revolutionary tract read aloud by Riais (Dominique Zardi) as Why and Frédérique approach the villa, and which concludes with the lines: 'La révolution, c'est un soulèvement, un acte de violence par lequel une classe en renverse une autre'.[9] It is against this ideal that Why's actions will be measured. At first it seems that Why is indeed planning to overthrow her bourgeois mistress: several scenes show her resentment at being treated as a sexual object-cum-servant. But as the *mise en scène* of the film makes abundantly clear, when the moment comes, Why does not achieve a true revolution. Far from overthrowing Frédérique, she copies her, wearing her clothes and speaking in her voice. In Chabrol's words, 'Why replaces Frédérique, but she does it by *becoming*

---

8 For more on these two examples, see the accounts of the two films, below, pp. 55 and 62.

9 'Revolution is an an upheaval, an act of violence by means of which one class overthrows another'

Frédérique' (Yakir 1979:9).[10] Revolution in *Les Biches* is thus simply a reiteration of the status quo, a repetition, in which the proletariat simply become the new ruling class. The point is driven home when Riais discovers Why dressed as Frédérique. To his assertion that 'Je suis un révolutionnaire, moi, quand quelque chose me déplaît, je renverse!', Why replies, 'Mais je suis très bien comme ça, moi'.[11] Her own reaction to the subservient position she finds herself in is not to revolt so much as to imitate (to become Frédérique). That Riais is in fact no revolutionary but merely a hanger-on, an annoying and parasitic dilettante, only increases the pessimism of Chabrol's political prognosis in the film. With Why simply a cheap copy of the bourgeois original, Paul a calculating social climber (trading up from Why to Frédérique), and Robègue and Riais (the intellectual revolutionaries)[12] nothing more than leeches, there seems to be no way of challenging the power of the bourgeoisie embodied by Frédérique. *Les Biches* was released in March 1968. Far from ignoring the political questions of the time, Chabrol might in fact be said to have made a very astute prediction about the outcome of the social unrest which swept France a few weeks later. For the 'events' of May 1968, although they brought about a great number of reforms, fell as far short of genuine revolution as Why does in *Les Biches*.

La Femme infidèle

The first film of the Hélène cycle, strictly speaking, is *La Femme infidèle* (1968). Charles (Michel Bouquet) is the straight-laced but decent husband and Hélène (Stéphane Audran) the inscrutable, unfaithful wife. Although there is no Paul, the role of charismatic playboy devolves to Victor (Maurice Ronet). Essentially, the triangle

10 Italics in original.
11 'I'm a revolutionary: when I don't like something, I overthrow it!' – 'But I'm fine like this'
12 Despite several evasive statements by Chabrol, it seems clear that these two characters are intended to lampoon French intellectuals of the time, and in particular Alain Robbe-Grillet ('Robègue–Riais').

established in *Les Cousins* remains, but with a twist. The male rivals are still analogous with Chabrol and Gégauff – Bouquet has said that his portrayal of Charles was based on the director's own personality – but this time Charles is the murderer not the victim.[13] The second, and more shocking twist, is that the husband's murder of his wife's lover actually resuscitates their dull marriage, and ironically reunifies their family even as he himself is taken away by the police. All the irony of this situation is captured in the superb and justly famous final shot, which will be discussed shortly. Written by Chabrol alone, *La Femme infidèle* none the less shows the influence of his three mentors, Paul Gégauff, Fritz Lang and Alfred Hitchcock. The characterisation of Charles and Victor, as we have noted, is Gégauffian. The plot also bears a resemblance, not just to the triangles of *Les Cousins* and *Les Biches* (both co-written by Gégauff), but also to another Gégauff screenplay, for René Clément's *Plein Soleil* (1959). Chabrol himself had originally wanted to film the source novel, Patricia Highsmith's *The Talented Mr Ripley*, but the rights were offered to Clément instead. The result was a cool and detached thriller which featured a typical Gégauffian anti-hero in Tom Ripley – deceitful, theatrical, but vulnerable. (The character of Ripley in *Plein Soleil* is also the spiritual father of Albin Mercier in Chabrol's *L'Oeil du malin* (1961): both men are defensive, lower-class hangers-on who are attracted by the wealth and leisure of their social 'betters'; they share a talent for manipulation and deceit, but also a vulnerability symbolised by their fear of water and inability to swim.) Like *La Femme infidèle*, Clément's *Plein soleil* features a sudden murder in everyday circumstances. In *Plein Soleil* Tom kills Phillip in mid conversation, during a casual game of poker; in *La Femme infidèle* Charles clubs Victor to death between whiskeys, also in the middle of a banal, if awkward, conversation. In both films, the complacent victim is played by Maurice Ronet. What distinguishes Chabrol's murder scene from Clément's is the exaggerated, parodic

---

13   This may explain why the Gégauffian figure is not called Paul, since Chabrol has stated that a Charles cannot be seen to kill a Paul. For more on this, see the analysis of *Que la bête meure*, below, p. 61.

banality of the conversation which precedes the murder, during which Charles asks Victor how many rooms there are in his apartment, and Victor advises Charles to move from Versailles to Neuilly. As in the excruciating pre-dinner conversation from *Que la bête meure*, the polite but meaningless small-talk of bourgeois etiquette is haunted by the threat of violence, the eruption of the same brutal desires it is designed to hold in check (Charles's murder of Victor, Paul's explosive entrance and angry outbursts).

Echoes of Hitchcock's *Psycho* (1960) have often been pointed out – and at times criticised – in the sequences of *La Femme infidèle* following Victor's murder, when Charles tries to dispose of the body.[14] A less obvious but more revealing Hitchcockian intertext is in fact *Notorious* (1946), a twisted love story which like *La Femme infidèle* centres on mutual guilt and mutual suspicion which threaten the potential happiness of a romantic couple. Chabrol wrote about the film in the book on Hitchcock he co-authored with Rohmer, and his comments throw light on the theme of speaking one's love in *La Femme infidèle*: 'The misfortune of the protagonists comes from the fact that as victims of their mutual preconceptions, they refuse to pronounce the saving "word". They fail to appreciate the virtue of this confession' (Rohmer and Chabrol 1957: 84). At the start of *La Femme infidèle*, the 'saving word' cannot be pronounced; it is blocked by Hélène's infidelity and Charles's suspicion. Thus, when he asks her if she loves him, she avoids the question. By contrast, and ironically by means of the murder of Hélène's lover, the word can be pronounced at the close of the film; hence the mutual declaration of love immediately before Charles is arrested: 'Je t'aime' – 'Je t'aime' – 'Je t'aime comme un fou'.[15] This narrative of redemption also recalls the plot of Lang's *Clash by Night* (1952), in which a marriage is saved when an unfaithful wife (May) witnesses the ferocity of her dull but decent husband Jerry's love for her, expressed by means of his violence towards her playboy lover (Earl). In Lang's film, the

---

14 Henri-Georges Clouzot's *Les Diaboliques* (1954) is also a probable influence here, as well as a precursor to *Psycho* in several respects.

15 'I love you' – 'I love you' – 'I love you madly'

murder of the lover is only figurative: May tells Jerry 'You're killing him!'; Earl becomes metaphorically dead for her soon afterwards. Chabrol takes this plot and pushes it to its logical extension, literalising the death of the lover. Characteristically for this period (reflecting the *embourgeoisement* of his settings and characters in the 1960s), he also replaces Lang's working-class, neorealist setting (a fishing village) with a deceptively glossy bourgeois setting (the family home in Versailles).

Accusations that Chabrol had become an apologist for the bourgeoisie inevitably dogged *La Femme infidèle* as they had *Les Biches* a year earlier. But although there is no exploration of class tensions in the former (the working class are completely absent, apart from very minor characters such as the housekeeper), the film is far from a simple celebration of the bourgeois lifestyle. Beneath the glossy image of Hélène and Charles's comfortable life in Versailles (including conspicuous consumption of food and drink, large house and garden, car, even the relative novelty of television) there lurks a feeling of unease. At times this is simply a question of suspense, or at others of narrative irony, as in the champagne toast to 'cette mémorable journée',[16] which Michel imagines is a celebration of his school report, but is for both Charles and Hélène a comment on her affair. But the prevailing sense of unease is also subtly and brilliantly evoked by Jean Rabier's camerawork and Jacques Gaillard's editing. *La Femme infidèle* begins with a tracking shot, from left to right, revealing a large house, with a family group gathered in the front garden: Charles, his mother, Hélène, and their son Michel, who runs up to them with a bouquet of flowers. The bourgeois family is apparently secure and idyllic. But as Charles says to his mother, 'Le moindre changement dans mon mode de vie pourrait troubler cette harmonie'.[17] In the credit sequence which follows, the seductive image of the family is blurred and then distorted beyond recognition, in a prelude to the explosion of suspicion and guilt which will shatter the illusion of harmony immediately after the credits

16   'to this memorable day'
17   'The slightest change in my lifestyle could unsettle this harmony'

(when Charles guesses the meaning of Hélène's secret phone-call). And when the status quo is threatened, it must be reasserted at any price. The camerawork, symbolism and the narrative function (alongside Charles himself) to achieve this return to harmony throughout the rest of the film. On the level of the narrative, this means that Victor, the source of the disruption, must be removed, so that Charles and Hélène can speak their love at the end. On the level of metaphor, it involves the symbolism of the missing jigsaw puzzle (the lack within the family which must be repaired) and the T.S. Eliot poem that Charles watches on television the day he follows Hélène to Victor's flat: 'Here the impossible union / Of spheres of existence is actual, / Here the past and the future / Are conquered, and reconciled'. On the level of *mise en scène*, it means that the camera movements in the film are all submitted to a similar logic of returning to the beginning. Thus the left-to-right tracking shots in the first half of the film, including the opening shot, are matched by tracking shots in the other direction in the closing stages. As Chabrol explains, this principle determined the shooting of the entire film: 'chaque mouvement est suivi de son inverse, si bien que tout finit par revenir à la même place. À chaque fois qu'il y a un travelling avant, il est suivi d'un travelling arrière ...; de même chaque panoramique gauche est suivi par un panoramique droite et ainsi de suite'[18] (Braucourt 1971: 92). Hence also the systematic use of shot / reverse-shot patterns in the dialogue scenes, and the breaking of the 180° rule,[19] for instance when Charles and Hélène embrace after the visit to the night-club.

Most unsettling are the tiny fissures in the editing, like cracks in the image of the idyllic family group at the start of the film. These miniature jump-cuts are most evident in the murder of Victor (as his body falls) and the cleaning of the blood in the sink.

18 'each [camera] movement is followed by its opposite, so that everything comes back to the point of departure. Each time there is a tracking forwards, it's followed by a tracking back; in the same way each pan to the left is followed by a pan to the right, and so on'

19 This is the classical realist convention that a scene, if shot from one side of its central axis (the 180 degree line), will not suddenly be shot from the other side (which would disrupt the construction of filmic space).

The editing of the first sequence after the credits is also troubling: as Charles bursts in on Hélène's phone conversation with Victor, the editing switches quickly and disconcertingly between a mid shot, a medium close-up, then a mid shot again, while the camera tracks rapidly from Charles to Hélène and back again. There are other scenes which suggest a latent violence or an emptiness beneath the glossy surface of the *mise en scène*: the long pause before Hélène appears in the doorway of Charles's office, or the moments, as Charles reflects on his wife's affair, when the ambient sound (traffic noises and so on) fades to be replaced by suspenseful music. These temporary disturbances are comparable to the break in the television programme that Charles watches early in the film. A message on the screen declares 'Veuillez nous excuser de cette interruption momantanée de l'image'.[20] But in *La Femme infidèle*, 'normal service' is only fully resumed in the doomed conclusion. There is a central irony here, as in *Juste avant la nuit*: bourgeois harmony, which must be preserved at all costs, is actually salvaged by murder. Thus the apparently calm and 'natural' status quo rests on behind-the-scenes violence (even if this violence is not explicitly politicised here, as it is in *Les Biches* and elsewhere). But there is an ambivalence in the film, as so often in Chabrol's work, since *La Femme infidèle* is also a dark romance, in which love is rediscovered at the last moment. This romantic element (the *Notorious* theme) is expressed by reference to another film of Hitchcock's. As Chabrol explains, the final shot in *La Femme infidèle* uses a technique which Hitchcock had developed for *Vertigo* – a simultaneous zoom forwards and tracking backwards – to show a final glimpse of Hélène and Michel, and to express the paradoxical situation in which Charles is emotionally reunited with them even as he is physically taken away from them by the police: 'C'est un plan qui se contredit lui-même! Mais c'est très beau, car c'est de là que venait ou non le happy end. Si le travelling arrière finissait avant le zoom avant, le film finissait bien puisqu'on se rapprochait de la bonne femme. Mais si le zoom avant finissait avant le travelling arrière, le film finissait mal

---

20 'We apologise for the temporary loss of picture'

puisqu'on reculait'[21] (*ibid.*: 92). The result is the most famous example of Chabrol's tendency to end his films with a moment of unsettling ambivalence rather than the expected narrative closure: 'people seem to think that the final shot explains everything when the contrary is true. It is a question mark' (Overbey 1977: 81).

Que la bête meure

Chabrol is a master of the pre-credit sequence, from the deceptively happy family group in *La Femme infidèle* to the triple suicide in *Dr M*. The twenty-shot sequence that begins *Que la bête meure* (1969) is a case in point: expressive, economical, terrible. The camera focuses on a young boy (Michel), then zooms back to show the beach where he is playing. Cut to a harbour scene with a road in the background. As a black car comes into view, a melancholy song by Brahms is heard. The car is driving very fast, from right to left. Michel begins walking in the opposite direction (the two opposing tracking shots suggest that these two movements will inevitably collide). The camera follows the car again, from right to left (a reversal of the direction of reading, of progression, hence implying death).[22] A shot of the radio as the driver changes gear shows that the song is coming from the car radio (rather implausibly, given what we will learn about the character of the driver, Paul). A shot of the road from above the speeding car shows a huge and ominous black bonnet; the top of the screen cuts off the

21 'It's a shot which contradicts itself! It's a tracking backwards with a zoom forwards! But it's very beautiful, since it's this shot which gives the film a happy ending – or not. If the tracking backwards finished before the zoom forwards, the film finished happily because you were getting nearer to the wife. But if the zoom forwards finished before the tracking back, the film finished unhappily because you were moving away.' Chabrol adds that in all three takes of this ending, the zoom finished first, so the film ends unhappily. I would suggest that the main effect, however, remains one of ambivalence. This is heightened by the question of point of view: is the camera here subjective (Charles's point of view) or objective?

22 See for example Susan Hayward's account of the right-to-left tracking shots in Varda's *Sans toit ni loi* (Hayward and Vincendeau 1987: 290).

road in the distance and the vanishing point, thus creating a sense of blindness, of ignorance in the face of fate, and also giving the impression that Paul will not see what is coming up. Michel leaves the beach and walks silently into the village. A shot of the passenger (Hélène) from the back seat; Paul puts his arm round her as the car enters the village. The sound of bells as the camera pans slowly along the village street from the church tower to Michel, walking in the middle of the road. The music is heard again, loudly, as in quick succession, the church comes into view and Hélène lurches across the car, grabbing the dashboard; Michel's face looms up; the car hits him; he falls to the ground (seen from above); Paul tells Hélène to shut up as she turns round and begins to scream. Finally, Hélène's point of view as she looks back at the scene of the accident. The sequence ends with a shot of Michel's body lying in the middle of the road as the car disappears. The shot is held, in silence. As well as the brutal fact of the accident itself (which provides the impetus for all that follows), several other things are concisely expressed here, most notably the mystery of the driver's identity (we see Hélène's face but only half of Paul's), the consequences of the crash for the two people in the car (the impact is experienced from Hélène's perspective rather than from Paul's; subsequently she will have a breakdown while he will deny that anything even took place); the sense of implacable fate and impending death (the song, the black car, the two movements that collide, the truncated shot of the road ahead, the glimpse of the church, the sound of bells). The premise of the revenge narrative, the idea of destiny and the almost inevitable process of loss – the essential themes and emotions of the film – have been expressed in less than three minutes.

The most perfect film of the accomplished Hélène cycle, *Que la bête meure* is a piece of fearful symmetry, in which terrible emotions and brutal actions are framed in a classical pattern. The emotional stakes are high, since the narrative concerns the killing of a child and the avenging of his death. The passions involved are controlled and accentuated by the poise of the *mise en scène* and the cyclical pattern of the plot. As Charles says at the close of the film, 'C'est digne d'une tragédie grecque. Un homme tue un enfant;

l'enfant de cet homme le tuera à son tour'.[23] *Que la bête meure* is in fact a Greek tragedy and a revenge narrative at once. On the one hand, the claustrophobic symmetry of the plot echoes classical drama, while the poeticising of death and revenge in Charles's diary is parodied by references to Homer's *Iliad*.[24] On the other hand, the emotions evoked, and the character of the righteous but ultimately indecisive and troubled avenger, recall Fritz Lang's *The Big Heat* (1953) and *Rancho Notorious* (1951), both of which tell 'the old story of hate, murder and revenge'.[25] But Lang and Chabrol qualify the act of revenge, so that he who confronts a beast risks becoming a beast himself. As a result, both *Que la bête meure* and *Rancho Notorious* subvert the cathartic act of vengeance on which the revenge narrative is predicated – and which takes place, for instance, in revenge westerns such as Mann's *Winchester '73* (1950). Vern in *Rancho Notorious* and Charles in *Que la bête meure* spurn opportunities to kill the men they have remorselessly hunted down. In the former case, Kinch is actually killed by Vern's friend Frenchy. In the latter, Charles may or may not kill Paul (both interpretations are possible), but the murder takes place off-screen and is therefore invisible, repressed (as were bloody events in classical tragedy). The similarities with *The Big Heat* are even clearer: like Charles in *Que la bête meure*, Bannion is caught in a circle of tragedy and repetition: destined to repeat the violence of his adversary, he is only redeemed thanks to the sacrifice of another (Debbie in *The Big Heat*, Philippe in *Que la bête meure*). In both films, the death of the hero's wife is compounded by the death (or loss) of her substitute (Debbie, Hélène). This is com-

---

23 'It's worthy of a Greek tragedy. A man kills a child; the child of that man kills him in turn.' Charles is referring here to Philippe's apparent confession to patricide. See below, p. 61, for the alternative explanation of Paul's murder.

24 James Monaco interprets these Greek allusions, and especially 'the image in *The Iliad* of a spear through the back of the head', as indicative of the 'paternal and platonic love' between Charles and Philippe. See Monaco: 1976, 273.

25 Quotation taken from the theme song of *Rancho Notorious*. There are also several echoes of *Rancho Notorious* in *Les Biches*, notably the sequences at Frédérique's villa in St Tropez, where she holds court much as Altar (Marlene Dietrich) does at the Chuck-a-Luck ranch. Riais rides Robègue at the soirée like Dietrich riding the deputy in the saloon steeple-chase.

pounded for Charles by the loss of his substitute son, Philippe. Chabrol makes several direct allusions to *The Big Heat*, notably the scene in the empty house, the enquiries at the garages, and Charles's cross-examination of Hélène about Paul (comparable to Bannion asking Debbie about Vince).

Que la bête meure pits an honourable and grieving Charles (Michel Duchaussoy) against the boorish and bullying Paul (Jean Yanne) responsible for his son's death. The apparent simplicity of the plot and the characterisation is gradually complicated, however. Charles is not above using Hélène (Caroline Cellier) as a means to enter Paul's family circle. Once there, he twice finds himself unable to kill Paul (either from cowardice or cunning, according to one's interpretation of the plot). Moreover, when Paul is at last horribly murdered, his son Philippe is either responsible for an action that Charles, for all his talk of vengeance, cannot actually commit or, just as damningly, is allowed to spend a night in the cells before Charles admits to the murder himself (again, both possibilities remain open). Ultimately, the film evokes a pervasive sense of loss, in which not just Michel but also Paul (for all his abrasiveness, a not entirely unsympathetic character), Hélène, Philippe and Charles himself are all destroyed by what has happened. Charles's final letter to Hélène emphasises the past conditional, the elegiac tense of the entire film: 'Si nous n'avions pas été emportés par tout cela, je t'aurais aimé ...'[26] The symmetry of both narrative and *mise en scène* makes this tragedy all the more apparent. Charles finds a surrogate wife in Hélène and a surrogate son in Philippe, only to lose both of them again. (The physical similarity between the two boys is striking. Michel is in fact played by Stéphane di Napoli and Philippe by his older brother, Marc.) Reminders of his dead son are everywhere, from the teddy-bear he cannot throw away to the spectral silhouette of Philippe which haunts the scene in Paul's garage. The narrative is in several ways repetitious, with the (off-screen) murder of Paul as the central point. On either side of this invisible apex, Charles loses both a

26 'If we hadn't been caught up in all this, I would have loved you.' There are three other examples of the past conditional in this short letter.

son and a wife; he watches a film about death (the home movie and the television report); he is involved in an attempt to solve a crime, in which a daring hypothesis proves to be true (Charles's suggestion to the police that the killer is a garage owner; the detective's suggestion to Charles that the diary is a deliberate alibi). To the love scene with Hélène early in the film corresponds the absence of love scene in the hotel at the end; the parallel with the former increases the sense of absence and loss in the latter. Pierre Jansen's superb, romantic music – often the soundtrack to Charles's diary entries – evokes the continuing trauma of Michel's death, since it presents a number of variations on the song from Brahms which plays during the fatal accident. There are also persistent splashes of red throughout the film, each of which recalls Michel's blood on the road at the end of the credit sequence: the pen with which Charles writes his vengeful diary, the tones of the Breton landscape, the lighting of the nightclub where he meets Hélène, the décor of Paul's living-room, the colour of Charles's sowester, and so on. Finally there is the camerawork, and in particular the use of the zoom.

Barely used before Chabrol's period of technical experimentation in the mid 1960s spy films, zooms are central to his film style in the Hélène cycle (see the final shot of *La Femme infidèle*, or the slow zoom in on the back of Hélène's head in *Le Boucher*). In *Que la bête meure*, the claustrophobic repetitions of narrative, music and *mise en scène* are mirrored by the patterning of the zooms, which tend to come in pairs, the second of which reverses the direction of the first. In other words, a zoom-in will be followed by a zoom-out, and vice versa. This is evident throughout the film, often as a means of framing a given action (when Paul slips on the clifftop, a zoom-in on Charles's face is followed by a zoom-out from the rocks below) or an entire sequence (the episode in Paul's garage is introduced by a zoom-out from a tree in blossom, and concludes with a zoom-in on the same tree). The tragic circle is completed in the sublime closing sequence, a recreation of the ending of Lang's *Moonfleet* (1955), in which a dying man leaves behind his surrogate son and sails alone into the dawn. Chabrol's film has come full circle in three ways. First, there is the return – after so many variations in the film score – of the Brahms song, the song of death. Second, the camerawork – a zoom-out from Charles as he sails away – repeats the opening shot, a zoom-out from Michel playing on the beach. And third, for the final shot, the camera actually sweeps in a huge circle over the sea before coming to rest on the crashing waves, thus encapsulating the movement of the film, and symbolising three deaths: that of Michel's mother (more or less absent from the film but present in the homonym *la mer/mère*),[27] that of Michel (who died walking home from the sea) and the potential death of Charles himself (as implied by the *Moonfleet* intertext and the quotation from Brahms: 'Il faut que la bête meure, mais l'homme aussi').[28]

This is not to say, however, that *Que la bête meure* is purely repetitious. There is a fundamental development within the film which concerns the question of perspective and identification. The pre-credit sequence, analysed above, is scrupulously objective, in that it avoids presenting the accident from any character's point of view (there is only one shot out of the twenty which is possibly identifiable as subjective: the glance back at the crossroads which may belong to Hélène; above all, Chabrol carefully avoids giving any shots from Michel's point of view). This objective style of filming, typical of Lang and of Chabrol at his most Langian, is however suspended after the credit sequence. From this point until the murder of Paul, Chabrol encourages the spectator to identify with Charles's perspective. This is facilitated by the emotive nature of Charles's position, and by the conventional use of point-of-view shots whereby we see what Charles sees. But Chabrol goes further than this in building up a subjective narration which – like Albin's story in *L'Œil du malin* – includes the use of music, commentary and camerawork. Hence the instances when Charles's diary entries are not only given in voice-over, but are also accompanied by Jansen's tragic score (based on Brahms) and by long, slow pans (usually from right to left, towards death) across the Breton countryside (itself bleak and red tinged, a pathetic fallacy to reflect Charles's state of mind). Immediately after the opening

27 *sea/mother*
28 'The beast must die, but the man also'

credits, the movement from objectivity to subjectivity is apparent: as Charles begins to write his revenge diary, we hear sombre music, and then the first entry, 'Je vais tuer un homme',[29] in voice-over. Charles's face is shot in close-up against a background of trees (moving right to left); although this is simply explained by his present situation (sat in a moving taxi), it also heralds the dramatic panoramas that will punctuate his search for the killer. There follows a shot of the taxi driver from Charles's point of view, and then in a simple but expressive movement, the camera shifts from Charles's face to the trees outside, suggesting that this landscape is to a degree subjective (the pathetic fallacy again).

Unexpectedly and crucially, although Chabrol films much of the hunt for Paul in this manner, he does not represent Paul's murder subjectively – in fact, it is not represented directly at all, while the police enquiry which follows is filmed objectively. Only in the coda – in which Charles repays Philippe's sacrifice and confession with his own – does the subjective narration (music, voice-over, slow pans) return. But the identification with Charles already established in the first half of the film enables Chabrol to pull off the major twist in the tale – Philippe's confession, and hence the possibility of two conflicting interpretations of the murder (revenge or patricide). Objectively speaking, Charles is the murderer: hence his boast to Paul that 'C'est comme si tu étais mort',[30] his hearty appetite when Paul has thrown him out and thus apparently thwarted him, and the uneasiness of Philippe's confession, during which he stares at Charles and refuses to look at the detective. But Charles's temporary connivance in Philippe's account, and the identification with Charles established by the subjective narration, encourages the spectator to make an erroneous (if plausible) interpretation and to accept Philippe's false confession in order to free Charles from guilt and imprisonment. Any confusion raised by Chabrol's remark that 'you'll never see a Charles kill a Paul' (Nogueira and Zalaffi 1971: 6) should be dispelled by two facts: first, the murder takes place off-screen, and second, Charles acts under his pen name, Marc Andrieu. In a quite brutal objective

29 'I'm going to kill a man'
30 'It's as if you were already dead'

sequence, Charles and Hélène's meal in the restaurant, the invisible murder is in fact symbolically expressed by the cutting up of a succulent roast duck. (We learn later that Paul was dying horribly from poisoning at this precise moment.) As Chabrol has written of Hitchcock, the subjective point of view is replaced by objectivity at the crucial moment in the plot (Chabrol 1976: 133–4). But by restoring Charles's perspective at the end of the film, Chabrol allows *Que la bête meure* to end with a renewed (if qualified) identification between spectator and avenger, and with a renewed (if qualified) depth of emotion. The righteous catharsis of the traditional revenge narrative is absent, but there is a sense of loss (instead of hatred) and of sacrifice (instead of triumph). The means may be the same, but Charles's subjective narration now expresses a much more poignant experience than the story he set out to tell, 'the old story of hate, murder and revenge'.

Le Boucher

Written quickly by Chabrol, simply constructed with only two main characters, *Le Boucher* was the most popular film of the Hélène cycle, and remains his most famous work to date. (The Parisian box-office figures for *Le Boucher* (1969) show 219,000 spectators, as opposed to 204,000 for *La Rupture*, 203,000 for *Que la bête meure*, and less than 200,000 for the other films of the cycle (Braucourt 1971:177). *Le Boucher* also did very well abroad, especially in the United States.) The film concerns the uneasy balance between two conflicting principles embodied by the two protagonists. On the one hand there is culture, education, civilisation, represented in the person of the schoolteacher, Mademoiselle Hélène (Stéphane Audran); and on the other nature, violence, sex and death, the hidden forces beneath the surface of society, personified by the butcher, Popaul (Jean Yanne). Although apparently schematic, this dichotomy fluctuates and surprises throughout the film. Not only are Hélène and Popaul in some ways as alike as they are opposite, but the film maintains the tentative possibility of romance and marriage between them – according to which one might see the schoolboy Charles as the potential couple's surrogate son – even after Popaul's murders come to light. The plot centres on Hélène's discovery (and ours) that Popaul is the serial killer operating in the village. The discovery is first made, then refuted, then confirmed again, by means of the lighter given to Popaul by Hélène. As Chabrol explains, the lighter is 'the only dramatic element' in the film, the marker of Popaul's guilt and the catalyst for the simple narrative pattern: '(1) The lighter is offered. (2) The lighter is found on the cliff-top [i.e. the crime scene]. So, the conclusion: it's the said lighter. (3) No, it's not the one. (4) Yes it is. So, it's very easy. I adore symmetry' (Yakir 1979: 4).

Like *Le Beau Serge* (1958), *Le Boucher* is set in a remote and enclosed French village (Sardent in the one, Trémolat in the other). The first quarter of an hour or so of *Le Boucher* is a naturalistic record of a village wedding, at which Hélène and Popaul are merely two guests among many. What emerges from this long first sequence is the centrality of marriage to the continuity of village life, and the suggestion (when they dance together, and when he serves her the roast) that the butcher and the school-teacher may follow suit. But almost immediately there are hints that things will not be that simple. Where the wedding sequence, and the theme of hope, continuity and community that it evokes, is introduced by the ringing of church bells, the second strand in the narrative – the thriller element, the theme of the traumatic past, of war and murder – is introduced by a glimpse of the war memorial and by the opening bars of Pierre Jansen's atonal score. After Hélène and Popaul stroll together through the village and then part, the camera remains fixed on the war memorial as the discordant music begins. Although the music lightens in tone and rises in pitch – in parallel with Hélène's ascent to her flat above the schoolroom – the sense of unease remains. Jansen's unsettling music returns throughout the film to underline the suspenseful or mysterious moments of the narrative – the arrival of the police, the discovery of the murder victims, and so on. Once it seems clear that he is the killer, Popaul is associated with the war memorial and the menacing music, in particular during the two nocturnal sequences when he approaches Hélène's flat. (The symmetry underlying the film is upheld here, but with a typical twist: in the first of these sequences, Popaul is seemingly proven innocent; in the second, he confesses he is guilty.) The church bells, meanwhile, are also heard repeatedly, signalling the rites of life and death (the wedding and the funeral) and structuring the everyday cycle of village existence (the time of day, the end of classes on the hour). A contrast is established between Hélène (order and continuity, the school, the church, the future of the village in the form of the children) and Popaul (the repressed violence on which Hélène's apparently tranquil order is based, the traumas and wars of the past, which spill over in the form of his reminiscences about the army and atrocities in Indochina, and ultimately in the form of the murders).

But in *Le Boucher* as in *Que la bête meure* the ostensibly simple, essentialist characterisation of the two leads is gradually broken down. Like the 'beast' played by Jean Yanne the previous year, Popaul may be a brute and a killer, but he is also a generous man who loves life (and Chabrol's favourite symbol of life, food). Hélène, although intelligent, graceful and cultured, is also presented at times as a cold, diffident figure, who has physically retreated from life, first by leaving Paris for Trémolat, second by locking herself in a tower high above the rest of the village. And to a degree, the two protagonists are comparable. Both have traumas in the past: Popaul his army experiences, Hélène a love affair ten years previously which ended in a breakdown. Neither can express their affection for the other in direct terms: Popaul does so by giving Hélène the leg of lamb and the cherries, Hélène by giving Popaul the lighter at the same time as refusing his kiss. This action is paradoxical, and as such represents Hélène's ambivalence towards Popaul, since the sexual connotations of the lighter – it lights his fire, and makes her 'une allumeuse'[31] – contradict the refusal of the kiss. (One might also compare the size of the two lighters given as gifts in *Le Boucher* and *La Femme infidèle*: the flame of Hélène's passion in the former is modest, in the latter it is exaggeratedly large.) Most crucially, and in contrast

31 'a tease'. The French word 'allumer' means to light up (a cigarette), but also to turn on (sexually).

with *La Femme infidèle* and *Notorious*, Hélène cannot kiss Popaul (in effect speaking the 'saving word' of love) until it is too late. In fact, she is only able to do so when she knows that Popaul is dying. It has been suggested in this context that Hélène's sexual frigidity recalls that of Hitchcock's Marnie (Braucourt 1971: 93). Certainly there are allusions to *Marnie* (1964) in *Le Boucher*, notably Hélène's need to bury the past by taking a new job (compare Marnie's interview at Rutland's, where she speaks of needing 'good, hard, demanding work'), her black-out at a critical moment (compare Marnie's reaction to the colour red), and her conjuring up of Popaul at the schoolroom window (compare Marnie's dream about the sailors tapping at the window because 'they want in'). But Hitchcock follows the development of a stereotypical, if warped, romance (red-blooded husband and frigid wife) to an implied point of resolution and consummation.[32] Chabrol, on the other hand, charts the tragic impossibility of such a romance. And as he himself has pointed out, sexual obsession is limited to the characters in his films, whereas it is in fact shared by Hitchcock (Jousse and Toubiana 1997: 27–8). Where Chabrol keeps Popaul's sexually motivated murders off-screen, Hitchcock cannot repress Mark's implied sexual assault on Marnie: the subsequent scene, in which Mark rescues Marnie from a suicide attempt by drowning, is shot exactly like a rape.

Although she is the object of Popaul's sexual obsession, Hélène in turn attempts to reconfigure what she knows of him to fit her own romantic desires. This is the motive behind her denial of his guilt, and her shattering relief when she is able to believe him innocent (the scene with the cherries and the lighter). The key to Hélène's romantic fantasies is provided in the early dictation sequence, during which she reads her class the following passage from Balzac while Popaul appears, as if summoned by the text, at the schoolroom window:

> En entendant ouvrir la porte de la chambre avec brusquerie, Hélène s'était levée du divan sur lequel elle reposait, mais elle vit le

32 Originally, the film was to have ended – rather like *La Femme infidèle* – with a love scene 'to be interrupted by the arrival of the police who came to arrest Marnie' (Truffaut 1984: 470).

marquis et jeta un cri de surprise. Elle était si changée qu'il fallait les yeux d'un père pour la reconnaître. Le soleil des tropiques avait embelli sa blanche figure d'un teint de brune, d'un coloris merveilleux qui lui donnait une expression de poésie, et il y respirait un air de grandeur, une fermeté majestueuse, un sentiment profond, par lequel l'âme la plus grossière devait être impressionée.[33]

The identification between the schoolmistress and Balzac's heroine is immediately apparent, and is underlined twice: first when the children laugh on hearing the heroine's name, and again when Chabrol cuts from Popaul back to Hélène at the mention of the heroine's 'coloris merveilleux'.[34] Popaul is first seen at the window when the text mentions 'les yeux d'un père'.[35] This seems to hint at voyeurism, particularly since Popaul is looking in at the children. But the last line of the dictation, after which Popaul is immediately ushered into the room by Hélène, associates him unequivocally with 'l'âme la plus grossière'.[36] This impression is confirmed when he proceeds to give Hélène a leg of lamb (rather than the expected romantic gift of flowers). None the less, in the rehearsal for the village fête, Hélène tries to recast Popaul as the archetypal romantic hero, the marquis. Popaul, like the school children but unlike Hélène, is dressed in period costume including hose and frilly cuffs. His costume presents an outward show of aristocratic refinement: ostensibly, he has become the marquis. But as it progresses, the dance sequence reveals a gulf between the two protagonists' fantasies of each other. Chabrol evokes Popaul's desire in a long, slow, subjective zoom on Hélène as the butcher watches her in silence. When she turns and, addressing the

33 'On hearing the bedroom door open abruptly, Hélène had risen from the divan where she was resting, but she then saw the marquis and gave a cry of surprise. She had changed so much that only a father's eyes would have recognised her. The tropical sun had lent her pale face an attractive tanned complexion, a marvellous colour, which gave her a poetic expression, and she radiated an air of grandeur, a majestic firmness, a deep emotion, which would have impressed the coarsest soul'

34 'marvellous colour'

35 'a father's eyes'

36 the coarsest soul'

camera, asks Popaul to join the dance, the brooding tension eases and there is a glimpse of romantic possibilities. These are swiftly shattered by what follows. Popaul's costume seems increasingly incongruous as he stumbles clumsily next to Hélène. The baroque music only heightens the absurdity and stresses how far he falls short of the figure of romantic hero. In fact, Popaul is characterised as a schoolboy rather than a potential lover (a parallel underlined here by the period costume and elsewhere by his habit of calling her 'Mademoiselle Hélène'). Hélène appears unable to swap sexual threat (butcher) for romantic ideal (marquis). Instead, she is here confronted with a seemingly desexualised and inept schoolboy (Popaul in costume), while elsewhere she will be confronted with the tragic, dying man of the closing scenes (too late), and the atavistic Cro-Magnon man (too threatening). Implicit from the opening credits onwards, this last parallel is emphasised in the central section. After the rehearsal, during which Popaul tells Hélène 'j'adore me déguiser',[37] she informs her class, on a trip to the prehistoric caves, that if Cro-Magnon man were alive today, 'Peut-être qu'il se transformerait pour vivre parmi nous, peut-être qu'il mourrait'.[38] There follows the grim proof that Popaul has yet to achieve this transformation: the discovery of the second murder victim on the cliff-top. As Hélène unwittingly suggests, it is Popaul's inability to transform himself (to submit his desires to civilised codes of behaviour) that will also result in his own death.

Ironically (and in keeping with the twisted symmetry of the film), it is in the schoolroom – the very place where she invoked the image of the romantic hero – that Hélène is finally confronted with Popaul-as-murderer. But the threat he poses is deflected in the suicide that follows. Crucially, Chabrol films Popaul from Hélène's point of view here: when she shuts her eyes in response to his approach with the knife, the screen fades to black. Consequently, as in *Que la bête meure*, the critical action is not actually shown, leaving room for different interpretations. Most logically, Popaul has stabbed himself while the screen was black. But there

37 'I love dressing up'
38 'Perhaps he would transform himself in order to live among us; perhaps he would die'

remains the suggestion that Hélène is, if not literally responsible, then at least morally responsible for his death. Not only does she shut her eyes to his desperate confession, one may infer that she fantasises his suicide, thus ultimately transforming him from threatening brute to subjugated romantic hero, and allowing her to accede to his dying demand for a kiss. Hélène also shuts her eyes in the hospital when the pulse of the red light ceases – instants before she is told Popaul is dead. As Michael Walker has noted, 'The whole section of the film between the two moments when she closes her eyes has an extra dimension – as if it were also, in some sense, her fantasy ...: an idealisation of "what might have been"' (Walker 1975: 51). As in *Que la bête meure* – which also ends with an evocation of what might have been – the symmetry of the narrative heightens the poignancy of the impossible romance. When Hélène kisses Popaul in the hospital, the spectre of that refused kiss in the woods returns, as does Popaul's hopeful comment 'J'aime bien vous regarder comme ça, avec les enfants'.[39] Just like Charles and Hélène in *Que la bête meure*, Popaul and Hélène could have loved each other (could even have had children) if they had not been carried away by more violent passions.

Chabrol defines accepted morality as 'Une règle du jeu qui arrange une classe dominante', and as a means of hiding the fact that 'Il n'est point d'âmes toutes noires, ni toutes blanches'[40] (Chabrol 1976: 53). In this context, Hélène is the good soul, the representative of dominant ideology and morality, while Popaul is the evil soul, a scapegoat for society's ills. He is the embodiment (via the psychological trauma of his war experiences, compulsively repeated in his words and his actions) of the violence which civilisation is built on but which it keeps repressed. As such, one could say that Popaul – the proletarian war veteran – is destroyed by Hélène as the official representative of the dominant class, the bourgeoisie. *Le Boucher* also bears comparison with both *La Femme infidèle* and *Juste avant la nuit* – films in which the status

---

39 'I love to look at you like this – with children'
40 'The rules of a game which suits the dominant class'; 'No soul is completely evil, nor completely good'. Chabrol adds that the concept of moral relativism is the single theme common to all his films.

quo is preserved by the absorption or repression of violence (the suicide of Popaul, the murder of Victor, the half-murder, half-suicide of Charles). But there is a difference here: the cost to Hélène. At the end of *La Femme infidèle* and *Juste avant la nuit*, Hélène is the focal point for the continuation of family life. In the former she is framed holding Michel, in the latter she is the centre of a family group (son, daughter, mother-in-law), with her dead husband already forgotten. But at the end of *Le Boucher*, Hélène is alone, faced with an uncertain future. Even if the village is now a purified community, from which the disruptive element, Popaul (like Victor in *La Femme infidèle* or Laura and Charles in *Juste avant la nuit*) has been expelled, there remains the question of Hélène's future place in it. Formally, Chabrol ends the film on another note of symmetry: 'Capri, petite île', the song from the wedding sequence, is heard over the final credits. But although the continuity of the village and its rituals is thus reiterated, Hélène herself is more removed from the life of the community than ever before. And where the film began with a series of establishing shots of Trémolat, each closer than the last, it ends with the reverse: a series of increasingly distant shots of the village in the morning mist, as if to evoke the distance that now separates Hélène (and Popaul) from the society where they first seemed to belong.

La Rupture

La Rupture (1970) crystallises the melodramatic tendencies of the Hélène cycle, and the inter-class tensions implicit in *Les Biches* and *Le Boucher*. On both counts, the film is unusually unequivocal. Chabrol's characteristic ambivalence is almost entirely absent, except – as ever – in the final shot. *La Rupture* pits absolute good against absolute evil, in the form of a custody battle between a working-class mother and her rich, megalomaniac father-in-law. The *mise en scène*, especially the expressionist use of colour, underlines this simple characterisation: warm, earthy, proletarian reds for Hélène (Stéphane Audran), cold blue and sinister black for Régnier (Michel Bouquet). It is above all the generic code of the melodrama which allows the expression of such extremes in *La Rupture*: 'The good people stay good. The villain stays bad. ... I wanted to make a melodrama, a real melodrama' (Noguiera and Zalaffi 1971: 5).

Melodrama and class are intimately related. But there are conflicting theories about the social origins of the genre. It has been linked with the proletarian entertainments of early cinema: 'Spectacle plébéien à l'origine, le cinéma s'était emparé des thèmes du feuilleton populaire et du mélodrame où se retrouvent ... hasards providentiels, magie du double (sosies, jumeaux), aventures extraordinaires, conflits oedipiens avec parâtre, marâtre, orphelins, secret de la naissance, innocence persécutée'[41] (Morin 1972: 22–3). According to others, however, 'the family whose drama the melodrama enacts is ... the bourgeois family', therefore 'The characters are neither the rulers nor the ruled, but occupy a middle ground, exercising local power, or suffering local power-lessness, within the family or the small town' (Nowell-Smith 1977: 70–1). The magical and menacing universe that Morin describes certainly seems nearer the world of *La Rupture* than the (American) small town environment identified by Nowell-Smith. Hence the presence in Chabrol's film of doubles (Sonia as 'l'autre Hélène'),[42] of Charles's Oedipal struggle with his cruel parents, of Hélène as the embodiment of persecuted innocence, and of a general air of magic and mystery, incarnated not only by the three old women (the three fates) but also by the balloon-seller and by the ghostly hand of destiny that is glimpsed in the tram-ride sequence.[43] Moreover, *La Rupture* concerns precisely those social categories absent in the bourgeois melodrama, 'the rulers' (Régnier) and 'the ruled' (Hélène). The only truly *petit bourgeois* characters are the

41 'Originally a working-class spectacle, the cinema had seized upon the themes of the popular serial and the melodrama, which combined chance happenings, the magic of the double (*doppelgängers*, twins), extraordinary adventures, Oedipal struggles with cruel father and mother figures, orphans, secrets of birth, and persecuted innocence.' For Chabrol's comments on melodramatic literature as authentically proletarian and left-wing, see Chabrol 1976: 48.

42 'the other Hélène'

43 A direct reference to Murnau's classic melodrama, *Sunrise* (1927).

Pinellis, who run the guesthouse.[44] But the assertion that 'patri-archal right is of central importance' (*ibid.*: 71) in the bourgeois melodrama is pertinent here. In fact, throughout *La Rupture* we observe patriarchal right in a literal battle with the matriarchal concerns of what has been called the maternal melodrama. In other words, the custody battle within *La Rupture* literalises a number of melodramatic motifs, both bourgeois and proletarian: not only good versus evil, but also mother versus father and more generally, the matriarchal (emotional warmth, the true family, the domestic sphere) versus the patriarchal (Régnier as the arch patriarch, Michel as his future heir and thus a potential continu-ation of his power). The central theme of the film, which holds all these strands together, is possession, in both a material sense (the custody battle, the Régnier inheritance) and also in a more occult sense (drugs, destiny, doubles).

For all the strident emotionalism, simple characterisation and melodramatic themes, *La Rupture* is as precisely structured as the rest of the Hélène cycle. It is by means of attention to narrative form and to *mise en scène* that Chabrol brings out the full impact of the melodrama. As in early melodrama, doubling is a key theme. Here it is present at the level of the narrative (the opening and penultimate sequences both concern a domestic breakfast which ends in an attack on Hélène, first by Charles, then by Paul) and above all in the characterisation. Sonia is not just disguised as Hélène late in the film, but acts as her 'evil twin' throughout. It is Sonia (who looks like Hélène even before wearing the wig) who enacts the illicit behaviour that Hélène is falsely accused of: dishonesty, slovenliness, sexual obsession, and ultimately the corruption of Élise with pornography and drugs. In a sense, Sonia is the sexualised (and hence demonised) side of Hélène, who herself, as Paul admits, is as white as the driven snow.[45] (There is also a doubling of characters from Chabrol's earlier films: when

---

44 The guesthouse is reminiscent of the *pension Vauquer* in Balzac's *Le Père Goriot*, and certain echoes of Balzac's melodramatic novel can be found in *La Rupture*.

45 Thus Hélène is the 'white woman' (desexualised mother) while Sonia is the 'red woman' (sexualised, threatening). For more on this traditional dichotomy in the representation of women, see Theweleit 1987.

Charles throws his mother down the stairs, he is revealed as an adult version of the son in *La Muette*; Monsieur Pinelli, an alcoholic since the birth of his mentally handicapped child, is an older version of Serge in *Le Beau Serge*.) As in most of his films, Chabrol uses *mise en scène* extremely effectively to externalise the characterisation. This is not just typical of Chabrol but also of melodrama, which relies on the 'externalisation of internal emotions and their embodiment within the *mise en scène* or décor' (Doane 1987: 72). In *La Rupture*, the emotions associated with the two lead characters are embodied by expressionist colour, as suggested above. For Régnier this means black and blue, signifying evil and coldness. His first appearance is notable in this respect: he enters the (largely white) children's ward wearing a black coat and tall black hat, thus resembling the archetypal villain of Victorian melodrama. (If Sonia is Hélène's evil twin, the thespian Gérard Mostelle, dressed also in black and given to melodramatic delivery and gestures, is Régnier's good twin.) For Hélène, it means warm, earthy reds and browns. Her son Michel is also associated with red, as is Charles during his convalescence, when he is clearly infantilised, and is mothered by Hélène (another example of the doubling of characters within the film).

The all-pervasive influence that Régnier exercises through his wealth is externalised in the shades of blue which seem to surround Hélène, particularly at crucial moments in the narrative. (Compare the use of blue to signify Why's descent into madness in *Les Biches* and to symbolise Philippe's oppressive and violent personality in *Une partie de plaisir*.) On her arrival at the *pension*, for instance, she is confronted by the cold and suspicious Madame Pinelli (a weak and petty character who will be influenced by Régnier's financial offer later in the film). While Hélène is framed on the right of the screen, dressed in reddish brown, with a similar-coloured background behind her, Madame Pinelli is framed on the left, dressed completely in blue, against a blue wall. Blue begins to surround Hélène from this point onwards: hence the overpowering décor of her room, the nocturnal scene where Paul makes his last desperate attempt to kidnap her, and the shot of Hélène standing alone outside Régnier's house, framed against a

dark-blue door. During the acid trip which threatens her sanity at
the close of the film, Hélène maintains an awareness of the real
threat to her son by repeating to herself the importance of the
colour blue. This insistence on colour in *La Rupture* expresses the
apparently simple conflicts of melodrama and of class war: red
versus blue, good versus evil, passion versus cunning, working
class versus upper class, and so on. It also underlines the meaning
of the quotation from Racine at the start of the film: 'Mais quelle
épaisse nuit tout à coup m'environne?'.[46] The night spoken of
here (and hinted at in the repeated shades of blue) is literalised
when Hélène is at her most vulnerable: night falls when she is
penniless and stranded at the airport. To this literal and moral
darkness is added a spatial and temporal obscurity which isolates
Hélène even further. Alone and seemingly friendless, she is in an
alien environment, a nameless town, sometime in the near
future.[47] The melodrama's typical longing for the past (expressed
in Hélène's reminiscences on the tram) is thus complemented by
a desire for spatial escape (to Paris). Because this is melodrama, it
is no surprise when Paul rather than Hélène succumbs to evil,
swallowed up by the black mirror at the end of the film. But
because this is also Chabrol, once also feels that the struggle
between Hélène and Régnier (in its socio-political implications, at
least) goes on.

Juste avant la nuit

The final film of the Hélène cycle, *Juste avant la nuit* (1971) was in
fact only made as an emergency measure, and as such brilliantly
illustrates Chabrol's pragmatism. Two weeks before shooting was
due to start on *Ten Days' Wonder*, Orson Welles – playing the male
lead – fell ill. The film was subsequently shot (with Welles but

46 'But what dark night suddenly surrounds me?' – spoken by Oreste in
   Andromaque.
47 The film is actually shot in Brussels. Hence Hélène's mantra about escaping to
   Paris. Of the future setting, Chabrol has said: 'It portrays the world as it will be
   in ten years time if ...' (Milne 1971: 9).

without the original female lead, Catherine Deneuve) in spring 1971. But in the meantime, and in order to avoid a massive loss by disbanding the waiting film crew, the producer André Génovès asked Chabrol to shoot another film from scratch. Chabrol gave Génovès three novels he considered suitable for adaptation, and Edward Atlyah's *The Thin Line* was chosen. Chabrol modified the story and then shot the film in seven weeks, in the winter of 1970–71.

Despite this far from ideal genesis, *Juste avant la nuit* provides a poignant inversion of the first film of the Hélène cycle, and functions as a conclusion to the cycle as a whole. Chabrol's robust defence of the film also serves to define its form: 'On m'a reproché de me répéter, d'avoir refait *La Femme infidèle*. Je défie bien quiconque de mettre un gant droit à la main gauche'[48] (Chabrol 1976: 175). *Juste avant la nuit* has essentially the same setting and plot as *La Femme infidèle*: a bourgeois family living in Versailles (Stéphane Audran as Hélène, Michel Bouquet as Charles) and an extra-marital affair brought to an end by Charles's murder of the lover. And each has a Hitchcockian sub-plot to fill out the narrative (the disposal of Victor's body and the affair of the thieving accountant, both reminiscent of *Psycho*).[49] But *Juste avant la nuit* inverts the central premise of the earlier film. Thus where Charles Desvallées rescues his marriage by killing Victor and feeling no guilt, Charles Masson imperils his marriage not by having an affair with Laura or even by killing her, but by feeling guilty about it. His desperate quest for judgement from his wife and his best friend (François, Laura's husband), is met with a benign acceptance and a refusal to condemn (itself perhaps a parody of Chabrol's own moral creed). In a typically ambivalent ending, Charles is killed by Hélène (possibly to prevent him from giving himself up to the police), but only after he has hinted to her that he wants to die. Consequently, where in *La Femme infidèle*, once dead, Victor is abruptly forgotten by both Charles and Hélène, in the final scene of *Juste avant la nuit* it is Charles himself who is quietly

48 'I was criticised for repeating myself, for having remade *La Femme infidèle*. I defy anybody to put a right-handed glove on their left hand'.
49 The opening sequence of *Psycho* is, moreover, replicated at the start of *Juste avant la nuit*.

erased from family history, his own mother telling Hélène 'les enfants commencent à oublier'[50] as they play happily on the beach.

Michel Bouquet has said that La Femme infidèle and Juste avant la nuit are 'deux films où Chabrol s'interroge lui-même'[51] (de Baecque 1997: 65). Bouquet's role as Charles Masson seems to represent Chabrol even more fully than his earlier performance as Charles Desvallées. Hence the physical resemblance (especially when wearing sunglasses early in the film), his 'hantise de devenir bourgeois'[52] and his desire to think of himself as an unconventional radical (he has written a novel, has a black au pair, wears paisley shirts, and above all, engages in a sadomasochistic affair with his best friend's wife). This is in a sense a version of Chabrol's own fascination with the controversial and provocative Paul Gégauff, a fascination played out in the realm of fiction by means of the collaboration with Gégauff on numerous screenplays, and in particular via the creation of the Charles and Paul characters. Although Juste avant la nuit does not exorcise Chabrol's fascination with Gégauff – that was to come three years later, with Une partie de plaisir – it does present a Chabrolian figure struggling with his Gégauffian fantasies. It is as if Charles wants to become a Paul, but then finds that he cannot maintain this change of image in reality (only in play). A poster in the advertising agency where he works declares that 'Toutes les fantaisies sont permises',[53] but this is only true as long as they remain fantasies. In his affair with Laura, and his lifestyle in general, Charles has been playing at breaking certain (rather small) taboos. But murder is a step too far. In reality, he cannot live with the consequences of his role-playing actions. The theme of gameplaying is associated explicitly with the extra-marital affair (itself parodied by the chaste game of Scrabble that Charles plays at home with Hélène). Described by Charles as 'une sorte de théâtre insensé',[54] what we see of the affair is a game of dominance and

50 'the children are starting to forget'
51 'two films where Chabrol asks questions about himself'
52 'fear of becoming bourgeois'. This is how François describes Charles in the film.
53 'All fantasies are permitted'
54 'a sort of insane play-acting'

submission, with Laura asking Charles to punish, rape and kill her. The theatrical metaphor is reiterated by the *mise en scène* throughout the film, which features the repeated use of curtains, walls or doors to frame the action. This is most explicit when the camera tracks forwards through open curtains to show François being interviewed by the police in the flat where the murder (and the affair) took place. In the subsequent sequence, the same camera movement (this time through an open doorway) reveals Charles and Hélène playing Scrabble. The visual parallel between Chabrol's filming of the illicit flat and the family home suggests a hidden similarity between them. The Massons' house – designed by François, who is an architect – although open-plan and made of glass, is none the less a place of secrets: hence Charles and Hélène's bedroom (like Laura's flat) can be screened off by means of a curtain. When, at the close of the seemingly optimistic Christmas interlude, Hélène is framed in the background, drawing the bedroom curtain (with Charles in the foreground, beside the Christmas tree), the implication is that the family secrets – the affair, the crime, and perhaps even marital sex,[55] – will be erased in order for the image of a happy family life to be preserved.

As with *Les Biches*, *La Femme infidèle* and *Le Boucher*, a political reading of *Juste avant la nuit* would centre on the preservation of the status quo by the expulsion (killing) of an unwanted element. This applies to Laura's death, but also to Charles's (although the latter is qualified by the suggestion that it might be aided suicide rather than murder). Both Laura and Charles threaten to stain the continuity of the blameless and conformist bourgeois family. Hence the discourse of guilt and innocence, expressed in metaphors of staining and cleaning, which dominates the film – as it dominates *Betty* (1992). In the very first scene, Laura wipes her kisses from Charles's face, telling him that no traces must be left. After her death, when the handkerchief she used has indeed become incriminating, Charles throws it into a drain. His overpowering sense of guilt is parodied, and associated again with dirt,

---

55 In contrast with the married couple of *La Femme infidèle*, Charles and Hélène in *Juste avant la nuit* sleep in separate beds. This only heightens the contrast in the film between partly-idealised family life and demonised, dangerous sexuality.

in the television advert for Culpa – a washing powder which, we are told, washes away evil. Ironically, it is because Hélène and François are fully prepared to whitewash his actions that Charles cannot be free from his burden of guilt, expressed by Chabrol in a number of compositions which place him behind bars, including one superb dissolve which superimposes the bars of François's gate onto a ghostly and despairing image of Charles. Ultimately confessing his crime to François, Charles declares that 'Il faut bien que je sois puni d'une façon ou d'une autre ... je ne peux pas supporter de ne pas être jugé'.[56] The Christian implications of his situation are challenged, however, by juxtaposition with the more pragmatic but materialistic values of the bourgeoisie, represented by Hélène and François, according to whom Charles's guilt is a self-indulgent and dangerous obsession which threatens all of them with scandal and tragedy. Not only is Laura's death materially useless, and dangerously dirty, but so too is Charles's guilt: hence the metaphor of the rat, which is linked with each in turn (Charles interrupts his son's story about the rat by revealing that Laura was strangled; the rat is caught in the trap in the middle of one of Charles's confessions). In this context, Charles and Laura are simply vermin to be destroyed by the clean-living bourgeoisie. Their affair associates them with sex, role-play, death and religious obsession (Laura's Catholic medallion and Charles's sense of sin): all elements which, according to Georges Bataille, conventional society considers to be transgressive and undesirable 'corps étrangers'[57] (Bataille 1970: 58). Therefore there is a need to be rid of them, even if it means murder and the rewriting of family history. Mixing metaphors, one might say that in order to live in glass houses, the bourgeoisie must appear whiter than white.

This interpretation is complicated, as usual, by Chabrol's ambivalence. Two areas in particular are open to debate: the representation of the bourgeois family and the question of Charles's death. With regard to the first, for all the cynicism and self-preservation personified by Hélène, there remains a strong sense of family unity and of friendship in the film. This is epitomised in the

56 'I must be punished one way or another. I can't bear not being judged'
57 'foreign bodies'. Italics in the original.

Christmas celebrations (in which François is included) and in the champagne toast that Hélène and Charles's mother make to 'a happy family'. As in the family compositions from *La Femme infidèle*, these scenes are undercut by the irony of terrible secrets (Hélène and Charles's affairs, Victor and Laura's deaths), but they are also to a certain extent representations of an ideal. It is in order to preserve this ideal (from which he is already absent during the champagne toast) that Charles has to die. When he makes his final confession on the beach, Hélène turns away to see a woman pushing a child in a pram. This bleak image of a lone mother corresponds to the spectral image of Charles behind bars earlier in the film: both are virtual representations of what will happen to the Masson family if Charles goes to the police. It is for this reason that the film cannot end, as did *La Femme infidèle*, with an optimistic arrest. Instead there is the pessimism of Charles's death, followed by the final image of the family group, without him, on the wintry beach. This image recalls two films by Luis Buñuel – *Un chien andalou* (1928) and *Belle de jour* (1967). If the ending of the former suggests that bourgeois marriage is like being buried in sand, Pierre and Séverine's walk on the beach in the latter has a wintry pathos which is similar to the beach scenes in *Juste avant la nuit*. Chabrol has in fact said that he and Buñuel have 'des relations identiques aux deux corps sociaux que sont la bourgeoisie et le clergé'[58] (Guérin and Jousse 1995: 30). For both directors the church, like the bourgeois family, is a subject of fascination and a target for satire. Returning to *Juste avant la nuit*, the priest's prayer at Laura's funeral is punctuated by the roar of passing traffic, just as the peasants' morning prayer in Buñuel's *Viridiana* (1961) is punctuated by the noise of lorries and cement-mixers.

As with *La Femme infidèle*, in *Juste avant la nuit* Chabrol mitigates the apparent cynicism of the ending (it is as if Charles and Victor had never existed) by introducing the theme of mutual understanding between husband and wife. The long sequence in *Juste avant la nuit* in which this understanding is reached plays on the title of the film, so that Hélène and Charles are in fact debating

---

58 'an identical position concerning the social institutions of the bourgeoisie and the clergy'

who will be 'just' before the coming of the night. When each has explained their position (Charles needing a release from his guilt but unable to confront suicide, Hélène dismissing him as acting 'comme un fou'),[59] a sudden and tacit pact seems to be reached (as it is with the burning of Victor's photo in *La Femme infidèle*), and Chabrol effects a circular tracking shot which physically encompasses both protagonists' point of view. Then Charles asks Hélène for something to make him sleep. She fills his glass with laudanum (something we have seen him do previously), but ensures that it is a fatal dose. At each gulp as he drinks the poison, she gives an involuntary start. Finally, they lie in their separate beds, holding hands (Charles in loud crimson, Hélène in innocent white). Charles asks his wife 'Fais la nuit',[60] and the image fades to black. What makes this scene, and the entire film, particularly ironic and sad, is that the love Hélène and Charles share has resulted quite simply in his death, and his disappearance from even his children's memory.

In the films of the Hélène cycle Chabrol undertakes a questioning of bourgeois values within the apparently reassuring form of classical realist cinema. There is ambivalence and disquiet here, but it is beneath the surface (the surface is glossy and appears unproblematic). But what is perhaps most unsettling about the cycle is the evasion of closure in the endings. Will Why kill Paul in *Les Biches*? Does *La Femme infidèle* end happily or not? In *Que la bête meure*, did Charles kill Paul and will he kill himself? Can Hélène ever return to her place in the village community of *Le Boucher*? Does *La Rupture* signal the end of Hélène's battle with Régnier? And in *Juste avant la nuit*, is Charles's death 'just' or not? Chabrol has said of his characteristically ambivalent endings that 'J'arrête toujours le film avant la scène finale. J'ai toujours préféré que la boucle de l'histoire ne se ferme pas complètement'[61] (Bocquet 1997: 96). The ambivalence is all the more disquieting

59 'like a madman'. Compare Charles's final statement to Hélène in *La Femme infidèle*: 'Je t'aime comme un fou [I love you madly]'.

60 'Make it dark'

61 'I always stop the film before the final scene. I've always preferred it when the story does not come completely full circle'

since Chabrol is operating within classical narrative cinema, and within the 'system' (of representation, production and distribution). This fact, and his use of popular genres (melodrama, thriller, even romance and vampire film) ensured that with the Hélène cycle Chabrol could reach (and subvert the assumptions of) a greater audience than his more experimental ex-new-wave colleagues. For instance, while Godard's *Tout va bien* (1972), although intended to attract audiences of 100,000 via the appeal of Jane Fonda and Yves Montand, was watched by only 30,000, Chabrol's *Que la bête meure*, *Le Boucher* and *La Rupture* (none of which could boast a major star) each attracted over 200,000 spectators in Paris alone (Braucourt 1971: 177). After the disappointments of the 1960s, when his films seemed to be either artistically successful (*Les Bonnes Femmes*, *L'Oeil du malin*) or commercially so (the *Tigres*, *La Ligne de démarcation*), but never both at once, the Hélène cycle brilliantly fulfilled both of these criteria, so fundamental to Chabrol's vision of cinema.

References

de Baecque, A. (1997), Une part du secret: Entretien avec Michel Bouquet, *Cahiers du cinéma*, Numéro spécial Claude Chabrol (October), 61–5.

Bataille, G. (1970), *Œuvres complètes, II: Écrits posthumes 1922–1940*, Paris, Gallimard.

Biette, J.-C., Daney, S., and Toubiana, S. (1982), Entretien avec Claude Chabrol, *Cahiers du cinéma*, 339 (September), 5–14.

Bocquet, J.-L. (1997), *L'Enfer*, d'un film l'autre, *Cahiers du cinéma*, Numéro spécial Claude Chabrol (October), 92–6.

Braucourt, G. (1971), *Claude Chabrol*, Paris, Seghers: Cinéma d'aujourd'hui.

Chabrol, C. (1976), *Et pourtant je tourne ...*, Paris, Robert Laffont.

Doane, M. A. (1987), *The Desire to Desire: The Woman's Film of the 1940s*, Bloomington, Indiana University Press.

Guérin, M.-A., and Jousse, T. (1995), Entretien avec Claude Chabrol, *Cahiers du cinéma*, 494 (September), 27–32.

Hayward, S., and Vincendeau, G. (1987), *French Film: Texts and Contexts*, London, Routledge.

Jousse, T., and Toubiana, S. (1997), Claude Chabrol de A à Z, *Cahiers du cinéma*, Numéro spécial Claude Chabrol (October), 7–31.

Kané, P. (1969), L'Organisation du désordre, *Cahiers du cinéma*, 211 (April), 53–5.

Milne, T. (1971), Songs of Innocence, *Sight and Sound*, 40:1 (winter 1970/1), 7–11.

Monaco, J. (1976), *The New Wave*, New York, Oxford University Press.

Morin, E. (1972), *Les Stars*, Paris, Éditions du Seuil, 3rd edn.

Nogueira, R., and Zalaffi, N. (1971), Chabrol [interview], *Sight and Sound*, 40:1 (winter 1970/1), 3–6.

Nowell-Smith, G. (1977), Minelli and Melodrama, *Screen*, 18: 2, 113–18, reprinted in C. Gledhill (ed.), *Home is Where the Heart Is: Studies in Melodrama and the Woman's Film*, London, BFI, 1987, 70–4.

Overbey, D. (1977), Chabrol: Game of Mirrors [interview], *Sight and Sound*, 46: 2 (spring), 78–81.

Rohmer, E., and Chabrol, C. (1957), *Hitchcock*, translated by S. Hochman as *Hitchcock: The First Forty-Four Films*, New York, Continuum, 1988.

Theweleit, K. (1987), *Male Fantasies, I: Women, Floods, Bodies, History*, Cambridge, Polity Press.

Truffaut, F. (1984), *Hitchcock*, London, Paladin.

Walker, M. (1975), Claude Chabrol: Into the Seventies, *Movie*, 20 (spring), 44–64.

Weiss, A. (1992), *Vampires and Violets: Lesbians in the Cinema*, London, Jonathan Cape.

Yakir, D. (1979), The Magical Mystery World of Claude Chabrol: An Interview, *Film Quarterly* (spring), 2–14.

4

Family plots

Chabrol's depiction of the middle classes usually concentrates on the family. The rituals of the bourgeois household, above all those of the dinner table, are the focus for his dissection of manners and morals in *A double tour* (1959), *La Muette* (1965), *La Femme infidèle* (1968) and *Que la bête meure* (1969). If the Hélène cycle as a whole tends to balance satire with idealisation, *La Muette* presents a resolutely satirical picture of the bourgeois family. This short film stars Chabrol and his wife, Stéphane Audran, as wealthy and egocentric parents who continually ignore their young son. (It is thus a preparatory sketch for the family crisis in *La Femme infidèle*.) Chabrol and Audran overact with relish, exaggerating the grotesque and self-obsessed nature of their characters. When the son returns home from school, his mother appears to ask him a number of questions about his day, until we see that she is actually speaking on the phone to a friend. The son is equally marginalised in the dinner scene, from which he seems at first to be absent (the focus is on the father's unsavoury manners) until a slight shift of the camera reveals him sitting silently at the table. The satire ends with deliberate malice as the son, having been ignored for so long, stuffs his ears so that he won't have to listen to his parents any longer; in the final scene, his mother falls down the stairs but he is unable to hear her dying cries and walks innocently out of the house.

As we saw in the last chapter, *La Rupture* (1970) is in several ways a sequel to *La Muette*, not least in its entirely negative portrayal of the *grande bourgeoisie*, here represented by the powerful Régnier household with whom the 'uneducated' and 'vulgar' ex-stripper and barmaid Hélène is engaged in a custody battle which seems more like class war. It is however in a number of films made after the Hélène cycle that Chabrol develops his depiction of the bourgeois family. In particular, the 1970s saw him repeatedly address the role of fathers within the family. Where the melodrama is traditionally associated with representations of motherhood, and is used by Chabrol to address questions of maternity in *La Rupture* and again later in *Une affaire de femmes* (1988), the thriller – with its conventional emphasis on male figures of authority – is the generic vehicle for most of the explorations of fatherhood we are about to consider.

Ten Days' Wonder

Ten Days' Wonder (1971) (also known as *La Décade prodigieuse*) invokes that basic paradigm of family tensions and of mystery thrillers, the Oedipus myth. Although it features a Charles, a Paul and an Hélène, it represents a break with the Hélène cycle in several ways. Filmed in English, with two major American stars in Orson Welles and Anthony Perkins, it concentrates not on any rivalry between Paul and Charles for Hélène, but on the nature of patriarchal authority, embodied by the omnipotent and tyrannical *pater familias*, Theo van Horn (Orson Welles). It is thus the first in a series of films – including *Les Noces rouges* (1973), *Une partie de plaisir* (1975), *Blood Relatives* (1978) and *Poulet au vinaigre* (1985) – which explore paternal role models (usually to find them wanting). Moreover, in the character of Paul Régis – a detective in the Ellery Queen source novel, recast by Chabrol as a philosophy professor – *Ten Days' Wonder* introduces the prototype of the detective-as-surrogate-father, a character who reappears in a less compromised form as Steve Carella in *Blood Relatives*, and as Jean Lavardin in *Poulet au vinaigre* and its film and television sequels.

Ten Days' Wonder has been described as 'the screen's first theological thriller' (Dawson 1972: 227). It concerns the machinations

of the powerful and god-like Theo to destroy his son Charles
(Perkins) in revenge for having an affair with Theo's wife, Hélène.
The outsider in this neurotic household, Paul (Michel Piccoli), is
just another pawn in Theo's plan – an intellectual called in to
witness Charles's erratic behaviour and the fascinating pattern of
his supposed crimes (Theo frames Charles so that it appears as if
he has broken each of the Ten Commandments in turn). The
Oedipal triangle in the film centres on father–son tensions rather
than mother–son incest (in fact, there is no incest as such, since
Hélène is Charles's step-mother). Theo is characterised as both
Zeus and the vengeful God of the Old Testament, while Charles
becomes alternatively Oedipus, Adam (naked in the garden with
Hélène as Eve) and Christ (abandoned by his father at the time of
his despair, and dying in a suicide which looks like a crucifixion).
Father–son relations in the film are also articulated by reference
to the work of Franz Kafka. Hence the stern, unforgiving father
and the rebellious yet timid and deeply unhappy son. Georges
Bataille has observed that 'Kafka wanted to entitle his entire work
"Attempts to escape the paternal sphere" ... What he really wanted
was to live within the paternal sphere – *as an exile*'[1] (Bataille 1990:
156–7). This expresses Charles's dilemma: striving to break free
from the authoritarian father, yet also in awe of him, declaring
that 'He gave me all he had.' A potential escape route is provided
by Paul, a rational, atheistic surrogate father who was responsible
in the past for breaking down Charles's faith and his fixation with
Theo ('I took your God away'). But although Charles and Paul are
identified with each other through dress, and later through the
one's confession to the other, Charles is unable – or unwilling – to
escape the paternal sphere. He chooses to return to the paternal
home from the alienating freedom of Paris. And once there, it is
ironically Paul just as much as Theo who drives him to his death.
The Kafkaesque resonance of *Ten Days' Wonder*, from the opening
scene of Charles waking in the hotel room to the central father–
son relationship, is enhanced by Chabrol's casting. The pairing of
Welles and Perkins evokes Welles's 1962 film of *The Trial*, in

1 Italics in original.

which Perkins plays the victimised Joseph K., while Welles himself is an omnipotent presence, both on and off-screen, in his role as the advocate (associated with 'the scriptures of the Law' just as Theo is with the Old Testament) and as the film's *auteur*. Welles's instantly recognisable voice closes *The Trial* – with the supreme *auteurist* statement 'I played the Advocate, and wrote and directed this film: my name is Orson Welles' – just as it introduces *Ten Days' Wonder*.

The *mise en scène* of *Ten Days' Wonder* is almost exaggeratedly baroque, with ornate camera movements, luscious photography and opulent décor. The action tends to be bathed in blue light (the opening sequence in Paris, the exterior and nocturnal scenes in Alsace) or set in heavily stylised and predominantly blue interiors (the van Horn mansion; the hotels where the blackmail sub-plot develops). These characteristics recall the formal *mise en scène* of the Hélène cycle generally, and specifically Chabrol's use of colour in *La Rupture*. Theo van Horn's all-pervasive patriarchal presence is expressed, even in his absence, by the ubiquitous colour blue, as is Régnier's in *La Rupture* and, later, Philippe's in *Une partie de plaisir*. Thus even when Charles van Horn is in Paris, miles from his father, he – and indeed the entire city – is shadowed in blue light, just as Hélène staying in the guesthouse is still subject to Régnier's influence, symbolised by the overpowering blue décor of her room. (Moreover, the blue décor of the hotels in *Ten Days' Wonder*, as much as the enigmatic voice on the telephone, suggests that Theo is the unseen blackmailer.) In some ways an exaggeration of Welles himself, Theo can also be seen as a hyperbolic parody of Chabrol-as-*auteur*, indulging his omnipotence in the manipulation of characters and the weaving of events into a formal pattern. In his later films on a paternal theme – notably *Blood Relatives* and *Poulet au vinaigre* – Chabrol uses the figure of the detective as a kind of alter ego. But in *Ten Days' Wonder*, Paul is far too compromised, both as a truth-seeking investigator and as a surrogate father, to fulfil that role. Asked by Charles and Hélène to listen to their confession but not to judge them, he cannot prevent himself from making a (disastrously wrong) judgement. Seduced by the formal pattern of the crimes he has witnessed,

Paul convinces Charles that he is guilty of Hélène's murder and thus provokes his suicide. When, a year later, Paul realises his mistake, he has to accept responsibility for Hélène and Charles's deaths. Like Theo, he too has been 'sitting in judgement on [his] puppets below'. Where in *Poulet au vinaigre* the detective will free his surrogate son from guilt by absolving him of a murder he did commit, in *Ten Days' Wonder* the detective kills his surrogate son by condemning him for a murder he did not.

Les Noces rouges

As we saw with regard to *Juste avant la nuit* (1971), Chabrol has compared his own attitude to the bourgeoisie with that of the surrealist film-maker Luis Buñuel. In 1972, Chabrol's wife, Stéphane Audran, appeared in Buñuel's *Le Charme discret de la bourgeoisie*, a satire about six well-heeled characters in search of a dinner party. Audran has said that after this film, she started telling Chabrol how Buñuel would have tackled a given scene: 'Je comparais: "Tiens, Buñuel aurait fait ci. Tiens, Buñuel aurait fait ça"'[2] (Grassin and Bernard 1991: 58). Whether as a result of his wife's prompting or not, when in 1973 Chabrol wrote and filmed *Les Noces rouges* (1973), he made it a satire on the bourgeoisie very much in the manner of Buñuel. The film stars four of the cast of *Le Charme discret de la bourgeoisie*, and combines a thriller plot derived from a real-life case (the Bourganeuf murders) with the portrayal of a corrupt Gaullist mayor. The film's release was delayed, on the pretext that it might prejudice the Bourganeuf murder trial. But as Chabrol points out, as soon as the elections of April 1973 had taken place, the film was mysteriously released (Chabrol 1976: 176). In fact, *Les Noces rouges* works most success-fully neither as a political comment nor as a realistic thriller, but as a satire on bourgeois adultery and as a hyperbolic version of *Le Charme discret de la bourgeoisie*.

---

2 'I used to compare: "Buñuel would have done it like this. Buñuel would have done it like that."'

In Buñuel's film, Stéphane Audran and Jean-Pierre Cassel (Paul Thomas from *La Rupture*) play Madame and Monsieur Sénéchal, a couple caught between the codes of bourgeois behaviour and the desires that lie underneath. Early in the film they ignore their newly arrived guests and climb down a trellis in order to have sex in the garden. When they return, brushing grass from their clothes and hair, their guests have disappeared (to be replaced by a bishop seeking a job as a gardener). In a later scene, Madame Thévenot (Delphine Seyrig) and the Ambassador of Miranda (Fernando Rey) engage in frantic foreplay under Monsieur Thévenot's nose. Both of these sequences are echoed in exaggerated form by the frenetic bourgeois adultery of *Les Noces rouges*. Saddled with undesirable partners (an impotent husband and a sickly wife), Lucienne (Audran) and Pierre (Michel Piccoli, the corrupt government minister in *Le Charme discret*), embark on a passionate affair. Chabrol increases the absurdity of this situation in several ways. Firstly, Lucienne's husband Paul (Claude Piéplu, the colonel from *Le Charme discret*) is the local mayor and also Pierre's boss. Hence the comic scene in which, immediately after the lovers have sex in the drawing-room of a château, Pierre has to sit next to Paul at a meeting while the mayor blames the desecration of the château on teenage tearaways. Moreover, Audran and Piccoli overact furiously in their love scenes, while Chabrol tends to shoot their affair with suspenseful music and sudden tracking shots. The sex scenes are never private and are often outside, as in the consummation of the affair by the lakeside, when Lucienne and Pierre are forced to hide in the bushes while a boat approaches. Chabrol had hinted at the farcical nature of bourgeois adultery in *La Muette*, where he himself played a *père de famille* having an affair with the maid. At the time, he remarked that 'il y a tout le côté folie sexuelle de la bourgeoisie. Les "folies bourgeoises", on pense que c'est de la rigolade, mais c'est vrai!'[3] (Braucourt 1971: 112). In the first half of *Les Noces rouges*, these 'folies bourgeoises' are more evident and more ridiculous than anywhere else in Chabrol's work.[4]

3 'there is the entire question of the bourgeoisie's mad sexual passion. You might think that "bourgeois passion" is a just a joke, but it's true!'

4 Except perhaps for the film of the same title. See below for an analysis of *Folies bourgeoises* (1976).

After Pierre kills his wife and Paul finds out about Lucienne's affair, *Les Noces rouges* changes in tone. Farce is swapped for suspense as the three central characters engage in a battle of wills. The shifting power relations of the Hélène cycle are again in evidence, as when Paul, to all intents and purposes an impotent cuckold, suddenly thanks Lucienne and Pierre for their 'discretion' and uses his new-found knowledge of their affair to blackmail Pierre into backing a crooked land deal. Although Paul is ultimately murdered as a result (in a fake car accident inspired – like the Bourganeuf murders – by James Cain's *The Postman Always Rings Twice*), from this moment on he is no longer a figure of fun. The impression created by the earlier sequences (in which he bounds across the lawn like a buffoon, or snores loudly on the couch) is qualified once it becomes clear how cleverly he has manipulated those around him. But those earlier scenes (in particular the shot of him snoring while his wife and daughter laugh at him) also reveal the weakness of Paul's position within his own family.

Far from being the authoritative father figure that a Gaullist mayor should be, and that Theo van Horn epitomises in *Ten Days' Wonder*, Paul is the butt of the family. This is partly because Hélène (Eliana de Santis) is only his step-daughter. But it is also because he represents a bourgeois pomposity that Lucienne and Hélène have both largely escaped, thanks to their lower social origins. Their alliance against Paul is both a light-hearted version of Pierre and Lucienne's murderous plot against him and a reminder of the closeness that, for Chabrol, characterises a non-bourgeois family. When Lucienne and her daughter sit together arm in arm on the couch to watch television, one is reminded of Chabrol's great affection for 'real' families: 'The bourgeois family is a farce, you realise? It doesn't exist. But a *real* family, that is something wonderful' (Nogueira and Zalaffi 1970: 6).[5] The 'real' family is personified by Hélène in *La Rupture*, and is also hinted at in the closing images of *La Femme infidèle* and *Juste avant la nuit*. Each time, the focus is on the mother. Father figures, however, are more problematic. At the end of *La Femme infidèle*, Hélène stands holding Michel while Charles is emotionally present but physically

5 Italics in original.

absent, as expressed in the *Vertigo* shot. The Paul of *Que la bête meure* terrorises his wife and son; even in his absence, the family group is frozen, awaiting his arrival with trepidation. And at the start of *La Rupture*, Hélène must literally fight Charles to protect Michel. For the rest of the film, Charles is incapacitated and replaced by his own father, the megalomaniac Régnier. In *Les Noces rouges*, Hélène again embodies the true family, but here she is the daughter not the mother (Eliana de Santis not Stéphane Audran). The father is again either absent (Hélène's biological father) or virtual (Paul, the step-father). If Pierre represents a potential second step-father after Paul's murder, it is Hélène who curtails this possibility by innocently bringing Lucienne and Pierre's affair to the attention of the police. By invoking the truthfulness of the 'real' family (which has characterised her relationship with her mother up to this point), Hélène destroys Lucienne and punishes her for lying about her 'folies bourgeoises' with Pierre.

Nada

In contrast with *Ten Days' Wonder* and *Les Noces rouges*, Chabrol's subsequent film does not concern murderous bourgeois families. Indeed, *Nada* (1974) might be said to posit a radical alternative to the family group: the terrorist cell. A group of left-wingers and anarchists, calling themselves Nada, kidnap the American ambassador in Paris. In the bloody police siege that follows, the ambassador and all but two of the terrorists are killed. But before the siege begins, an alternative family seems to be established at the gang's hide-out in the countryside. Chabrol contrasts almost idyllic pastoral sequences (the tentative affair between Epaulard and Cash, images of rabbits and wheatfields) with the violent urban world that has been temporarily left behind: police brutality, suicide, paranoia. The treatment of Epaulard and Cash also contrasts with the absurd but murderous passion of Lucienne and Pierre in *Les Noces rouges*. Here, the affair is tender and poignant; it is not even consummated. But apart from this brief interlude, there is in fact no mutual understanding among the terrorists. From the beginning, they act from different motives (desperation at the everyday struggle of living, fatalistic despair, revolutionary anger, drunken self-hatred), and even before the kidnap, the intellectual of the group, Treuffais (Michel Duchaussoy) pulls out. The gradual fragmentation of the group, their bloody destruction one by one, and the persistent comparison Chabrol establishes between their violent and confused actions and those of the police against whom they are fighting, all heighten the sense of nihilism implied by the title. Moreover, as one might expect, Chabrol portrays the state security apparatus as both farcical and chilling. If, in Buñuel's *Le Charme discret de la bourgeoisie*, the cynical political manoeuvrings of the Ministre de l'Intérieur are comically elided (drowned out by the noise of aeroplanes and typewriters), in *Nada*, Chabrol shows them at length. Ultimately, *Nada* also shows the recuperation of terror by the state, as predicted by Treuffais's manifesto assertion that 'le térrorisme gauchiste et le térrorisme étatique sont les deux mâchoires du même piège à cons'.[6]

Chabrol had already suggested in the Hélène cycle that murder cannot shake the social status quo. In his own words, 'The state is the master of he who destroys it, not its supporters. Another phrase which applies to *Nada* is: the state prefers its own destruction, and the death of all, to the revolution' (Yakir 1979: 9). By the end of the film, the French state has turned the murder of the American ambassador and the very existence of the Nada group to its own political advantage. Indeed, as the Assistant Minister explains, allowing the terrorists to kill the ambassador both alienates potential left-wing support for Nada and allows the government to replace the American with a more amenable candidate. This picture of the state's power to assimilate and neutralise its enemies recalls the theories of Jean Baudrillard. In *Le Miroir de la production*, published the year that *Nada* was filmed, Baudrillard describes France (and capitalist society in general) as characterised by 'la logique de l'appropriation, l'impossibilité de la dépense,

6 'leftist terrorism and state terrorism are the twin jaws of the same trap'

du don, de la perte, l'inexorabilité de la loi de la valeur'[7] (Baudrillard 1973: 125). In such a society, even death and terrorism are recuperable, and only revolution is not. The revolution, however, never happens: it is indefinitely deferred, as in *Nada*, where the kidnapping is merely the means to raise money for a potential uprising at some time in the future. And even if it were to take place eventually, would not the new order be reminiscent of the old? As Chabrol has said of *Les Biches*, 'It's a revolution: the replacement of one class by another – Why replaces Frédérique, but she does it by *becoming* Frédérique' (Yakir 1979: 9).[8]

Nada is not, however, quite as nihilistic as first appears. Chabrol does not go as far as Buñuel in dismissing all ideologies as equally futile. In *Le Charme discret de la bourgeoisie*, Florence points out that the rallying sign for the feminist movement is 'un signe idiot, comme tous les autres: fasciste, communiste, victoire, et le Christ est notre maître'.[9] Similarly, the acronyms of the fictional terrorist groups cited at the end of Buñuel's *Cet obscur objet du désir* (1977) are all equally ludicrous: POP, PRIC, GRIF, RUT, GAREJ, PAF and STIC. Chabrol, by contrast, does not laugh at the Nada group. Their principles are right, it is their terrorist practices which are wrong. This becomes clear when Diaz (Fabio Testi), having escaped from the siege, tapes a message to the press reiterating Treuffais's manifesto and renouncing terrorism as a mistake, an action 'consumable' by the state. Chabrol's *mise en scène* here is suggestive: Diaz wears white, not his usual nihilistic black, as he tapes his statement (see Milne 1974). In the finale that follows, Diaz is confronted by the police chief Goemond (Michel Aumont). The latter has taken a hostage of his own, Treuffais, and anticipates that Diaz will kill his former colleague in response to a rumour that Treuffais is a police informer. This eventuality would only confirm Treuffais's pessimistic prediction with a brutal

7 'the logic of appropriation, the impossibility of spending, of giving, of losing, and the relentless nature of the law of value'. Compare Chabrol on the political films of Costa-Gavras: 'Tout est récupéré [everything is recuperated]' (Chabrol 1976: 319).

8 Italics in original.

9 'an idiotic sign, like all the others: Fascist, Communist, Victory, and Christ is our lord'

irony: he himself would become the victim of violence at the hands of both the state and the terrorists. But Diaz's final act is to kill Goemond and save Treuffais, at the cost of his own life. The pragmatism and solidarity celebrated in this ending seem to reflect Chabrol's own ideology of the time, as explained to *La Revue du cinéma* in December 1973: 'je me borne à accepter des dogmes pour des temps limités: par exemple, en ce moment, je me dis qu'après tout, le marxisme–léninisme n'est pas plus con qu'autre chose ...! Donc, partons de celle-ci en ne se faisant aucune espèce d'illusion'[10] (Magny 1987: 124). Two decades later, after the fall of the Berlin Wall and the supposed death of Marxism, Chabrol was to resume, playfully, this position with *La Cérémonie* (1995).[11]

Les Innocents aux mains sales; Folies bourgeoises

Les Innocents aux mains sales (1975) shares with *Les Noces rouges* a plot derived from *The Postman Always Rings Twice*, elements of farce, a concern with sexual power and impotence, and actors fresh from working with Buñuel. Here, the latter play minor characters: both François Maistre (the detective Damy) and Jean Rochefort (the aptly named lawyer, Albert Légal) had appeared the year before in Buñuel's *Le Fantôme de la liberté* (1974). Their droll commentaries and eccentricities lend Chabrol's film a farcical edge, which is particularly strong in the pairing of Maistre and Pierre Santini as two comic detectives. Moreover, the phone conversation gag at the end of the film is taken directly from *Le Charme discret de la bourgeoisie*, where again it features Maistre as an incredulous policeman. But the comedy in *Les Innocents aux mains sales* remains peripheral to the central plot, a convoluted and blackly ironic story of adultery and murder. For all its comedy turns, *Les Innocents aux mains sales* is also a *film noir*.

10 'I limit myself to accepting a dogma for a certain length of time only: for example, at the moment, I tell myself that a Marxist–Leninist position is, after all, no more stupid than any other! So, let's start from that position, without having any illusions about it'
11 See Chapter 7.

Although it can be defined, historically speaking, as a film movement limited to Hollywood in the 1940s, *film noir* has proved extremely influential on subsequent generations of film-makers, including those of the French new wave. The main legacy of *film noir* is found in certain character types – the vulnerable and confused private eye, the seductive but dangerous *femme fatale* – and in the use of expressionism – looming shadows, unsettling camera angles – to evoke a chaotic and amoral universe. *Film noir* 'founds itself upon the absence of the family', and presents 'family relations as broken, perverted, peripheral or impossible' (Harvey 1980: 25). It is peopled by impotent or crippled husbands and childless couples (*ibid.*: 29, 33). In short, the family in *film noir* is a sterile and sick place. For wanting to escape this claustrophobic, desexualised family space and to fulfill her own ambitions (be they sexual or economic), the strong woman (the *femme fatale*) is usually condemned to imprisonment, suffering or death. Even this brief account of *film noir* conventions suggests how closely *Les Innocents aux mains sales* follows the model. In fact, Chabrol's film could be described as an exaggerated version of *film noir* – or rather, a hybrid of *film noir* and farce, in which each genre competes with the other. The film centres on a childless couple – a rarity in Chabrol's work – made up of an alcoholic and impotent husband, Louis (Rod Steiger), and his beautiful, unsatisfied wife Julie (Romy Schneider). From the start, the emphasis is on Louis's powerlessness and Julie's sexual power. When a handsome young stranger, Jeff, enters their lives, Julie fulfils her potential as *femme fatale* and decides to murder her husband. (She is filmed in a typical expressionist composition at one point, with the shadows of trees looming around her, signalling duplicity and menace.)[12] After a series of convoluted plot twists, Louis dies, Jeff is arrested and Julie is punished for her transgression. As the genre demands, Chabrol's film 'damns the sexual woman and all who become enmeshed by her' (Place 1980: 36).

As the film develops, so too does Julie's suffering: Louis's apparent death is followed by Jeff's disappearance. Julie finds herself confronted by a series of men (Légal, the detectives, Georges)

12 This image is in fact taken from Clouzot's *film noir Le Corbeau* (1943).

intent on mocking her grief for her husband's death, and on testing its sincerity. The final test is provided by Louis himself, miraculously back from the dead. In one of Chabrol's blackest ironies, no sooner has Julie passed this test – reversing her earlier choice of Jeff over Louis, and choosing to stand by the husband she had attempted to murder – than she is denied her second chance by Louis's second death. (A real death from a real heart attack, rather than the fake death and the fake heart trouble that Louis had simulated at the start of the film.) The film concludes with Julie grieving, friendless and alone. Her husband's wealth is now hers, but it has become meaningless. And in an echo of Cain's *The Postman Always Rings Twice*, having originally been found innocent of her genuine attempt to murder Louis, she is now implicated in his accidental death. The final sequence formally marks a return to the beginning. *Les Innocents aux mains sales* began with a left-to-right tracking shot across the coastal land- scape to Julie and Louis's villa, the camera movement expressing Jeff's invasion of the couple's crumbling private space. Chabrol begins the final scene with an identical camera movement but this time at night, tracking from the distant lamp of the lighthouse to the silent villa. Is the lighthouse calling to Julie somehow, or is she hearing the voice of her dead husband? Her face illuminated and livid against a black background, she rises from the couch, and with a kind of traumatised composure walks into the night towards the flashing white light of the lighthouse. The camera tracks forwards into darkness and the light is fixed in a freeze- frame as the credits begin. In this hallucinatory moment, Julie and Louis have become comparable with the tragically separated couples at the end of *La Femme infidèle*, *Le Boucher*, and *Folies bour- geoises*, and are in stark contrast with the adulterers so absurdly and literally shackled to each other in the final shot of *Les Noces rouges*. But Julie's isolation and imprisonment here remains a punishment, an excessive version of the typical *film noir* ending in which the *femme fatale* 'must be confined' (*ibid.*: 46). It is excessive and poignantly ironic because Julie – unlike, say, the *femme fatale* in *Mildred Pierce* (1945) – has no husband to return to, yet wishes she had.

Like *Les Noces rouges*, and many of Chabrol's films since *Les Biches* in 1967, *Les Innocents aux mains sales* explores the changing power relations within a triangle of characters. A new edge is provided not only by the exceptional number of twists in the plot, but also by the erotic charge of the film. *Les Innocents aux mains sales* is about sexual power, and conveys this with as much eroticism as anything in Chabrol, whose habitually reserved representation of sex has been commented on by critics (Wood and Walker 1970: 104). Although sexual power at first resides with the *femme fatale*, it is later transferred to her once-impotent husband. The key to the depiction of desire in the film is scopophilia, the power of the gaze. Hence where Paul, the cuckolded and impotent husband in *Les Noces rouges*, regains his control over his wife and her lover by means of political blackmail, in *Les Innocents aux mains sales* Louis does so simply by spying on them. And although both men end up dead, Paul dies without ever having regained his sexual potency, while Louis achieves a complete sexual rebirth through voyeurism. As he tells Julie on his return from the grave, Jeff and Julie's plan to murder him has in fact only resulted in his rejuvenation: 'grâce à vous je suis vivant. Et j'aime la vie.'[13] Cured of his impotence, he proceeds to institute 'des relations nouvelles'[14] in their marriage and, for all his cynicism and cruelty (he pays Julie to have sex with him), he thereby cements a new bond of sexual and emotional depth between husband and wife. The real mystery in the film is ultimately not the startling reappearance of first Louis and then Jeff when each was supposed dead, but the restoration of Louis's sexual power through the act of looking.

The theme of sexual predation and Julie's status as the object of male desire is expressed in the first scene, where Jeff's kite (a red bird of prey) lands suggestively on her as she lies sunbathing naked. This is followed by Jeff's visit to the couple's home in the evening. Both of these scenes end with a close-up of Julie's naked back as the opening credits roll. Finally, the third and crucial part of the credit sequence sees a brief and, it is later revealed,

13 'thanks to you two, I'm alive. And I love life'
14 'a new relationship'

deliberately exaggerated exposition of Louis's impotence and alcoholism in front of Jeff. Once Louis has staggered upstairs to bed, Jeff and Julie have sex on the rug, during which Chabrol's signature ('Un film de Claude Chabrol')[15] is superimposed on a facial close-up of the two lovers. What makes this last scene so important to the plot of the film and indeed to an appreciation of Chabrol's film-making technique in general, is the nature of the camera shot used. As Julie walks on to the rug and lies down on it, pulling her dress up over her thighs, Chabrol shoots from a high angle not used before in the film. Moreover, he zooms in on Julie's face as Jeff climbs on top of her and they begin to have sex. Both the intensity of the zoom (suggesting heightened emotion of some kind) and the precise angle of the shot (seemingly filmed from the top of the staircase) may appear just a little curious, but none the less the impression remains that the scene is still being shot objectively, from the point of view of the camera rather than that of a particular character. But what appears as objective camera here is later revealed as subjective (just as Steiger's slightly hammy performance in the first sequence is later revealed as an act intended to test his wife). On his reappearance towards the end of the film, Louis tells Julie that he suspected her and Jeff's intentions from the beginning, and that he watched them make love from the top of the stairs. This is the cue for a flashback of the sex scene, again seem from the high angle which is now identified as Louis's point of view. As Louis explains the ruse by which he escaped murder and apparently killed Jeff himself, the camera circles round the staircase, now the site of power in the film. It was here that Louis turned from a drunken victim to a cunning voyeur, and it is also from a superior position on the stairs that he reveals the truth to Julie, who stands below him. He explains that his sexual impotence was cured by this act of voyeurism, and then requires Julie to have sex with him in the very same place, on the rug. In a prediction of the closing sequence, the *femme fatale* has been 'confined', put back in her place.

Les Innocents aux mains sales was the last of Chabrol's films to be produced by André Génovès, whose company Les Films La

15   'A film by Claude Chabrol'

Boétie had helped to finance all of Chabrol's work between 1967 and 1975. It might therefore be said to bring to a close a particular chapter in his career, one which, most critics agree, stands as his most consistently successful period. This sense of closure is heightened by *Folies bourgeoises* (1976), a little-known and little-liked film which in fact parodies the thematic and formal concerns of the Génovès years. More precisely, *Folies bourgeoises* is an outlandish parody of *Les Innocents aux mains sales* and *Les Noces rouges*: hence the plot centres on a love triangle and an impotent husband. The eroticism and the hallucinatory final vision of *Les Innocents aux mains sales* are here exaggerated to the point of the grotesque in several fantasy sequences, particularly one set at the Crazy Horse strip club, where William (Bruce Dern) finally achieves an erection only to imagine his wife Claire (Stéphane Audran) cutting him down to size with a pair of scissors. As Bruce Dern remarks of the soup he is served immediately after one such sequence, 'it's a bit overdone'. None the less, and again as in *Les Innocents aux mains sales* among other films of the Génovès period, Chabrol achieves a dramatic shift in tone in the closing scenes, from hysterical (though largely unfunny) farce to a remarkable poignancy. Such mixing of registers has been described by Chabrol as something foreign to French cinema: 'Il n'y a qu'en France qu'on ne mélange pas les tons. On n'y a pas le droit de démarrer drôle et de terminer tragique ou vice-versa. Ça vient d'une notion de goût'. He continues: 'J'aime bien ce que font les Italiens (comme Germi, Risi, Salce, Ferreri, Festa-Campanile), c'est très fort. Je crois que j'en serais capable de faire l'équivalent français, si c'était possible en France'[16] (Braucourt 1971: 119). It is fair to say that *Folies bourgeoises* is as close as Chabrol has come to this ideal of a supposedly tasteless cinema of the sublime and the grotesque. The film is also the last in his long line of Italian co-productions, which includes twenty films from the 1960s and

16 'It's only in France that one doesn't mix different tones. Here, you don't have the right to start off funny and end up tragic or vice versa. This comes from a notion of taste ... I really like what the Italians do (like Germi, Risi, Salce, Ferreri, and Festa-Campanile), it's very strong. I think I'd be capable of making the French equivalent if it were possible in France.'

1970s. But in the final analysis, *Folies bourgeoises* is more than a self-parody or an exercise in bad taste. It is also the study of a married couple wavering frantically on the brink of separation. Suspicious, neurotic and unfaithful, Claire and William finally manage to reach out to each other, with very little hope of making contact. The film ends with one of Chabrol's most moving scenes (and one he would rework a decade later in *Poulet au vinaigre*), as the camera circles round two statues in a wintry garden, forever reaching out to each other but never touching. Thus *Folies bourgeoises* marks not only the end of the Génovès years but also the end of Chabrol and Audran's marriage.

Blood Relatives

The generic police thriller *Blood Relatives* (1978) (also known as *Les Liens du sang*) was shot in Montreal, in English, during the summer of 1977, at a time when Chabrol was also preparing his major project *Violette Nozière* (1978). Both films introduce the question of incest into the apparent security of the *petit bourgeois* family, and they do so by emphasising the spatial constriction of the family home. If Muriel in *Blood Relatives* and Violette in *Violette Nozière* become entangled in incestuous relationships (the former with her cousin Andrew, the latter implicitly with her father), the suffocating closeness of the family home seems to be the cause. As Chabrol has noted, the family unit is a source of great physical tension: 'What's frightening is that there's a father, a mother, and children – they are all pressed together – it's disgusting. ... I don't see how people can live that way – and yet it has such strength. It's masochistic; they're unhappy but it endures' (Yakir 1979: 8). Confronting their own teenage desires, Muriel and Violette attempt to negotiate a private, sexualised space away from their unhappy families. In *Blood Relatives*, Muriel lives with her uncle and aunt, the Lowerys, and has to share a bedroom with her cousin Patricia; Muriel and her male cousin Andrew consummate their affair in a boat offshore from the rest of the family; her desire to escape the family is evoked in a slow, desperate tracking shot away from the meal table and down a corridor while her voice-over tells us 'I hate this house'. She later plans to move into a hotel or even an apartment with her boss (himself just another surrogate to replace her dead father and her guardian–uncle). Blood ties ensure that she never leaves the family space: she is murdered by Patricia before she can escape. In *Violette Nozière*, the projected escape is put into practice, with Violette leaving behind the cramped flat she shares with her parents to indulge in sexual adventures in nocturnal Paris. And, of course, Violette is not the victim of murder but its perpetrator; she kills her father and disables her mother.[17] But in *Blood Relatives*, each daughter figure (of whom Muriel is only one among four) remains subject to the moral and physical hold of one or more father figures, who offer various personifications of patriarchal authority.

The father may be absent from *La Rupture* and *Les Noces rouges* (as the mother is from *Les Cousins* and *Que la bête meure*), but in *Blood Relatives* he proliferates into a number of characters. The alternative father–daughter relationships presented in the film vary from the obsessively patriarchal to the paedophiliac. That each is in fact a reflection of the others is apparent from the basic similarities in each case: these actual and virtual fathers are all in their forties, and the girls all teenagers. Chabrol thus suggests a number of possible models of paternal behaviour. Ironically, the most satisfactory of these relationships is that between the detective and the killer. Firstly, as a yardstick for comparison, there is the conventional relationship between detective Steve Carella (Donald Sutherland) and his daughter Helen, aged twelve. Although Helen remains in the background throughout the film, largely supplanted by Patricia as an object of Carella's interest and even affection, the single scene between her and her father is crucial. Chabrol shoots the two of them strolling arm in arm across a park in Montreal. As they approach the camera, Helen says, 'I like it when I hold you like this ... Dad, we're like lovers'. Carella's response is gently to correct her misapprehension and to maintain that their relationship is a safe, asexual, familial one: 'Ah no, we have something else.' His correction is important: Helen's

17 For further analysis of *Violette Nozière*, see Chapter 6.

reading of things finds its logical extension in the liaison between the paedophile Doniac and his thirteen-year-old lover Jean. As for incest, that too will be portrayed in the film, although in the much more ambiguous light of sex between cousins. But the 'something else' that Carella and Helen share will be replaced by the shifting game of trust and confidence played between cop and witness–suspect, in which fifteen-year-old Patricia becomes Carella's surrogate daughter.

Chabrol added the character of Helen to the Ed McBain source novel, no doubt to allow the identification between the detective's two daughters (one real, one virtual), an identification which he himself underlines when describing the subject of the film as 'the relationship of a 40-year old cop with his daughter ..., but it's not even his daughter' (*ibid.*: 7). This process is confirmed when Chabrol shoots Carella and Patricia walking arm in arm across the meadow, exactly as Carella and Helen had crossed the park earlier. There are two other scenes in which Chabrol's *mise en scène* associates Carella with Patricia. In his first appearance, the detective is framed in the archway where the murder took place; Muriel lies dead where she stood in the pre-credit sequence, while Carella stands in Patricia's position – on the right and shot in profile. Later, at the identity parade, Patricia identifies the man she is looking for (in fact a fantasy since she herself was the killer) as 'the second man from the left': Chabrol's shot of the two-way mirror shows Carella's reflection as occupying that position. But for all the growing rapport between Carella and Patricia (a rapport which is ironically fuelled by his suspicions and her lies), the composition of their final meeting identifies the detective with Muriel and against her killer. By now, Carella has read Muriel's diary, and has come to understand that Patricia committed the murder. In another side-on shot which echoes the murder scene, Chabrol shows Carella crouching on the left of the frame opposite Patricia, who is again on the right. His assumption of Muriel as a second surrogate daughter is thus not only moral (his investigation into her death and his reading of her words) but also spatial (he assumes her position *vis-à-vis* Patricia). It is at this point that the kaleidoscope of family ties in the film is finally pulled into focus and that Carella, correcting his paternal relationship with Patricia, solves the murder.

If the paedophile Doniac represents one pole of paternal behaviour with regard to daughters and sex, Lowery represents the other. (Muriel's boss Armstrong is an unsettling figure who combines elements of each; while projecting the image of a conventional family man, he uses his authority over her to suggest that they begin an affair.) As Muriel's uncle and Patricia's father, Lowery is the family patriarch, a God-fearing Christian who proudly tells Carella that 'family's a sacred thing' and that he vetted each of Muriel's boyfriends by inviting them into the house and asking them to shake his hand and look him in the eye. But the very household that he ruled in this way is the seat not just of adolescent desires but of incestuous ones too. Although Muriel and Andrew are cousins, they are referred to as brother and sister on several occasions, by the Lowerys and Patricia. The incest taboo which they themselves feel (Muriel tells Andrew 'It wouldn't be right for us to have a baby – we're blood relatives') is hence all the stronger. And it is Patricia's repugnance at the sight and sound of their sexual acts that prompts her to kill Muriel and then incriminate Andrew. Her imaginary account of the murder simply recasts the violent oral sex scene she witnessed as a killing: 'They were cousins – almost like brother and sister – and he was forcing her to do this!'. In a sense, by punishing Muriel for breaking the family taboo on sex between blood relatives, Patricia is merely the instrument of her father's will. Her last words in the film reaffirm the hierarchical importance of family ties even as they imply an incestuous desire of her own: 'He's got to love his sister more than his cousin.'

The theme of repetition which characterises Chabrol's representation of fatherhood in *Blood Relatives* is echoed in the narrative structure. The film is framed by the Hitchcockian device of the lying flashback, made famous in *Stage Fright* (1950). As Chabrol's account of that film points out, however, 'lying flashback' is in fact a misnomer. It is not the flashback images of the murder that mislead the spectator, but the voice-over applied to them: 'In Hitchcock films, the images never lie, though the characters do. The same sequence shown without the soundtrack can illustrate the true version of events. It is the commentary that makes it false, that lies' (Rohmer and Chabrol 1957: 105). Chabrol himself is equally scrupulous not to cheat the spectator in *Blood Relatives* (and also in the flashback regarding Jeff's supposed murder in *Les Innocents aux mains sales*). Muriel's murder is shown in part during the pre-credit sequence. It is then retold (falsely) twice by Patricia, without any flashback images. Finally the murder is shown in flashback, without any voice-over, but as a visual representation of Patricia's confession to Carella at the farm. Even here, in the true version, the theatricality of the gestures, enhanced by slow motion, renders the murder as unreal as ever.

The murder scenes which frame the film, the family plot, the narrative repetition, the flat *mise en scène* and the kitsch décor all combine to create an impression of claustrophobia in *Blood Relatives*. But Chabrol provides a glimpse of other possibilities in the character of Carella. In contrast with the bad fathers of this film and others – *La Rupture, Ten Days' Wonder, Les Noces rouges, Une partie de plaisir* – Carella is some kind of role model. Unlike Charles in *Que la bête meure*, who only appears to be a virtuous father, but is in reality 'full of shadows', Carella is 'a virtuous man' (Yakir 1979: 12, 5). As Chabrol has suggested, it is in his ability 'to just let things be' rather than to judge that Carella's virtue is most apparent (*ibid.*: 5). Hence, despite his initial revulsion, Carella is actually quite lenient with Doniac, and refuses to pass comment on Armstrong or Lowery. Coupling a professional regard for the truth with a refusal to judge (unlike the Paul of *Ten Days' Wonder*), Carella seems to reflect not only a Chabrolian ideal of fatherhood but also a projection of the film-maker himself. This is even more explicitly the case with Carella's 1980s avatar, Inspecteur Lavardin, surrogate father, detective, and Chabrolian alter ego.

Poulet au vinaigre; Inspecteur Lavardin

In a sense, the laconic Inspecteur Lavardin came to Chabrol's rescue in the mid-1980s. The first Lavardin film, *Poulet au vinaigre*

(1985), came at a low point in the director's career, after a number of poorly received projects including *Le Cheval d'orgueil* (1980) and *Le Sang des autres* (1984). The eventual producer of *Poulet au vinaigre*, Marin Karmitz, tells how Chabrol had failed to find anyone to finance the film. Karmitz agreed to do so, as long as the budget was cut from the French average of the time – twelve million francs – to six. The result was the relaunching of Chabrol's career, with Karmitz marketing *Poulet au vinaigre* as the director's 'second first film', much as he had Godard's *Sauve qui peut (la vie)* six years earlier (Jousse and Toubiana 1997: 73). Although it would be more accurate to describe *Poulet au vinaigre* as Chabrol's third first film – after *Le Beau Serge* (1958) and *Les Biches* (1967) – the relaunch worked. The critical and popular success of the film resulted in a sequel, *Inspecteur Lavardin* (1986), and a television series for TF1, *Les Dossiers de l'inspecteur Lavardin*.

Jean Lavardin (Jean Poiret) is a virtuous variant on the Chabrolian intruder, in search of 'un petit peu de vérité'[18] in a provincial town and specifically within a single household. *Poulet au vinaigre* is essentially a film about a house: the Cunos's ramshackle home is not just the site of Filamo's intended purchase but also, as Lavardin tells Louis (Lucas Belvaux), the place where the deaths of Delphine and Filiol, the disappearance of Anna and the cryptic notes from Tristan all intersect. But the crucial death haunting the film remains that of Monsieur Cuno, an event which has turned the Cuno house into the realm of the dead father. Hence the wedding anniversary dinner where three places are set, one for Madame Cuno (Stéphane Audran), one for Louis, and one for the invisible guest. Like the van Horn mansion in *Ten Days' Wonder*, although for different reasons, the family home has become a shrine to the past. When Lavardin enters the house (the only character to do so, apart from Louis himself and the firemen at the end of the film) Madame Cuno invokes the ghost of her dead husband, telling Louis to throw the detective out, 'ou j'appelle ton père!'.[19] It is in fact Lavardin alone, in his role as replacement for

18 'a little bit of truth'
19 'or I'll call your father!'

the dead man and as surrogate father, who can free Louis from the house. To this extent, Lavardin succeeds and corrects Paul Régis from *Ten Days' Wonder*: Lavardin will free his brow-beaten protégé from the family sphere, where Paul killed his. At the conclusion of *Poulet au vinaigre*, Louis may have lost his mother (Madame Cuno is taken to hospital having set fire to the house) but he has gained a surrogate father in Lavardin and a girlfriend in Henriette. It is Lavardin himself who sends Louis to Henriette, both granting him freedom from the childhood home, and absolving him of Filiol's murder. In other words, he lets Louis go twice over, once in his role as detective and once in his role as surrogate father. Lavardin's virtue is that he only finds out guilt to absolve it; he only assumes paternal authority to relinquish it. However, not even he seems to realise that in liberating Louis from one emotionally possessive maternal figure (Madame Cuno), he is simply delivering him to another (Henriette). The ending is thus characteristically double-edged.

In *Inspecteur Lavardin*, the detective makes a second appearance as a surrogate father. Arriving in Brittany to investigate the murder of hardline Catholic author Raoul Mons, Lavardin (again played by Jean Poiret) discovers that the victim's widow Hélène (Bernadette Laffont) is an old flame of his. Gradually, Lavardin assumes Raoul's position within the household, in particular with regard to Hélène and to Véronique, her daughter by an earlier marriage. This paternal role is only dissolved at the end of the film, when the lone cop makes his escape under the pretence of returning to his own family (showing Véronique a fake family photo). Not only does Lavardin assume Raoul's patriarchal place in the household, he even begins to take on the latter's authoritarian moral position. Just as Raoul is revealed as a hypocritical libertine in moralist's clothing (trafficking in drugs and sex at Max's nightclub), so Lavardin becomes involved in a moralistic quest to close down the club and to correct the activities of Raoul and Max. Lavardin's new-found patriarchal authoritarianism is best shown when he tells Véronique to take off her make-up (she has been to the night-club in secret) so as not to let her mother see her looking like a whore ('une pute'). Identity is inverted throughout *Inspecteur Lavardin*, and it is not just Lavardin and Raoul who are involved. The entire film is structured on a series of reversals: the lone cop becomes a family man and the puritan a bigot; the gay Francis is in fact straight; the dead come to life (Véronique's father Pierre Manguin, suspected dead, reappears as Peter Guinman)[20] and the living appear dead (the recurrent shots of Hélène sitting or lying, deaf, mute and staring into space as if comatose); the guilty are innocent (Lavardin absolves Véronique and Claude of responsibility for Raoul's death) and the innocent guilty (Max, the target of Lavardin's moralistic quest, is framed for the murder). And the anti-authoritarian rogue cop of *Poulet au vinaigre* comes in *Inspecteur Lavardin* to represent *la loi du père*, the power of the patriarchal law.

Thematically, the decade or so after the Hélène cycle sees Chabrol working through family plots and exploring different models of fatherhood. In particular, he represents the family as a paternal space. Only in *Les Noces rouges* is the bourgeois home conventionally represented as matriarchal. In *Ten Days' Wonder, Une partie de plaisir, Blood Relatives, Poulet au vinaigre* and *Inspecteur Lavardin*, the house is a patriarchal space. Even when the father or husband is absent, dead or supposed dead, as in *Les Innocents aux mains sales, Poulet au vinaigre* and *Inspecteur Lavardin*, the family home remains permeated by his presence. Thus the surviving mother–wife (Julie, Madame Cuno, Hélène), like the house itself, is haunted by the departed male.[21] The husband's possession of the domestic space even in his absence, expressed by the family and guests' ominous wait for Paul's arrival in *Que la bête meure*, is almost exactly replicated by Theo's first appearance in *Ten Days' Wonder*, and is later developed in the spatial composition of *Les Innocents aux mains sales*, where Julie's lonely wandering through house and garden is anchored by the iterative shots of the spiral staircase, the site of Louis's voyeuristic power and invisible presence.

20 The actual process of reversal is encapsulated in the scene where Lavardin reveals Pierre's change of name from Man-guin to Guin-man.
21 In *Inspecteur Lavardin*, Hélène is in fact haunted by her first husband, the supposedly dead Pierre, rather than by her second, the actually dead Raoul.

The association of male authority with the power of looking is elaborated in a number of later thrillers by Chabrol, notably in the patriarchal protagonists of *Masques* (1986) and *Dr M* (1990). Invisible, all-seeing and manipulative, they control family, entourage and television audience by means of an omniscient, divine gaze, as we shall see shortly.

References

Bataille, G. (1990), *Literature and Evil*, translated by A. Hamilton, London and New York, Marion Boyars.

Baudrillard, J. (1973), *Le Miroir de la production*, Paris, Casterman.

Braucourt, G. (1971), *Claude Chabrol*, Paris, Seghers: Cinéma d'aujourd'hui.

Chabrol, C. (1976), *Et pourtant je tourne ...*, Paris, Robert Laffont.

Dawson, J. (1972), Ten Days' Wonder, *Sight and Sound*, 41:4 (autumn), 227–8.

Grassin, S., and Bernard, R. (1991), Le cinéma, c'est rien que de l'amour, *L'Express*, 2078 (10 May), 54–8.

Harvey, S. (1980), Woman's place: the absent family of film noir, in E. A. Kaplan (ed.), *Women in film noir*, London, BFI, 22–43.

Jousse, T., and Toubiana, S. (1997), Masques et bergamasques: Entretien avec Marin Karmitz, *Cahiers du cinéma*, numéro spécial Claude Chabrol (October), 72–7.

Magny, J. (1987), *Claude Chabrol*, Paris, Cahiers du cinéma: Collection 'Auteurs'.

Milne, T. (1974), Nada, *Sight and Sound*, 43: 2 (spring), 119.

Nogeira, R. and Zalatti, N. (1971), Chabrol [interview], *Sight and Sound*, 40:1 (winter 1970/1).

Place, J. (1980), Women in film noir, in E. A. Kaplan (ed.), *Women in film noir*, London, BFI, 35–54.

Rohmer, E., and Chabrol, C. (1957), *Hitchcock*, translated by S. Hochman as *Hitchcock: The First Forty-Four Films*, New York, Continuum, 1988.

Wood, R., and Walker, M. (1970), *Claude Chabrol*, London, Studio Vista/Movie Paperbacks.

Yakir, D. (1979), The Magical Mystery World of Claude Chabrol: An Interview, *Film Quarterly* (spring), 2–14.

5

The power of the gaze

While analysing *Rear Window* (1954) in the book on Hitchcock which he co-wrote with Chabrol, Eric Rohmer gives an account of cinematic voyeurism which is worth quoting at length:

> the theme concerns the very essence of cinema, which is *seeing*, *spectacle*. A man watches and waits while we watch this man and wait for what he is waiting for ... In a manner of speaking, the crime is desired by the man who expects to make of his discovery his supreme delectation, the very sense of his life. The crime is desired by us, the spectators, who fear nothing so much as seeing our hopes deceived. (Rohmer and Chabrol 1957: 124–5)[1]

According to Rohmer, this 'theory of spectacle implies a theory of space' (*ibid.*: 124). In other words, the voyeur is outside looking in at a framed image. To the spatial power of the outsider looking in – and in Chabrol especially, looking down too, as in *Les Innocents aux mains sales* (1975) or *La Cérémonie* (1995) – is added the emotional power of fantasy or desire, which motivates the voyeur's gaze. Hence the subjective nature of what the voyeur sees (or claims to see): the windows the photographer looks at in *Rear Window* become 'the projections of the voyeur's thoughts – or desires; he will never be able to find in them more than he had put there' (*ibid.*: 126). This concept clearly informs *L'Œil du malin* (1961), Chabrol's first exploration of voyeurism, but also Forestier's perception of Juliette at her window in *Le Cri du hibou*

---

1 Italics in original.

(1987) and Paul's visions of Nelly's infidelity in *L'Enfer* (1994). In these films, as in *Rear Window*, the voyeur's 'passion to know, or more exactly to see, will end by suffocating all other feelings' (*ibid.*: 125). Apparently in accordance with psychoanalytical film theory, the obsessive male gaze, dynamised by varying degrees of pathological desire, objectifies (and even kills) the voyeur's female victims. In Chabrol's cinema, this gaze operates not only within the voyeuristic thriller, but also, as we have seen, within the family plot, where the victim may be male or female: witness *Ten Days' Wonder* (1971) and *Les Innocents aux mains sales* (1975). It is this spatial and, ultimately, political power of the patriarchal gaze over a family, a community, and indeed a whole city, which Chabrol elaborates in *Masques* (1986) and *Dr M* (1990).

Masques

The gaze simultaneously demonised and celebrated in *Masques* (1986) is that of the apparently all-powerful game-show host, Legagneur (Phillipe Noiret). Like Theo's in *Ten Days' Wonder*, Legagneur's name is suggestive of his status and his authority over an awed entourage.[2] Here, this includes willing servants and helpers as well as Catherine (Anne Brochet), his drugged and docile god-daughter. The intruder-cum-detective (the equivalent of Paul Régis in *Ten Days' Wonder*) is Legagneur's supposed biographer, Wolf (Robin Renucci). As Wolf's investigation develops, the rivalry between the two men becomes a battle to claim possession of Catherine and her huge inheritance. Although increasingly deadly, the contest is never wholly serious, the ludic element (the rivals play tennis and chess, and share a love of wordplay) tending above all to reveal the similarities between Legagneur and Wolf. Ultimately Catherine, like Louis in *Poulet au vinaigre* (1985), escapes from the control of one possessive (god-) parent only to submit to the control of a younger version. As a result, like many of Chabrol's films, and above all *Que la bête*

---

2 Legagneur means 'the winner' and Theo means 'god'.

meure (1969), which also concerns the apparent defeat of a monster by a seemingly virtuous hero, *Masques* can be read two ways. Superficially, Legagneur is a crook and a bully, while Wolf is a white knight riding to Catherine's rescue. But Wolf is perhaps just as materialistic and unscrupulous as Legagneur (just a younger version). Hence the parallels established between the two, particularly in the cross-cutting between them during the garden scene, and in Legagneur's final warning to Catherine to beware of Wolf, 'jeune loup aux dents longues'.[3]

The overriding discourse in *Masques* (expressed both verbally and visually) is the discourse of looking. This is particularly true of the relations between Legagneur, Catherine, and Wolf, in which power is equated with the gaze and impotence with blindness. Wolf's purpose, as he tells her, is to open Catherine's eyes to her godfather's true nature (without of course appearing in anything other than a good light himself). His own self-regarding nature is reflected in a series of compositions that show Wolf looking at himself in the mirror. By contrast, Catherine is unable to control her own gaze. Her eyes, apparently damaged, are protected by dark glasses. This poor sight is paralleled by a metaphorical blindness towards Legagneur's machinations. When she does express her own sense of self, it is as blind and vulnerable (the sculpture of herself, blindfolded) or as the object of a predatory male gaze: when she and Wolf kiss for the first time, she tells him, 'Embrassez-moi, en me regardant très fort'.[4] Ultimately, having transferred her naïve affections from Legagneur to Wolf, she declares that 'Vos yeux sont entrés dans les miens et je vois clair maintenant'.[5] But for most of the film, Wolf's gaze is no match for Legagneur's. The television host's authority, originally derived from his manipulation of the visual medium, manifests itself as a gaze so unbearably powerful that he has to sleep blindfold, with the windows closed and the curtains tightly drawn. Like Theo in *Ten Days' Wonder*, he seems to watch over his household even when absent. But where Theo expresses this possibility hypothetically

3 'the voracious young wolf'
4 'Kiss me, staring at me very hard'
5 'Your eyes looked into mine and I can see clearly now'

(saying to Hélène 'I wish I could always watch you – and you not know I'm there'), the camerawork in *Masques* grants Legagneur this power literally. In a crucial meal-time scene, from which Legagneur is absent, Wolf begins to ask questions about his own sister's mysterious disappearance from the house. The secretary's response that 'Il faudrait demander à Monsieur Legagneur'[6] is the cue for a switch of camera angle from one side of the table to the other, breaking the traditional 180° rule, as Chabrol gives us the host's point of view, shot from his vacant chair. The suggestion here that Legagneur possesses a divine gaze, invisible, ubiquitous, and disconnected from his corporeal presence, is underlined when Wolf warns Catherine to beware of 'la figure de Dieu. C'est une figure très commune, et très dangereuse'.[7] Not only is Legagneur Catherine's godfather, he also assumes the ostensibly beneficent authority of God the Father in his own household, and plays a (falsely) paternal role as host to contestants in their second childhood on his game-show *Bonheur pour tous*.

To these patriarchal connotations, again reminiscent of the characterisation of Theo in *Ten Days' Wonder* (although handled more lightly) is added the technical significance of the invisible gaze in the construction of filmic space. In the scene under discussion, the absent Legagneur (denoted by the point-of-view shot) assumes the traditional site of the camera – known as the 'invisible guest' – in the composition of classical meal-table sequences. Thus Legagneur's gaze is at once the gaze of God and the gaze of the camera, two figures that Chabrol also combines in the portrayal of the nightclub owner Max from *Inspecteur Lavardin* (1986) and the media megalomaniac Marsfeldt from *Dr M* (1990). In all three cases, the conflation of the eye of God and the eye of the camera is associated with the power of television. The metaphor is first introduced in *Inspecteur Lavardin*, when Chabrol tracks slowly towards the ceiling in Max's studio to reveal a hidden video camera in the centre of the canopy. The perspective from this hidden camera, looking down on Claude as he discovers the

6 'You will have to ask Monsieur Legagneur'
7 'the face of God. It's a very common face, and a dangerous one'

crime scene, has been described by Chabrol as 'comme le point de vue de Dieu'[8] (Chevrie and Toubiana 1986: 12).

In *Masques*, television is not just the seat of Legagneur's power but also an Orwellian weapon which subjugates the viewer: 'Dans ce dispositif télévisuel idéal, on ne regarde plus, on est regardé. On est situé par l'autre, incapable de se situer et de le situer'[9] (Magny 1987: 184). Hence Legagneur's refusal to watch *Bonheur pour tous* (or any other programme, it seems). As he tells Wolf, his own television audience (like the elderly contestants) are passive and weak, needing 'protection' (read: control). The clips of the game-show that punctuate the film show that television exercises control largely through direct audience address: hence the shot of a contestant singing directly to the camera that starts the film, the flashing sign reading 'Applaudissez'[10] which follows, or the frontal shots of Legagneur. In all of these cases, and most obviously in the final scene of the film, Chabrol exploits the ambivalence of the frontal composition: it is not just the game-show audience (in the studio and in front of the television), but also the cinema spectators of *Masques*, who are being addressed. This allows Chabrol to have Legagneur, on the point of being arrested on air during his last show, to insult not only the television audience but the cinema audience too: 'Mesdames et messieurs, il ne me reste qu'une chose à vous dire, du fond du cœur: je vous emmerde!'.[11] The direct address to camera here works not just as a revelation of the host's true feelings, but also as a parodic exaggeration of film theory which posits the spectator as a passive object of manipulation by the medium. Beginning with Hitchcock's well-known thoughts on controlling the *Psycho* audience – 'I was directing the viewers. You might say I was playing them, like an organ' (Truffaut 1984: 269) – this tendency, in its most extreme form, results in the conclusion that 'The visible is essentially pornographic, which is to say that it has its end in *rapt, mindless*

8 'like God's point of view'.
9 'In this ideal televisual mechanism, one no longer watches, one is watched. One is positioned by the other, unable to position oneself or them.'
10 'Applaud'
11 'Ladies and gentlemen, there remains only one thing for me to say to you, from the bottom of my heart: bugger you!'

fascination' (Jameson 1990: 1).[12] But in Chabrol it is only ever television (and never cinema) which is seen to objectify the spectator in this way, often to deadly effect, as in *Dr M* and *La Cérémonie* (1995).

Le Cri du hibou

Masques continued Chabrol's mid-1980s renaissance under the auspices of the producer Marin Karmitz. But Karmitz refused to produce or even distribute three of Chabrol's next four films, *Le Cri du hibou* (1987), *Dr M* and *Jours tranquilles à Clichy* (1990). While his judgement is certainly borne out by the latter, a decidedly limp adaptation of Henry Miller's novel, and undoubtedly one of Chabrol's worst films, both *Le Cri du hibou* and *Dr M* develop in various ways the exploration of voyeurism and power begun in *Masques*.

Le Cri du hibou begins as *Masques* ends, with a framed image from which the camera slowly tracks back to reveal the presence of a spectator. In this case, the image is of a young woman, Juliette (Mathilda May), seen at the window of her house by Forestier (Christophe Malavoy), a voyeur hiding in the darkness of the garden. Just as the meal-table shot in *Masques* mimics the classic construction of filmic space, so this typically significant pre-credit sequence refers to the dreamlike space of the cinema experience. Psychoanalytical film theory has long compared the experience of watching films in a darkened cinema with the process of dreaming and fantasising. Chabrol's composition here – like the murder scene in *L'Œil du malin* (1961) – evokes just that synthesis of looking and dreaming via the darkened space between the spectator in the foreground and the image of the girl illuminated and framed in the background. Juliette thus assumes the reassuring and dreamlike beauty that the filmstar holds for the cinemagoer. But as Forestier belatedly realises, 'Les images de

12 My italics. Linda Williams cites this as an example of how film theory has tended to vilify 'the gaze' in her seminal 1993 lecture, Visual Culture and Spectatorial Discipline.

rêve sont destinées aux rêves. Il ne faut pas les introduire dans la vie'.[13] The 'zone mixte et confuse' between 'le spectacle et la vie'[14] traditionally inhabited by filmstars (Morin 1972: 8) will, in *Le Cri du hibou*, be the site of a fatal confusion. Like the professor in Fritz Lang's *The Woman in the Window* (1944), Forestier, by projecting his own fantasy on to the image of a woman, will generate a vortex of violence and death.

This deadly process begins when Forestier introduces himself to Juliette and admits that he has been spying on her for three months. Divorced, psychologically unstable and prone to depression, he has found an apparent symbol of happiness and normality in the image of Juliette: 'Cette image de vous derrière la fenêtre, enfin, pour moi, c'était une image très belle, très rassurante'.[15] But his interpretation of what he sees is purely subjective, and is refuted by Juliette herself. His comment that 'Vous aviez l'air heureux dans votre maison, avec votre fiancé'[16] is met with a reply which encapsulates Chabrol's attitude to appearances: 'Il y a des airs qui trompent'.[17] Forestier believes Juliette to be happy and satisfied when, objectively, she is nothing of the sort. Moreover, he has inadvertently destroyed what little happiness and stability she had. After meeting Forestier, she grows dissatisfied with her fiancé Patrick and increasingly fascinated by the enigmatic voyeur. And while she represents for Forestier the essence of life (home, family, happiness, stability, continuation), Juliette is in fact drawn towards death by her growing friendship with the voyeur. His reserve and mystery serve to feed her own morbid obsessions: she shows him photographs of her dead brother, and finally comes to believe that Forestier is the personification of death. His morbid persona is enhanced by Malavoy's detached performance, which is based on the theory that Forestier is a man back from the dead (Toubiana 1988: 8). For all his charm and restraint, Forestier is indeed a bird of evil omen, a bird of prey like those he habitually

13 'Dream images are meant for dreams. One must not introduce them into life'
14 'mixed and confused space' between 'spectacle and life'
15 'That image of you at the window, well, for me, it was very beautiful, very comforting'
16 'You looked happy in your house, with your fiancé'
17 'Appearances can be deceptive'

draws and photographs. (When he tells Juliette they must not see each other any more, it is under the gaze of a huge photograph of an eagle hung on his wall.) These predatory and nocturnal connotations are complemented by the association of Forestier with the owl, whose fateful cry is heard on the deaths of Juliette, Patrick, and Véronique (for all of which Forestier is indirectly responsible.) Just as, in *L'Œil du malin*, Albin's perception of the Hartmanns as presenting 'un univers rond, parfait, où tout est harmonieux'[18] is only the prelude to Hélène's murder by her husband, so, by the end of *Le Cri du hibou*, Forestier's projection of 'une image très belle, très rassurante' on to Juliette has resulted in her suicide and three other violent deaths. The gaze of the voyeur, apparently detached and innocent, is nothing of the sort: it is the gaze of the Medusa, killing all it sees.

Within this portrayal of predatory voyeurism is a secondary account of the power of looking, which concerns the reversal of Forestier's gaze. Although for most of the film Chabrol's use of subjective camera gives Forestier's point of view, as events begin to spiral out of control the voyeur becomes an object of the gaze rather than its bearer. This is first apparent when, in a repetition of the pre-credit sequence, the camera tracks back from a shot of Forestier and Juliette together inside her house to reveal a voyeur, Suzie, watching from outside. By abandoning his position of power and entering the house, Forestier has made himself the object of a hostile gaze. The principle is repeated when Patrick watches Juliette and Forestier in the latter's house at night. According to the 'theory of space' which Rohmer applies to *Rear Window*, by moving inside, the former voyeur submits himself to an outside gaze, and to the powerful desires that motivate that gaze. In this case, the gaze is overtly malicious (rather than simply misguided, as is Forestier's). Suzie and Patrick represent the judgemental gaze of the local community, which has decided that Forestier is a deranged criminal. (Chabrol's choice of setting is relevant here: Vichy has become synonymous with the paranoia and suspicion of the Occupation; *Le Cri du hibou* might almost

18 'a round, perfect universe where everything is in harmony'

have been called *L'Œil de Vichy*).[19] The culmination of this theme comes when, shot and wounded in the arm by Patrick, Forestier lies on a couch as a crowd of neighbours peer in at the window. Vulnerable and immobilised, he is explicitly objectified. In the previous scene, he had complained to the police that 'On a bien le droit de regarder les gens'.[20] But, as the vicious gaze of his neighbours and the fatal consequences of his own voyeurism both bear out, in *Le Cri du hibou* looking is a crime after all.

Dr M

Dr M (1990) was conceived as a tribute to Fritz Lang, whose film *The Testament of Dr Mabuse* (1933) first made Chabrol want to work in cinema. Released to coincide with the centenary of Lang's birth in 1890, *Dr M* was shot on the same site in Berlin as *Dr Mabuse, the Gambler* (1922) and *The Thousand Eyes of Dr Mabuse* (1960) and is in part a homage to Lang's *Mabuse* series. Hence the all-seeing megalomaniac villain, the gambling references, and the importance of expressionism in the *mise en scène*. Chabrol's film is also a topical investigation of its time, as were both the first and second *Mabuse* films (decadence in the Weimar Republic and the rise of Nazism, respectively). *Dr M* features AIDS (the 'sickness' or 'epidemic' of the 'suicide virus'), the power of television, the manipulation of female icons (Sonia) and images of children (Marsfeldt's broadcast *à la* Saddam Hussein), the psychobabble of new-age therapies (Club Theratos), and, most strikingly, the future reunification of Germany. Shot in autumn 1989, immediately before the fall of the Berlin Wall, the film is prophetically set in a partly unified Berlin.

The conflation of the gaze of God and the gaze of television, explored by Chabrol briefly in *Inspecteur Lavardin* and at length in

19 *L'Œil de Vichy* is actually the name of Chabrol's 1993 anthology of propaganda and newsreels from the Occupation. *Le Cri du hibou* also features poison-pen letters, written to Forestier's employers by Patrick – an echo of Clouzot's portrayal of wartime denunciations in *Le Corbeau* (1943).
20 'One does have the right to look at people'

Masques, is embodied in *Dr M* by the media tycoon Marsfeldt (Alan Bates). In Lang's *The Thousand Eyes of Dr Mabuse* the 'eyes' are in fact TV screens used by Mabuse to monitor the other characters' movements. Similarly, in *Inspecteur Lavardin* Max uses surveillance cameras to spy on the clientele (especially the young women) in his nightclub. And in *Dr M*, Marsfeldt controls Berliners by televisual means. Not only does his position as head of Mater Media give him a practical monopoly over the city's television channels, he also manipulates the masses through the huge 'video-boards' positioned throughout the city. His nightclub, Tod ('Death'), features two balconies, vantage points from which he can look down upon the dancefloor and the roulette wheel as his video screens look down upon Berlin. Marsfeldt himself is part man, part robot – at Lang's suggestion (Legrand 1991: 41) – and is dependent on a life-support machine. As a consequence, he has to retreat periodically inside a technological cell, where a bank of televisions feed him images of war and death, as well as surveillance pictures from the streets of Berlin.

Whereas in *Le Cri du hibou* the gaze of the voyeur inadvertently causes Juliette's suicide, in *Dr M* the gaze of the television screen has become explicitly deadly. Marsfeldt uses his control of the medium to precipitate a wave of suicides, and hence to generate TV images of deaths with which to sustain himself. As detective Hartmann (Jan Niklas) discovers, the trigger for the suicides is a subliminal message in the video adverts for Marsfeldt's holiday group, Club Theratos. And, in a variation on the figure from *Masques* of the patriarch controlling his female ward, Marsfeldt is the adoptive father of the videostar Sonia (Jennifer Beals), 'The "Time To Go" Girl' whose image looks down on Berlin. Throughout the film Sonia, like Juliette in *Le Cri du hibou*, is the focus for a recurrent tension between appearance and reality. She is in one sense the Angel of Death, bearing the gaze of the Medusa: her image is both the trigger for the recurrent deaths and, often defaced with the eyes blacked out, the only clue left by the suicides. In one striking shot, her silent gaze stares directly at the spectator from the glossy surface of a 'video-card'. But she is also a manipulated orphan, whose submission to her surrogate father is reflected in a series of compositions which show her kneeling or sitting beneath him. Through her character and its multiple representations (photographs, drawings, paintings, moving images on videoboards, TV screens, and the video-card) Chabrol explores the unreliability of representation as a measure of truth. Even Sonia's mirror image is a lie, since in *Dr M* the mirror is not a reflection of the truth but a false surface which manipulates the viewer, as in the two-way mirror at Club Theratos. First seen in her disembodied form, addressing Berlin from a huge screen, Sonia only manages to replace her own representation with her real self in the climactic scene of the 'final broadcast', when she 'goes out live'. For, like an inversion of Juliette, Sonia is in fact an embodiment of life whose image erroneously suggests death.

For all its faults – Alan Bates's hammy performance as Marsfeldt, the dubbing of several German actors into English, and the formulaic basis for the plot, in which a lone cop, thrown off the case, confronts a web of corruption and manipulation – *Dr M* is a fascinating film and a brilliant example of how Chabrol follows Lang in matching style to substance. The film is realised in a flat, glossy style which tends to rely, like Lang, on a limited number of (mostly static) shots. This Langian economy of style – particularly evident in the pre-credit sequence detailing three different suicides – is also reminiscent of television, as Chabrol has admitted:

> Le principe de départ était un pur hommage à Lang et au fur et à mesure je me suis aperçu que c'était impossible. Et j'ai trouvé une autre solution, ... c'était de montrer comment un style pur ne peut que se dégrader, comment il peut se transformer en un style de feuilleton télé. Car tous les feuilletons-télé – en particulier Kojak – ont le style abâtardi des films de Lang.[21] (Jousse and Toubiana 1992: 35)

21 'The starting-point was a pure homage to Lang, and then as things developed I realised that that was impossible. And I found another solution ...; it was to show how a pure style can only deteriorate, how it can turn into the style of a TV series. Because all TV series – especially Kojak – have a style which is a bastardised version of Lang's films'. See also Chabrol cited in Gristwood 1990: 'Lang is an example I try to follow ... Not to use two shots when you only need one. No movement when you can do without it'.

With its directness, simplicity, and televisual (rather than cinematic) nature, Chabrol's shooting style in *Dr M* is immediate and effective. Combined with the dark, other-worldly music of Hindemith[22] (a rare use of symphonic score rather than the film music of Pierre Jansen or Matthieu Chabrol) and an expressionist attention to architecture, the result is a polished but Germanic quality which again harks back to Lang. The thematic significance of the expressionist *mise en scène* is especially apparent in the extended sequence which sees Sonia and Hartmann make love in his bedroom while Marsfeldt satisfies himself with images of death in his studio-cum-cell. While the cross-cutting between the two scenes establishes an ironic parallel between sex and death (comically underlined when Marsfeldt, sated, lights up a post-coital cigar), the décor emphasises a shared sense of imprisonment. As Marsfeldt later declares, Berliners lead an 'existence defined by the idea of escape' (here the fact that the city of the film is only partially unified allows Chabrol to exploit the metaphor of the Wall). In short, Sonia, Hartmann and Marsfeldt, like all Berliners, are living in a box. The expressionist presentation of this theme involves the visual motif of black boxes or checks on a white background, a pattern which is repeated in the banks of TV screens at Club Theratos and the design of the police station floor. In the sequence in question, the black-and-white box motif occurs in at least ten individual shots, principally in the pattern of the duvet and the screen in Hartmann's bedroom and in the barred glass walls of Marsfeldt's cell, but also, more subtly, in the static shots of Berlin which immediately follow: Sonia's image framed on a video-board on the walls of various buildings; a newspaper hoarding with the photographs of six dead children set out in rows; lines of cars in a traffic jam; a row of square windows in a block of flats. Ultimately, the entire city is assimilated to a screen, a box, a prison.

---

22 Hindemith's works, like those of Lang, were banned in Nazi Germany. Like Lang in 1934, Hindemith fled Germany for the USA in 1940.

L'Enfer

Dr M and L'Enfer (1994) reflect two distinct approaches to the theme of the gaze, as well as two distinct approaches to cinema, via the respective influences of Chabrol's masters, Lang and Hitchcock. Where the Langian Dr M concerns the socio-political theme of surveillance, encapsulated in the metaphor of the two-way mirror, the Hitchockian L'Enfer explores the personal realm of fantasy, expressed by the metaphor of projection (in both senses of the word). And where in Dr M the touchstone was Lang's Mabuse series, in L'Enfer it is Hitchcock's Vertigo (1958), already reworked by Chabrol thirty years earlier in L'Œil du malin. In particular, the scenes in which Paul (François Cluzet) trails his wife Nelly (Emmanuelle Béart) recall both Scottie following Madeleine in Vertigo and Albin following Hélène in L'Œil du malin. The genesis of L'Enfer also has a more direct source in the aborted film of the same name, begun by Henri-Georges Clouzot in 1964 but abandoned after a month due to the director's heart trouble. In 1993, Clouzot's widow offered the rights to Marin Karmitz, Chabrol's producer, and the project was resurrected. But while for Clouzot hell is to be found in 'la relation sadomasochiste entre l'homme et la femme'[23] (Jeancolas 1994: 65), for Chabrol hell resides in the gulf between reality and one man's obsessive fantasies.

In terms of both style and theme, L'Enfer is cinematic where Dr M is televisual. Stylistically, key sequences such as those in which Paul follows Nelly provide 'de magnifiques moments de cinéma ... qui soudent le spectateur bouche bée au défilement des images'[24] (Taboulay 1994: 36–7). Thematically, the crucial, filmic metaphor of projection is established early on when Paul, alerted by the flashes of the projector, catches Nelly and Martineau (Marc Lavoine) watching slides together in the dark. This discovery first arouses Paul's suspicions about his wife's infidelity. From this point on, he moves rapidly from being the object of filming (when Monsieur Duhamel shoots him with his movie-camera) to creating his own hallucinatory film-cum-fantasy, with Nelly as the supposedly

23 'the sado-masochistic relationship between men and women'
24 'magnificent cinematic moments ... which unite the spectator, open-mouthed, with the stream of images'

adulterous protagonist. At first it seems that his jealousy is actually anchored in reality, given Nelly's flirtatious demeanour and eva-sive responses to his questions. Accusing his wife of persisting in her supposed affair with Martineau, Paul tells her that his jealousy is logical. She replies that 'C'est 'logique, mais c'est pas vrai'.[25] For Chabrol, who tends to film the truth no matter how illogical it seems – witness especially the *fait divers* films such as *Landru* (1963) and *Violette Nozière* (1978) – Paul's 'logical' untruth is a terrible error. As *L'Enfer* progresses, the slippage between truth and fiction, between objective reality and Paul's subjective fantasy, becomes increasingly apparent.

Chabrol's meticulous recording of Paul's paranoia involves sounds as well as images. In fact, it is the soundtrack which provides the first indications of his mental instability, and which most frequently leads us into his fantasy world. Where Clouzot's original screenplay spoke of 'le fracas des trains qui passent en hurlant sur l'immense viaduc de fer'[26] (Jeancolas 1994: 64), Chabrol uses the roar of jets passing overhead, complemented at various times by the crying of Paul and Nelly's baby son, the buzz-ing of bees or flies, Paul's own interior monologue, and even the comically apt song *L'Enfer de mes nuits* ('Je t'attendrai toute la nuit / jalousie pour toute compagnie').[27] The first sign of Paul's anxiety, and the first instance of interior monologue, is in reaction to his son's crying, while both the slide-show scene and Duhamel's filming of Paul are heralded by the sound of jets. That Paul's 'film' of Nelly's infidelity has its own soundtrack as well as imagery is made clear when, returning from town in the car, his memory of the sound of her footsteps is the prelude to a fantasy sequence. Later, when he follows her from the shore of the lake, his pursuit is punctuated by a cacophony of buzzing insects, roaring jets and a snatch of *L'Enfer de mes nuits*. This attention to sound effects as an index of the imaginary recalls Luis Buñuel's *Belle de jour* (1967). In the ambiguous ending of *Belle de jour*, the sound of bells alone denotes that we are seeing Séverine's fantasy, while the image

25 'It's logical, but it's not true'
26 'the roar of the trains screaming by on the huge iron viaduct'
27 'I'll wait for you all night / alone with my jealousy'

track offers no obvious clue. Like Chabrol, Buñuel asks what is real and what is simply a projection of the protagonist's desires. But for the surrealist Buñuel, the implication is that the solipsistic realm of fantasies and desires is just as vital as what is known as reality. For Chabrol, by contrast, no illusion or dream (be it personal or political) is worth fostering at the expense of a lucid realism.

The course of Paul's descent from jealous anxiety to murderous paranoia is charted by half a dozen fantasy sequences interspersed throughout the narrative. These sequences in effect mark half a dozen stages in 'la destruction du bonheur d'un couple qui visait précisément à donner une trop belle image du bonheur'[28] (Taboulay 1994: 36). The deceptively reassuring images of harmony in *L'Œil du malin* and *Le Cri du hibou* are destroyed by the intrusive voyeurs Albin and Forestier. But in *L'Enfer*, the typical Chabrolian triangle is reduced to the couple, and the image of domestic bliss is eroded from within. This is a process not without its moments of black humour. As Paul dashes through the town, following Nelly to some imagined rendez-vous with Martineau, he passes a wedding scene as idyllic as his own at the start of the film. And the family enjoying a picnic by the side of the lake as Paul rushes past, again in pursuit of his wife, are a parody of the happy picture his family made before his jealousy took hold. In the crucial film-show sequence, Paul replaces the objective images of Nelly (shot by Duhamel and shown to the assembled guests in the hotel) with his own imaginary home movie (complete with paranoid voice-over, and *L'Enfer de mes nuits* as theme song). The filmic nature of Paul's paranoia is reiterated during the storm, when the flashes of lightning recall the slide-show and the film-show, and thus precipitate the projection of Paul's fantasies once more.

L'Enfer concludes with two endings, one in which Paul kills Nelly, and one in which he fantasises her murder, then recovers his lucidity long enough to realise that he can no longer tell what is real and what is imagined. But the clear encoding of fantasy throughout the film implies that, unlike the cryptic ending of

28 'the destruction of a couple's happiness, precisely for having wanted to present a too beautiful image of happiness'

Buñuel's *Belle de jour* – or indeed of several of Chabrol's films, including *Le Beau Serge* (1958) and *Que la bête meure* (1969) – the ending of *L'Enfer* is not totally ambiguous. That the murder of Nelly is a fantasy seems to be made clear by the roaring of jets and the wailing of sirens on the soundtrack, coupled with a burst of flash-back images which combines objectively filmed events with scenes from Paul's previous hallucinations and glimpses of the apparent murder. The most obvious parallel is in fact with *Folies bourgeoises* (1976), another film which details the destruction of a married couple from within, and towards the end of which William (Bruce Dern) fantasises that he has murdered his wife Claire (Stéphane Audran). Here, the fantasy is signalled as such by a whited-out screen in the preceding shot, and by the continuation of the narrative, which reveals that Claire is still alive and that William is merely in the act of brushing his teeth (just as Paul is shaving while he appears to imagine killing Nelly). But where William is lucid, and thus able to embark on the tentative reconciliation that closes *Folies bourgeoises*, Paul is not, and consequently cannot be sure (even if the spectator is) that he has not killed Nelly. In *Le Cri du hibou* Chabrol reveals that what the voyeur chooses to see is a projection of his own fantasies. By the end of *L'Enfer*, Paul's fantasies have been interiorised to the point that the blurring of projection and reality is complete, and potentially fatal. He can no longer trust what he sees. Ironically, as the final image – Paul's view out of the rain-covered window – blurs, and he tries to make sense of what has happened, the last word in *L'Enfer* is 'Voyons ...'[29]

The weakest point in *L'Enfer* is the portrayal of Nelly as a bouncy, two-dimensional extrovert (and, in the later stages, as an equally two-dimensional victim of rape and, possibly, murder). Although there are narrative reasons for this – to give Paul's jealousy a plausible origin and a terrifying outcome – it remains evident that Chabrol's characterisation of Nelly as simply an object (of fantasy, desire and paranoia) is a shortcoming. As the scriptwriter of Clouzot's version says,'Seul le point de vue de l'homme est pris en

29 'Let's see ...'

compte. La femme est un personnage qui vit dans la tête de son mari'[30] (Bocquet 1997: 95). Such characterisation of women is generally uncharacteristic of Chabrol, but typical of what has been taken to be classical cinema's gender-specific portrayal of the power of the gaze. As first posited in the mid-1970s (Mulvey 1975), film theory has maintained that in conventional cinema at least, the gaze is male and the object of desire female. This generalisation appears to be borne out by the power relations between Legagneur and Catherine in *Masques*, Forestier and Juliette in *Le Cri du hibou*, Marsfeldt and Sonia in *Dr M*, and Paul and Nelly in *L'Enfer*. But these are knowing explorations of the nature of power rather than unquestioning examples of cinematic voyeurism. As we have seen with regard to *Masques* and *Dr M*, the paradigms of voyeurism (male voyeur and female object) and of the family (father controlling surrogate daughter) are also complemented by a wider concern with the nature of television and spectatorship. In all three areas, power is shown to be in the hands of men, even if it involves self-destruction ultimately (for Legagneur, Forestier, Marsfeldt, and even Paul to a degree).

As his own comments make clear, Chabrol is strongly aware of historical power relations between the sexes: 'If there are men, women are the victims' (Yakir 1979: 9). But this has not prevented him from portraying a number of female protagonists as confronting patriarchal power rather than submitting to it. This is already evident in *La Rupture* (1970), where Hélène is celebrated for fighting against a bourgeois patriarch. The theme returns in several later films, made concurrently with those explored in this chapter, but detailing the female experience with all the depth and subtlety missing from *L'Enfer*.

---

30 'Only the man's point of view is taken into account. The woman is a character who lives inside her husband's head'

References

Bocquet, J.-L. (1997), *L'Enfer*, d'un film l'autre, *Cahiers du cinéma*, Numéro spécial Claude Chabrol (October), 92–6.

Chevrie, M., and Toubiana, S. (1986), Attention les yeux! Entretien avec Claude Chabrol, *Cahiers du cinéma*, 381 (March), 9–13.

Gristwood, S. (1990), Mabuse returns: Chabrol pays his respects, *Sight and Sound*, 59:2 (spring), 74.

Jameson, F. (1990), *Signatures of the Visible*, London and New York, Routledge.

Jeancolas, J.-P. (1994), Enfer ou damnation, *Positif*, 397 (March), 64–5.

Jousse, T., and Toubiana, S. (1992), Entretien avec Claude Chabrol, *Cahiers du cinéma*, 453 (March), 31–7.

Legrand, G. (1991), Impasse de l'extinction, *Positif*, 359 (January), 40–3.

Magny, J. (1987), *Claude Chabrol*, Paris, Cahiers du cinéma, Collection 'Auteurs'.

Morin, E. (1972), *Les Stars*, 3rd edn, Paris, Éditions du Seuil.

Mulvey, L. (1975), Visual pleasure and narrative cinema, originally published in *Screen*, Autumn 1975, republished in C. Penley (ed.), *Feminism and Film Theory*, London and New York, Routledge, 1988.

Rohmer, E., and Chabrol, C. (1957), *Hitchcock*, translated by S. Hochman as *Hitchcock: The First Forty-Four Films*, New York, Continuum, 1988.

Taboulay, C. (1994), L'enfer me ment, *Cahiers du cinéma*, 476 (February), 35–7.

Toubiana, S. (1988), Dialogue: Isabelle Huppert–Claude Chabrol, Retour à la bien aimée, *Cahiers du cinéma*, 407/8 (May), 4–10.

Truffaut, F. (1984), *Hitchcock*, rev. edn, New York, Simon and Schuster.

Yakir, D. (1979), The Magical Mystery World of Claude Chabrol: An Interview, *Film Quarterly*, (spring), 2–14.

6

Stories of women

In 1995, Chabrol said that 'Finalement, je ne m'intéresse qu'aux personnages, et plus ça va, plus je ne m'intéresse qu'aux personnages féminins'[1] (Guérin and Jousse 1995: 28). In the same interview, he added: 'Plus on cherche à comprendre, moins on comprend. Le vertige que cela procure me plaît beaucoup'[2] (*ibid.*: 32). This 'vertigo' – as in Hitchcock's films, including *Vertigo* (1958) itself – is felt most strongly in the representation of female protagonists. It is expressed most succinctly in the dreamlike images of women's faces suspended in space which dominate Chabrol's films about women, from the coda of *Les Bonnes Femmes* (1960), via the endings of *Le Boucher* (1969) and *Les Innocents aux mains sales* (1975) to *Violette Nozière* (1978), *Betty* (1992) and *La Cérémonie* (1995). It seems that Chabrol chooses more and more to base his films on stories of women because he shares the traditional (male) view that they are more enigmatic than men. But aside from the Hélène cycle – in which Stéphane Audran as Hélène is a personification (half satirical, half idealised) of the bourgeoisie – Chabrol does not use his female characters to represent abstracts or to symbolise absolutes; they remain socially and historically defined individuals. There is thus a degree of Marxism as well as mystery in their depiction. Women in Chabrol's work

1 'In the end, I'm only interested in the characters, and the more I go on, the more I'm only interested in the female characters'
2 'The more you try to understand, the less you understand. I really like the sense of vertigo which that causes'

are often trapped, frustrated or disadvantaged, and this is often a matter of social class. But the power relations between the sexes, although exacerbated by poverty, transcend class. The prevalence of patriarchal power structures means that even Chabrol's bourgeois women are generally dominated by men. As Chabrol says, 'If there are men, women are the victims' (Yakir 1979: 9). This is evident in the relations we have noted between autocratic patriarchs and their young female wards – Legagneur and Catherine in *Masques* (1986), Marsfeldt and Sonia in *Dr M* (1990) – and also in the marriages shown in *Que la bête meure* (1969), *Ten Days' Wonder* (1971), *Une partie de plaisir* (1974) and *L'Enfer* (1994). In these examples, the female characters are usually objects (of desire, of exchange, of fantasy). This trend culminates with Nelly in *L'Enfer*, Chabrol's least convincing female character, whose life (and death) is defined by her husband's fantasies. But conversely, as his 1995 statement suggests, recent years have also seen Chabrol develop an ongoing interest in women as subjects rather than objects.

Given that in Chabrol's cinema women are often lacking in financial or social power, there are limits to the ways in which they can either define themselves or escape their situation. This is spelled out most clearly in *Les Bonnes Femmes*, where the potential escape routes are (in order of appearance in the narrative) sex, marriage into the bourgeoisie, a career, romance, or death. Several of these alternatives – notably sex, romance, and marriage into the bourgeoisie – also arise in *Violette Nozière* and *Betty*. Even the bourgeois love affairs in *La Femme infidèle* (1968), *Les Noces rouges* (1973) and *Les Innocents aux mains sales* are essentially dreams of escape which do not provide a solution. The persistence of frustration in a middle-class marriage is also portrayed in *Une partie de plaisir*, where Philippe torments his wife Danielle by suggesting she break the confines of marital fidelity, only to punish her when she does so. Eventually he kills her for leaving him. But he also punishes her for seeking her own escape route from their claustrophobic marriage: a career. When she says she is looking for a job, he accuses her of 'bovarysme'. By comparing his wife to the heroine of Flaubert's *Madame Bovary*, Philippe is accusing her of sheltering from reality in a romantic dream. But he is also establishing a key point of reference for many of Chabrol's female characters: the importance of the imagination as a means of escape. Although he did not film Flaubert's novel until 1991, Chabrol in a sense had already made several versions of it, all of them in fact better than the adaptation itself! For Jacqueline in *Les Bonnes Femmes* and Violette in *Violette Nozière*, dreaming is their prime means of autonomy; like Emma Bovary, they dream themselves away from their lives by reading into their affairs a possibility of escape which will prove illusory. This is true of career ambitions as well as well as romantic ones: witness Ginette in *Les Bonnes Femmes* and Marie in *Une affaire de femmes* (1988), both of whom dream of being singers. The importance to women of negotiating a new identity (be it through dreams or action) is emphasised in *Les Biches* (1967) when Why, dressed as Frédérique, tells Paul that she always wanted to 'changer de peau'.[3] Paul replies that he cannot see the point, to which Why responds: 'Parce que tu es un homme'.[4]

Violette Nozière

Throughout his career, Chabrol has shown a recurrent interest in the *fait divers* or real-life crime story. This is most obvious in *Landru* (1963), which tells the story of the infamous serial killer, and *Une affaire de femmes* (see below, p. 133), based on the case of the last woman to be guillotined in France. The *fait divers* also informs the references to Weidmann's execution in *Les Bonnes Femmes* and the Bourganeuf murders in *Les Noces Rouges*, and the implicit parallel with the Papin sisters in *La Cérémonie*.[5] Even *Madame Bovary* could be said to have a *fait divers* at its origin (the suicide of a local woman was the basis for Flaubert's novel). The case of Violette Nozière, which Chabrol filmed in 1978, is notable in that – unlike the others – it concerns the relationship between a young woman and her family. In 1933, at the age of eighteen,

3 'turn over a new leaf' (literally, to 'change my skin').
4 'Because you're a man'
5 For an analysis of *La Cérémonie* and of the *fait divers* in general, see Chapter 7.

Violette poisoned both her parents, killing her father while her mother survived. In Chabrol's film, the crime is presented as a mystery, irreducible to the socio-historical context or to individual psychology. Violette herself is a totally opaque and ambivalent figure: was she a heartless, lying murderer, a greedy opportunist and a nymphomaniac, or a gullible young girl, duped by her boyfriend, and the victim – and avenger – of incestuous abuse by her father? As Chabrol's own voice-over reveals at the end of the film, the hysterical condemnation of Violette during her trial, and her subsequent death sentence, were followed by clemency, a reduction in her sentence due to good behaviour, and ultimately by her release, a pardon, and an apparently conventional family life as wife and mother. She thus came to represent what – according to the surrealists' interpretation, at least – she had tried to destroy: the normal, everyday *petit bourgeois* family. As the sensational trial and press coverage of 1934 made clear, the threat to the established order posed by Violette's crime could not be dismissed as originating in the working or supposedly 'criminal' classes. Instead, it 'came from within the very ranks of the respectable classes and crystallized around the spectre of female sexuality within the family' (Walker 1995: 94).This recalls Chabrol's depiction of sexual tensions, incest and murder within the *petit bourgeois* family in *Blood Relatives* (1978), the film he made immediately before *Violette Nozière*. Indeed, the French title for that film, *Les Liens du sang*, may have been suggested by one of the surrealist poems written to celebrate the Nozière case: 'Violette a rêvé de défaire / A défait / L'affreux nœud de serpents des liens du sang'[6] (*ibid*.: 98).

Chabrol's increasing concern with female characters as individuals rather than as types or as embodiments of class is illustrated by the characterisation in *Violette Nozière*. Gone is the symbolic Hélène role played by Stéphane Audran (usually the personification of the bourgeoisie, but also in *La Rupture* (1970) of the

---

6 'Violette dreamt of undoing / Undid / The hideous nest of snakes that is blood relations'. The poem is by Paul Eluard and was published in December 1933. For more on *Blood Relatives*, see Chapter 4.

working class). Now the female lead passes to Isabelle Huppert who, as Violette, plays the first of several central roles in Chabrol's more recent films. (Audran plays her mother Germaine and Jean Carmet her father Baptiste.) As Violette, Huppert portrays an ultimately unknowable individual. The ambivalence of all human psychology (as Chabrol sees it) is paralleled in the film by the competing explanations for Violette's notorious crime. While the narrative addresses the possible explanations – psychosexual, financial, moral, political – without reaching a definitive conclusion, so too the camerawork and the editing appear to suggest answers, but with the same result. The repeated close-ups on Violette's face and the flashbacks to her childhood suggest that we are going to learn something concrete about her motives, but we never do. As she tells the police, and as her impassive, mask-like make-up implies, 'Il n'y a rien à comprendre'.[7] Violette and her crime have to be accepted but cannot be understood: she is as unfathomable as her pale, made-up face, as intangible as her ghost-like presence hovering in the night.

The tiny, constricted family flat is a recurrent metaphor for the narrow horizons of the middle classes, the claustrophobic closeness of the family unit (also evoked in *Blood Relatives*), and the possibly incestuous proximity of Violette and her father. Like Emma Bovary, Violette repeatedly dreams of an escape from her confined life to broader, more romantic spaces. She tells her manipulative boyfriend Jean (himself a downmarket version of Count Rodolphe just as Violette is a downmarket Emma Bovary) that 'C'est mesquin, s'ennuyer, c'est petit. Moi, j'aime la grandeur'.[8] And when her parents force Violette to write to Jean asking if he will marry her, she calls them 'des nains'.[9] Although tiny, the Nozières' flat is a place of many secrets: caches of money, letters and photographs are hidden all over the flat. The identity of Violette's real father (Monsieur Émile), her affair with Jean, her parents' sexual activity, her father's desire for her and even the murder itself are all poorly-hidden secrets which are stumbled

7 'There is nothing to understand'
8 'Being bored is petty, it's small-minded. What I love is greatness'
9 'dwarves'

upon in the confines of the family space. It is as if the brutal
Freudian urges of the family – the jealous hoarding of money, the
search for one's origins, the taboo desires of incest, the violent
hatred of one's parents – cannot be repressed for long in such a
tight space. The theme of repression is most brilliantly evoked
when Violette appears to leave home after the discovery of her
affair with Jean. The screen is split in half by a partition: on the
right-hand side, her parents busy themselves tidying up and
restoring the 'normal' family order; on the left-hand side, un-
noticed, Violette silently appears and stands in the doorway.
Apparently invisible to her parents, she is the 'abnormal' spectre
of the taboo desires that haunt the family and cannot be success-
fully repressed. Although on this occasion she slips away again,
her next intervention in the family space will be to attempt the
murder of her parents.

Before she commits her crime, Violette is associated more
strongly with fantasy than with action, as indeed are most of the
film's characters. Where the men dream of power (either financial
in the case of Jean, or political, in the case of the young Fascist
seen at the start of the film), the women mostly dream of escape:
Violette's friend Maddy of going to California; Violette of driving
to the coast with Jean in a Bugatti sportscar. Monsieur Émile
appears at times to be less a real character than a fantasy of escape
into a higher social class, both for Germaine and for Violette. In
the restaurant scene where Violette begins to blackmail him,
Monsieur Émile is in fact shot as if he were an image in her head:
she is shown in a facial close-up, with her real (or imagined?)
father's face hovering, reflected, in the mirror behind her.[10] Most
images in the film of dreams and fantasies are, as here, mirrored
compositions. Numerous shots of Violette show her staring at her
reflection, as when she tells Maddy that 'Je veux qu'on parle avec
des mots qui me fassent rêver',[11] or when she play-acts in front of
the mirror in her hotel room, kissing it and pretending it is an
image of Jean. Photographs also play a role in evoking fantasy. A

10 Compare the composition at the hospital in *Le Boucher*, where the doctor
   appears to spring from Hélène's imagination.
11 'I want people to speak to me with words that will make me dream'

photo of Lilian Gish, the great Hollywood actress of the silent era (associated with melodrama and with innocent suffering) is pinned to the mirror in the hotel room. Ironically, although at this stage in the film Violette seems the polar opposite of this role model, by the end she has herself attained a kind of martyrdom. Another photograph in the hotel room, showing waves crashing on rocks, acts as a catalyst for Violette's romantic imaginings. It is from staring at this that she conjures up the image of Jean, in a prophetic dream, rising from the sea (like a male version of the mythical birth of beauty).[12] Hence also the recurrent dream of driving to the sea with Jean, and his divine status in her eyes as a kind of romantic god (when he is in fact literally screwing her for money). In these dreams and above all her false image of Jean, Violette is revealed not as a violent monster but as a gullible and naïve young woman. (This image is again reversed, however, by her promiscuity where other men are concerned.)

The mirror images of Violette act, like the contrasting glimpses of her personality throughout the narrative, to fragment our picture of her rather than to confirm it. Which is the real Violette? Or are we only seeing partial versions, reflections of different aspects of her identity? Time and again the camera switches away from what we had supposed was Violette's 'real' face to reveal that we were looking at an image in the mirror. Our view of her is thus always being revised. In the same manner, the flashbacks to her childhood that punctuate the closing stages of the film qualify our impression of Violette without ever proving definitive. They simply add another layer to her mystery rather than peeling one away. Chabrol's attitude to Violette might be compared with Violette's to her (equally enigmatic) mother, of whom she says, 'Je l'aime parce que je ne la comprends pas'.[13] The final ironic twist is provided by Violette's gradual change from guilt to innocence, from sickness and dirt (she is afflicted with syphilis) to purity, from the sexually-active, dirty and murderous 'red woman' (an unwelcome spectre in the family home) to the rehabilitated,

12 According to classical mythology Venus, goddess of love and beauty, was born from the waves.

13 'I love her because I don't understand her'

family-oriented 'white woman' (carer, wife and mother).[14]

This development begins with the hospital sequence in which Violette, in her habitual black coat and hat, confronts two nurses dressed in white from head to foot. Both the *mise en scène* and the narrative (Violette has just committed her crime; she is visiting her poisoned mother) underline the contrast between the supposedly good women and the supposedly evil one. But from this point on, Violette becomes associated with innocence and selflessness rather than guilt: she gives her watch to an old woman in the hospital corridor; she is betrayed to the police by a passer-by; at the trial, she spares both her mother and Jean (by refusing to betray the former's secret about Monsieur Émile or to incriminate the latter in the theft of a ring). Finally, in prison, she becomes a saintly figure: washing her cell-mate's feet (an allusion to Mary Magdalene), giving away her food and, in the last sequence, singing while embroidering a white garment. (It is not just the colour of the garment which is symbolic. The act of embroidery is associated culturally with the 'white woman' and, in the films of Luis Buñuel, with the dutiful bourgeois wife – see especially the ending of *Belle de jour* (1967), another film about the potential rehabilitation of a 'red woman' – in this case, a wife who turns to prostitution.) It is over yet another facial close-up of Violette (this time, devoid of her pale, mask-like make-up, and apparently at her most real, natural and innocent), that Chabrol reads the closing voice-over, in which the destroyer of the family is rehabilitated as a model wife and the mother of five children. The 'spectre of female sexuality' has been domesticated once more. And – as in many of Chabrol's films, including *Juste avant la nuit* (1971) and *Nada* (1974) – the threat to the status quo seems to have been absorbed and neutralised.

14 The terms 'red woman' and 'white woman' are taken from Theweleit 1987. See also the account of *La Rupture* in Chapter 3.

Une affaire de femmes

In many ways, *Une affaire de femmes* (1988) is a companion piece
or sister film to *Violette Nozière* – a *fait divers* in which a woman is
found guilty of a crime against the family. Both women are played
by Isabelle Huppert, and they share a certain naïvety and an
ignorance of the ideological ramifications of their actions. Both
crimes are set against a background of political tensions (the rise
of Fascism in the early 1930s; the German Occupation of France
during the Second World War). *Une affaire de femmes* could even
be considered the sequel to *Violette Nozière*, not just because
embryonic Fascism has now developed into a fully-fledged Fascist
state – Vichy – but more precisely, because ten years separate both
the films (1978–88) and the real-life crimes they involve (1933–43).

Where the two films differ is in the importance of genre and of
political history. Neither has a major role in structuring *Violette
Nozière* (the film is about a murder case but is not a thriller;
history and politics remain in the background and cannot explain
the case). *Une affaire de femmes*, by contrast, is essentially a melodrama[15] which ends up confronting the ideology of the period (as
Marie herself has to do). In July 1943, Marie Bayon became the
last woman to be guillotined in France. Her crime was the illegal
practice of abortion. Under the wartime Vichy regime, a crime
against the family could be construed as a crime against the state.
Marie is tried by the Tribunal de l'État because abortion contravenes Vichy ideology, expressed in the motto *Travail, famille, patrie*.[16]
Thus the reasoning behind her execution, as Chabrol demonstrates,
is political. She is made an example of because she contravenes
the Vichy model of the family (and the key role of the mother
within it) as the cornerstone of the Fascist state. It is here that the
film's concerns with history and genre overlap: motherhood is the

15 I would therefore disagree with Christian Blanchet's comment, in an otherwise
   excellent account of the film, that there is no genre in *Une affaire de femmes* and
   hence no distancing of the *auteur* from his subject (Blanchet 1989: 179).
   However, the distancing effect of the melodrama is certainly transcended in the
   closing stages concerning Marie's trial and execution.
16 'Work, Family, Country'. Under Vichy, this replaced the Republican motto
   Liberté, égalité, fraternité.

crux of the Vichy case against Marie, and of melodrama as a genre. It is perhaps natural, then, that *Une affaire de femmes* should be for the most part a maternal melodrama.

Maternal melodrama is most strongly associated with the 'weepie' or 'woman's film' made in Hollywood during the 1940s. In her study of the genre, Mary Anne Doane has defined melodrama and the maternal as 'two discourses of the obvious'. Melodrama makes it clear that 'Everyone has a mother, and furthermore, all mothers are essentially the same, each possessing the undeniable quality of motherliness' (Doane 1987: 70–1). This discourse of the obvious is identifiable in Chabrol's *La Rupture* (1970) which, as we have seen, concerns a good mother in her battle with her son's evil father-in-law. Although overlaid with strong political implications, *La Rupture* remains a straight melodrama, characterised by its moral absolutes, its obviousness and its 'will-to-transparency' (*ibid.*: 71). *Une affaire de femmes* is a much less straightforward case, and as such is more characteristic of Chabrol's cinema in general. Here, the discourse is one of ambivalence rather than obviousness. This is because the generic conventions of maternal melodrama are complicated by two connected factors: the historical and political context, and the unstable, ambivalent status of motherhood in the film. There is nothing obvious about definitions of the mother in *Une affaire de femmes*. Under Vichy, motherhood is a contested sign, an everyday reality subjected to an extreme political definition. Marie is punished for attacking that definition (albeit in ignorance of the definition itself) by her practice of abortion. What she perceives as a favour or a helping hand for women 'in trouble', the state perceives as an action against motherhood. But Marie is not just an abortionist – she is also a mother to her two young children, Pierrot and Mouche. Moreover, as in the typical maternal melodrama, she brings up her children alone, without their father's help, and directs all of her efforts towards improving their quality of life. (One can easily compare Marie buying chocolate, jam and biscuits for Pierrot and Mouche with the money from one of her first abortions with the similar scenes from the classical melodrama *Mildred Pierce* (1945), where Mildred buys piano and dancing lessons for her daughters with the money she earns – also secretly – as a waitress.) So is Marie a good mother or not?

Within the generic code of the maternal melodrama, women are often punished for becoming bad mothers – usually for seeking a role outside the home.[17] In *Mildred Pierce*, for example, Mildred (Joan Crawford) begins the story as a good wife and a good mother. She is identified solely with child-rearing and domesticity: 'I was always in the kitchen. I felt as though I'd been born in a kitchen, and lived there all my life, except for the few hours it took to get married. I married Bert when I was seventeen. I never knew any other kind of life – just cooking and washing and having children'. This is the starting-point for her (ultimately dangerous and doomed) flirtation with life outside motherhood. It is also the starting-point for Marie's story and, as one of her clients makes clear, it is the reason why the abortions she provides are in demand. (Jasmine tells Marie that she has six children, that she hasn't been happy since she was sixteen, and that 'j'ai l'impression d'être une vache'.)[18] This anti-maternal (and therefore anti-Vichy) discourse is expressed by Marie herself, symbolically in her actions as abortionist and independent woman, and verbally when she describes herself as more than just 'une petite femme au foyer'.[19] It is most explicit in the bitter mock-prayer she offers to the Virgin Mary at the end of the film: 'Je vous salue Marie, pleine de merde, le fruit de vos entrailles est pourri'.[20] In *Mildred Pierce*, Mildred's deviation from good motherhood (her divorce, her remarriage, her career in the restaurant business) is seen to bring about her downfall: she loses both her daughters, her second husband and her business. Similarly, Marie in *Une affaire de femmes* is punished for moving out of the domestic and into the entrepreneurial realm. It is increasingly for herself rather than her

17 The same is true of the representation of women in *film noir*. *Mildred Pierce* is in many ways a hybrid of *film noir* and melodrama.

18 'I feel like a cow'

19 'a little house-wife'

20 'Hail Mary, full of shit, rotten is the fruit of your womb'. Blanchet suggests that this can be read two ways – as anti-Christian or as Christian – according to whether the prayer is addressed to the Virgin or to Marie herself (Blanchet 1989: 183, n.2).

children that she wishes to move to bigger and better apartments and to have more money; she aspires to be a singer, and takes lessons; she starts an affair with a young collaborator while encouraging the maid to sleep with her husband; and she rents the prostitute Lulu a room in which to bed her clients. Above all, she expands her booming business as an abortionist. Marie's abortion business fulfils exactly the same function as Mildred's restaurant business: originally a means of providing for their children, in time it becomes a kind of career, a means of economic independence and self-definition away from the family home. It is for this move away from the maternal role that both are punished.

But Marie's generic punishment as a bad mother (as decreed by the conventions of maternal melodrama) is doubled by her political punishment (her execution as decreed by the Vichy state). This can be related back to her dual status as abortionist and as mother. The ideological weight of the former (under Vichy) is emphasised in the later stages of the film. But even in the earliest sequences, Marie's status as a good mother – and in particular her relationship with her son Pierrot – is problematised. Pierrot (like his father Paul) is consistently ignored or marginalised by Marie, who favours her daughter Mouche. For all the celebration of female friendship and solidarity in the film (especially in Marie's relations with Rachel and Lulu but also with her own daughter) there remains the suggestion (again, typical of the maternal melodrama) that Marie is destabilising the family by marginalising her weak husband and her neglected son. The patriarchal power structures which condemn her to death – from her own husband, who denounces her to the police, to the male judges and also Vichy itself, personified by its leader Marshal Pétain – do so because she has sought to live outside male society and the roles it assigns to women. (It is also implicit that she is punished in order to make defeated France – symbolised by her husband Paul – feel stronger.) As Marie approaches her downfall in all innocence, at first it is only generic expectations that come into play. A growing sense of unease is linked to her dream of becoming a singer. Just when it seems as if she might be able to fulfil her ambition, her world falls apart – as one would of course expect in a melodrama.

Thus she is arrested on her return from a triumphant singing lesson. But there are also hints throughout the narrative at the excessive (political) nature of Marie's fate. As she becomes ever more daring in her affairs (both romantic and business), Chabrol implies that the guillotine is awaiting her: hence the scene with the decapitated goose, the death of the Resistance fighter in front of her, and Pierrot's strange (possibly prophetic) wish to become an executioner.

The final section of the film is introduced by a voice-over from the adult Pierrot, looking back on his mother's death. This has the effect of mitigating the more reactionary implications that *Une affaire de femmes* shares with maternal melodrama. In other words, the sense that Marie is being punished for neglecting her husband and son is qualified by her son's commentary. The harrowing prison sequences – culminating in the shocking execution – that follow fulfil two key functions. Firstly, they satirise (in the blackest of tones, but with a touch of humour in the ludicrous rhetoric of the trial judge) the hypocrisy and cruelty of the Vichy regime (which, as Marie's lawyer helpfully reminds us, deported Jewish children to their deaths while executing Marie for crimes against the unborn). Secondly, they allow Chabrol to comment not just on the cruelty of Marie's executioners but also, less explicitly, on the cruelty of the genre as well. The normal outcome of the maternal melodrama has been exaggerated to the point of excess: Marie is executed for being a supposedly bad mother. And, as made clear in both the closing legend – 'Ayez pitié des enfants de ceux qu'on condamne'[21] – and the film's most brutal scene (where Mouche cries out and Pierrot starts banging his head against the bedroom wall as Marie, sentenced to death, shakes uncontrollably in her prison cell), the mother–child relationship has been totally lost in the equation.

21 'Have pity on the children of those condemned to death'

Madame Bovary

Both *Une affaire de femmes* and *Les Innocents aux mains sales* (1975) turn genres against themselves in their portrayal of women, exposing the cruelty that the melodrama directs against bad mothers and the *film noir* against the *femme fatale* by exaggerating the punishment the female characters ultimately undergo. But there is no such gap between generic conventions and their exploitation in Chabrol's heritage film *Madame Bovary* (1991). This is despite the fact that Isabelle Huppert (who plays the lead once again) has identified in Flaubert's original novel 'un petit décalage ... qui juxtapose le cliché et la critique du cliché'[22] (Boddaert *et al.* 1991: 133). In truth, Chabrol's *Madame Bovary* does not distance itself from the clichés of the heritage genre in the way that, for example, Yves Angelo's Balzac adaptation *Le Colonel Chabert* (1994) does.[23] Hence *Madame Bovary* is characterised by fidelity to a literary source, luscious costumes and décor, the depiction of public space (the town square) and reliance on set pieces (the ball, the wedding banquet). It thus remains largely a genre piece, with little – except for the dark humour – to distinguish it from French period dramas such as Claude Berri's *Germinal* (1993). The central theme of the film – female desire and its failure to find satisfaction in a claustrophobic social environment – is expressed in several other films by Chabrol, from *Les Bonnes Femmes* to *Une affaire de femmes* and beyond. Emma Bovary's perpetual dissatisfaction at whatever fantasy she tries is even comparable to Jeanne Decourt in *Que la bête meure* (1969) – dabbling self-indulgently and unsuccessfully in painting, music, poetry, and eastern religion – and to Hélène escaping into yoga in *Le Boucher* (1969).

All of this raises the question of why Chabrol chose to film Flaubert's novel, and to add his adaptation to those of Jean Renoir (1934) and Vincente Minnelli (1949). He had planned the project

---

22 'a little shift, which juxtaposes the [romantic] cliché with the critique of the cliché'

23 Angelo inverts the conventions of heritage camerawork by using slow and graceful tracking shots to reveal impoverished and sordid – rather than wealthy – surroundings. The film itself is about the dignity of poverty in the face of hypocrisy and greed.

for years, but the deciding factor was the excellent working relationship he built up with Isabelle Huppert on *Violette Nozière* and *Une affaire de femmes*. Without Huppert in the lead, Chabrol would never have filmed this story of a country doctor's wife whose romantic and financial escapades end in her suicide. By the time he actually came to shoot *Madame Bovary*, Chabrol may also have found that it chimed with the themes he had explored in his other films starring Huppert: the place of female desire, and the punishment of its expression. Isolated in a dull marriage, a small provincial town and a bourgeois, male-dominated society, Emma Bovary is always dependent on men for the satisfaction of her desires – be it her prosaic husband Charles (Jean-François Balmer) for her family life, the comically down-to-earth priest for her spiritual longing, the cynical Monsieur Lheureux for her elegant wardrobe, or Count Rodolphe and the lawyer Léon for her sexual passion. Each, in his way – including her decent but limited husband – fails her. In Huppert's words, 'C'est de cela que meurt Madame Bovary: de ne pas avoir été reconnue comme une personne désirante'[24] (*ibid.*: 126). Emma may be frustrated as a desiring subject, but her desires are also represented as romantic clichés – unoriginal, fluctuating and at odds with reality. (Stereotypical romantic passion is mocked during the 'Comices' scene, when banal speeches and the mooing of cows from the agricultural show are heard as Emma swoons in Rodolphe's arms.) Like Marie in *Une affaire de femmes*, she is never satisfied with what she has: hence the scenes in both films where the purchase of a new house promises the start of a new chapter in the heroine's life, only for the novelty to quickly wear off. But unlike Marie, Emma cannot express her desires through independent or entrepreneurial action, only through the cultural stereotypes she has learned from her reading (romantic heroine) or her upbringing (dutiful wife and mother). It is between these two poles – which we may term the 'red woman' and the 'white woman' (Theweleit 1987) – that Emma oscillates with increasing desperation in her search for an authentic and fulfilling identity.

24 'That's what Madame Bovary dies of – not being recognised as a person with desires'

Emma's fragmented sense of identity is comparable to Violette's in *Violette Nozière*. Her desires – like Violette's – are repeatedly signalled by mirror images. Mirrors might be said to represent Emma's ideal self, her fantasy of herself through the looking-glass. They are associated with her romantic experiences: hence the mirrored compositions of her and the vicomte after they waltz together, and the almost identical post-coital mirror images of her with Rodolphe and with Léon. The most revealing example of this kind of shot comes in Emma's first private conversation with the haberdasher Lheureux. In a composition reminiscent of the restaurant scene in *Violette Nozière* – where Monsieur Emile appears reflected above Violette's head – Emma faces towards the camera as she speaks to Lheureux (off-screen). On the wall behind her a mirror shows the reflection of her own head. Also visible in the mirror (but not outside it) are the shiny dresses that Lheureux is trying to tempt Emma into buying. The effect of the framing here is to suggest that in the realm of her own fantasy – the looking-glass – Emma is captivated by the dresses and the elegant lifestyle that they evoke. But for once she repudiates her romantic fantasies and declares 'Je n'ai besoin de rien'.[25] When Lheureux has left, Emma turns to the mirror and tells her fantasy self 'Comme j'ai été sage'.[26] For the moment, the spectre of the romantic 'red woman' has been kept at bay. In her final meeting with Rodolphe, to ask him to pay off her debts, Emma is again framed in a mirror. This time, the 'red woman' is in full sway. Emma has in fact recreated her passionate image – wearing a black dress and red lipstick[27] – from the time of her affair with Rodolphe, in order to persuade him to perpetuate her fantasy existence and to pay off the demands of reality. (After all, romantic images have worked this magic before in the film. The picture of a ball on the wall of the Bovarys' first house functions in this way: the image precedes the reality, and appears to summon it up. Immediately after Emma has gazed wistfully at the picture, Charles announces that they have been invited to a ball at the

25 'I don't need anything'
26 'Wasn't I good?'
27 This is also the image recreated on the film poster.

château.) But her attempt fails. The gestures and swoons she practised in the garden earlier now become frantically genuine, and culminate in her impulsive suicide.

Colour functions symbolically throughout *Madame Bovary* – although this can be related not just to Chabrol's expressionism, but to other heritage films, such as Alain Corneau's *Tous les matins du monde* (1992), which contrasts warm reds with cold blues. Chabrol similarly evokes the emotional connotations of red and blue in *Madame Bovary*. Hence red dominates in the scenes of Emma's affairs – her dresses and lipstick, and also the décor of Rodolphe's château and of Léon's rooms in Rouen. Red is also used – as Hitchcock uses it in *Marnie* (1964) – to express the protagonist's state of mind at a moment of crisis. Where Hitchcock shows Marnie, after she has had to shoot her injured horse, against a background of red carpets and walls (suggesting blood but also 'seeing red' and a loss of all self-control), so Chabrol shows Emma against a bright red background as Rodolphe tells her he has no money and she realises there is no way out. Blue, meanwhile, is used to signify the threat of death – as it does for instance in *Les Biches* (1967), *La Rupture* (1970) and *Une partie de plaisir* (1975). Emma's suicide is bathed in blue – from the décor and lighting of the pharmacy where she swallows arsenic to the colour of her bed and even of the dark liquid that she vomits at the moment of death. But colour in *Madame Bovary* also has a cultural significance relating to stereotypes of female behaviour, according to which, as we have hinted, red is contrasted with white.

Red signifies female sexuality encoded as a threat, as illicit passion (the 'fallen woman' or the 'scarlet woman'). White, on the other hand, denotes the 'white woman', the good wife and mother, the carer – desexualised and domesticated. Emma switches between these two roles in her attempt to define herself, and the *mise en scène* emphasises the dichotomy. Red – with black – dominates the décor and Emma's costume during her planned elopement with Rodolphe, her liaisons with Léon and, as we have seen, her final attempt to raise some money. But these phases as the 'red woman' alternate with sudden periods of repentance, in which Emma assumes a dutiful family role. While she is playing the good wife and mother – attending to her little daughter Berthe, encouraging Charles to be ambitious, even sewing on his buttons – her clothes and the surrounding décor are invariably white or an associated pale colour (cream, grey, light green). But when this fantasy wanes, as when Charles's misconceived operation on a club-foot goes horribly wrong, Emma reverts to her role as scarlet woman – in this case resuming her affair with Rodolphe the same night, and appearing incongruously at breakfast next morning (beside the drab Charles and his aged mother) in a splendid red dress. In a sense, it is her inability to keep the two mutually exclusive roles apart (with the 'red woman' visibly invading the pale domestic space more and more frequently) which precipitates her death.

The patriarchal society she inhabits can also be implicated in Emma' s death – but Chabrol makes no attempt to emphasise a feminist reading of the film. This is due to his desire to remain absolutely faithful to Flaubert and to refrain from introducing a (conscious) twentieth-century perspective in the film. It remains clear, however, that Emma's dissatisfaction stems in part from the constraint she is under, as a woman, to conform to one or other of a very limited number of roles. She cannot see beyond those roles, but nor is she encouraged to do so by the men who surround her. Emma is also inhibited by her social status. Like Violette,[28] she is constricted emotionally and physically by her middle-class surroundings: hence the small, drab home she shares with Charles, and especially the cramped dining room (which is juxtaposed regularly with wider spaces like the château where the ball takes place, or the fields and woods where she goes riding with Rodolphe). While Emma dies within these social restrictions, and Violette is finally recuperated into them, the contemporary protagonist of *Betty* (1992) frees herself and is able to simply exist outside them (in a way that a nineteenth-century woman like Emma could not). Only in the world of the *grande bourgeoisie* (a vestige of the nineteenth century) does Betty suffer the identity crisis that Emma suffers throughout her life.

28 The parallel is emphasised when Violette's parents suggest that she should marry a middle-class professional – a chemist (like Homais in *Madame Bovary*) or a doctor (like Charles Bovary).

Betty

Betty (1992), like *Madame Bovary*, is a faithful adaptation of a
novel, telling the story of an unsatisfied young woman who seeks
to define herself outside the social and familial roles offered her.
But there are three crucial differences. Firstly, the film escapes
easy definition as a genre piece: its likeliest description is as a
psychological drama, but it is resolutely anti-psychological (we are
given questions about the characters, not answers), while the only
dramatic event, as Chabrol admits, is 'la signature du papier'[29]
(Jousse and Toubiana 1992: 31). Secondly, unlike Emma in *Madame
Bovary* (and Marie in *Une affaire de femmes*), Betty triumphantly
survives: 'C'est la revanche de Madame Bovary, sa triomphe
finale. Si Emma avait été comme Betty, elle s'en serait tirée'[30]
(*ibid.*). And thirdly, this is undoubtedly one of Chabrol's best films.

Betty is Chabrol's second adaptation from Georges Simenon,
following *Les Fantômes du chapelier* in 1982. Even more so than
Balzac, Simenon is a novelist who bears close comparison with
Chabrol, and with whom he identifies (Chabrol 1976: 348). They
share a prolific output (Simenon wrote over two hundred novels,
including seventy Maigret stories), an interest in criminal and
anti-social behaviour, and a detached perspective. Chabrol's objective camerawork, like Simenon's neutral writing style, presents
case studies of human action without making any moral judgements. *Betty* follows a young woman (Marie Trintignant) on a
drunken binge from which she is apparently rescued by an
enigmatic mother figure, Laure (Stéphane Audran).[31] Betty slowly
reveals to Laure how she married into the *grande bourgeoisie*, but
was driven out and forced to sign away her rights to see her two
daughters when her numerous affairs were discovered. Sticking
closely to the structure and the dialogue of the source novel,
Chabrol's film is fragmented, shifting backwards and forwards

29 'the signing of the paper'
30 'It's the revenge of Madame Bovary, it's her final triumph. If Emma had been
    like Betty, she would have escaped'
31 Chabrol comments on the fact that Stéphane Audran could almost have been
    Marie Trintignant's mother in real life, since Audran's first husband was
    Marie's father, Jean-Louis Trintignant (Jousse and Toubiana 1992: 34).

between the present and the past. There is however no sense of deliberate formal patterning here – as there is, say, in *À double tour* (1959) or *Les Bonnes Femmes* (1960). The flashbacks, which include repeated glimpses of Betty's signing away of her children, and – in a flashback within a flashback – a Freudian 'primal scene' in which she sees her uncle having sex with the maid, are all subjective and, so to speak, organic. They develop from Betty's present situation and state of mind. In this regard they are closer to the fluid temporality of stream of consciousness than to the usual role of flashbacks in cinema – to explain the present by reference to the past. The flashbacks are traditionally anchored by close-ups of Betty's face, but they are motivated not by any narrative function so much as by Betty's own inability to follow the thread of the present conversation. Bored and drunk, she claims to be listening to Laure, and in fact we often continue to hear Laure's voice droning on in the background, as images from the past drift into Betty's mind and onto the screen. Even when the central enigma in the film is resolved – how and why has Betty got into the state she's in at the start? – a second is posed regarding her relationship with Laure and with the latter's boyfriend, Mario. It is no coincidence that the film ends with a close-up on Betty's mysterious smile, shot through the misty waters of an aquarium. Like the Hélènes of *La Femme infidèle*, *Le Boucher* and *Juste avant la nuit* (played of course by Stéphane Audran), she remains obscure.

The close-ups on Marie Trintignant's face throughout the film – like the flashbacks – invert their conventional role in cinema. Where flashbacks are meant to explain, here they complicate matters. (For instance, does the scene between her uncle and the maid really explain Betty's promiscuity? Or is it a red herring, or at the most, simply one stage in the development of her sexuality?) Where facial close-ups on an actress are usually associated with sacred beauty or eroticism, here they reveal Betty as ravaged, exhausted and drunk, seemingly mechanical in her indifference to everything except ordering the next whisky. (The unsparing photography is not limited to Trintignant: Stéphane Audran complained that the chief cameraman had ruined her appearance throughout the film.) Like Violette, Betty is presented as fragmented, irreducible to one single reading. She is always seen from the outside (hence the opening credit sequence where we watch through a window as she drinks in a bar), even if the flashbacks are subjective. Again as in *Violette Nozière*, the camera pans back from an apparently real image of the protagonist's face to reveal it as a reflection in the mirror. This raises questions of how Betty's identity is defined.

The dual nature of Betty's identity makes the film one of Chabrol's most incisive comments on the position of women in a male-dominated society. (A position which is – again – exacerbated by social class: Betty is a lower-class woman in a male-dominated and bourgeois-dominated society.) 'Betty' is the protagonist's natural self: anti-social, alcoholic and fascinated by sex. 'Elisabeth' is her artificial self: a culturally defined identity as bourgeois wife and mother, socialised and subservient. Even more than the loss of her two small daughters and her expulsion from the bourgeoisie, it is the traumatic collision of these two identities which is dramatised in the scene of the paper-signing – the narrative crux of the film, to which we are returned again and again by Betty's remembering of it. As the first flashback reveals, Betty originally signs the paper 'Betty', but this is spotted by her mother-in-law (the personification of the *grande bourgeoisie* and a character who only ever refers to Betty as Elisabeth). Corrected by the lawyer, Betty signs as 'Elisabeth Étamble', giving her maiden name, age, (lack of) profession and so on. That this is felt as some kind of betrayal of her real self is evident from her account of the event. In her drunken misery at the memory of what she has done, she sobs that she has sold her children, and also that 'J'ai marqué "Elisabeth" au lieu de "Betty", et puis j'ai pris un chèque'.[32] It is not just her daughters that Betty has sold, but her own identity. Viewed in this light, the spiral of drinking and casual sex which follows the signing of the paper is Betty's means of reasserting her identity, and an act of defiance against the legalistic and reductive definition of her recorded in the document. The first proof of this comes when she signs to have her belongings transferred to Laure's hotel in Versailles: in a reversal of the document scene, she begins to write

32 'I put "Elisabeth" instead of "Betty", and then I took the cheque'

'Elisabeth', but changes the 'E' to a 'B' and signs as 'Betty'. The final proof – as we shall see shortly – is her betrayal of Laure and her running off with Mario.

If sex and alcohol characterise Betty's natural behaviour, then marriage and motherhood characterise her culturally acquired identity. Flashbacks to her bourgeois existence with Guy Étamble and his insufferable mother reveal the extent to which she is required to deny her true personality and to become – like Jasmine in *Une affaire de femmes* – little more than a womb. Her role is to provide children but she is also, paradoxically, denied the chance to rear them – that is the nanny's job. As in *La Muette* (1965) and *La Rupture* (1970), it is the coldness of the bourgeois family that Chabrol satirises most violently. In a scene added to the original novel, Chabrol contrasts the marginalisation of Betty's children by the Étambles – they are brought in to say goodnight but not allowed to spend even five minutes with their mother – with a television gameshow watched by Madame Étamble, in which the contestant warmly declares, 'J'embrasse toute me famille – ma femme, mes enfants ...'[33] Betty is also confronted with the bourgeoisie in the slightly seedy form of Laure. There is a kind of doubling here, in which Laure is an older version of Elisabeth (Betty's bourgeois self). Like Debbie and Bertha in Lang's *The Big Heat* (1953), they are 'sisters under the mink'. During the long sequences in Laure's hotel room, the two women tell each other about their past – each using exactly the same form of words to assure the other that they really are listening when they are not. Like Betty, Laure has tried to drown a previous existence as a bourgeois wife in an alcoholic binge. But whereas Betty never felt that she belonged to bourgeois society ('Je ne pouvais pas être comme eux'),[34] and precipitated her own expulsion from it (she is discovered having sex with her lover in the middle of the drawing-room), Laure was a willing partici-pant: 'Mon univers, c'était mon mari, ma maison'.[35] Laure regrets

33 'I send my love to all the family – my wife, my children ...' With typical malice, Chabrol has Madame Étamble suddenly fall asleep in front of the television, as if struck dead by a heart attack.

34 'I couldn't be like them'

35 'My world was my husband and my house'

her husband's death, her isolation from the bourgeoisie and her new, rootless status. She is lost without a social role to fulfil (hence perhaps her mothering of Betty). She therefore represents what Betty risks becoming if the latter fails to reassert her true, anti-social and anti-bourgeois identity. This identity is characterised by her survival instinct and her sex drive, which allow her to overcome the falsity of her bourgeois life and eventually Laure's claustrophobic maternal attentions. Rather than the female solidarity of *Une affaire de femmes*, the relationship between Betty and Laure is reminiscent of the power struggles between Charles and Paul in the Hélène cycle (with Mario the object of desire and exchange). Betty wins, and Laure goes away to die. The final line of the film, read by Chabrol, declares that 'Laure Lavancher en définitive était morte parce que Betty avait survécu. C'était l'une ou l'autre, et Betty avait gagné'.[36] But it is also Elisabeth – the tamed, civilised and constrained bourgeois self, the subservient wife and mother – who has died, allowing Betty's true self to survive.

If female sexuality is spectral in *Violette Nozière* and illicit in *Madame Bovary*, in *Betty* it is unclean. Betty is portrayed as dirty (in both senses) throughout the film: at school she has to write on the blackboard 'Je suis une petite sale';[37] when she meets Guy for the first time, she spills coffee all over his clean suit; later he tells her 'C'est effacé'[38] when she confesses to a promiscuous past. As she herself says, 'J'ai passé ma vie à salir'.[39] This complies with the conventional, patriarchal representation of sexually active women (particularly those from the lower classes, like Betty) as unclean: 'the bodies of erotic women, especially proletarian ones, become so much wet dirt' (Theweleit 1987: 421). But Betty's sexuality is not condemned in the film so much as celebrated – as an affront to prudish bourgeois manners and as a defining fact of her own existence. (Chabrol himself is fond of metaphors – like 'getting

36 'Ultimately, Laure Lavancher had died because Betty had survived. It was one or the other, and Betty had won'
37 'I am a filthy little girl'
38 'It's wiped clean'
39 'I dirty everything I touch'

your hands dirty' – which link life with dirt.) The Étambles perceive Betty as a sexual threat, and try to redefine her as a desexualised wife and mother – the 'white woman'. But her sexuality cannot be repressed. The white suit she wears on the day she signs the document becomes crumpled and stained in the bars and hotel rooms she visits later that night. In the final triumphant scene – when she has escaped with Mario to his suggestively named restaurant Le Trou[40] – she wears black, with red lipstick. As the credits roll, a final close-up on her face centres on the sexual symbol of her bright red mouth. Where Emma Bovary's 'red woman' fantasy of eloping with Rodolphe fails, Betty's elopement with Mario succeeds. (The parallel is emphasised by the *mise en scène*: both women wear black with red lipstick in the climactic scenes.) Alternatively, like Laura in *Juste avant la nuit* (1971) – another sexually voracious woman associated with dirt – Betty has been expelled from the apparently spotless bourgeoisie, but where Laura is killed (and her murder effaced), Betty survives, resolutely sexual and anti-social to the last.

Popular film genres seem to entail the punishment of the sexualised woman: hence the fate of the *femme fatale* in *film noir* (Julie in *Les Innocents aux mains sales*) and the bad mother in melodrama (Marie in *Une affaire de femmes*). Chabrol, as we have seen, is fully aware of this convention and foregrounds it through exaggeration. His adaptation of *Madame Bovary* elaborates the main theme – women punished for having desires – of the genre pieces just mentioned. The case with *Violette Nozière* and *Betty* is complicated, however, by the fact that these are not genre films (they are only distantly related to the thriller). Both avoid the brutal closure of the others, and allow their eponymous heroines to survive beyond the last frame. If in *Violette Nozière* this survival is at the price of a rehabilitation into the conventionally feminised space of domesticity, in *Betty* the situation is reversed: Betty has to leave her children behind along with the unreal upper-class world of the Étambles family. If it thus seems impossible for the women in these films to have their cake and eat it (to have a family and a

40 The Hole

sexualised, independent identity), this is largely because of the determining influence of social class (bourgeois codes of morality in *Madame Bovary* and *Betty*) and of patriarchy (the male jurors cursed by Violette, the Vichy state which condemns Marie). (It might also be noted that all four films end with the voice of a male narrator: Chabrol in *Violette Nozière*; Chabrol again, reading Simenon, in *Betty*; Marie's son Pierrot in *Une affaire de femmes*; and François Perrier reading Flaubert in *Madame Bovary*.) None the less, the spirit of dissatisfaction and rebellion incarnated at least temporarily by Violette and Emma, and almost incessantly by Marie and Betty, remains – to be given a further, defiantly Marxist, twist in *La Cérémonie* (1995).

References

Berthomieu, P., Jeancolas, J.-P., and Vassé, C. (1995), Entretien avec Claude Chabrol, *Positif*, 416 (September), 8–14.

Blanchet, C. (1989), *Claude Chabrol*, Paris, Rivages.

Boddaert, F., de Biasi, P.-M., Eliacheff, C., Laporte, A., Mouchard, C. and Versaille, A. (1991), *Autour d'Emma: Madame Bovary un film de Claude Chabrol*, Paris, Hatier, Collection Brèves Cinéma.

Chabrol, C. (1976), *Et pourtant je tourne ...*, Paris, Robert Laffont.

Doane, M. A. (1987), *The Desire to Desire: The Woman's Film of the 1940s*, Basingstoke, Macmillan.

Guérin, M.-A., and Jousse, T. (1995), Entretien avec Claude Chabrol, *Cahiers du cinéma*, 494 (September), 27–32.

Jousse, T., and Toubiana, S. (1992), Entretien avec Claude Chabrol, *Cahiers du cinéma*, 453 (March), 31–7.

Theweleit, K. (1987), *Male Fantasies*, I: *Women, Floods, Bodies, History*, Cambridge, Polity Press.

Walker, D. H. (1995), *Outrage and Insight: Modern French Writers and the 'Fait Divers'*, Oxford and Washington, DC, Berg.

Yakir, D. (1979), The Magical Mystery World of Claude Chabrol: An Interview, *Film Quarterly* (spring), 2–14.

Master of *Cérémonie*

Chabrol's forty-ninth film, *La Cérémonie* (1995), can be considered the pinnacle of his career so far. Described by *Cahiers du cinéma* as 'le plus grand film du cinéma français depuis longtemps'¹ (Strauss 1995: 26), it finally confirmed his long, slow rehabilitation by the intellectual strand of the French film press. In contrast with the critical reception in France for much of Chabrol's work from the 1960s, the 1970s and even the early 1980s, he was now considered 'le plus moderne de tous les auteurs issus de la Nouvelle Vague'² (Jousse 1995: 35), and possibly the greatest French film-maker ever.³ Although this reassessment involved a very brief glance back at his earlier films, it was principally on the evidence of *La Cérémonie* that Chabrol was adjudged to be a master at work.

Based on a Ruth Rendell crime novel that Chabrol updated and modified (adding in particular an emphasis on television which was absent from the book), the film relates the gradual tensions that surface in the power relations between a wealthy bourgeois family, the Lelièvres, and their new maid Sophie (Sandrine Bonnaire). The two catalysts for the bloody finale, in which the family are shot dead in cold blood, are Sophie's sense of powerlessness – exacerbated and symbolised by her inability to read – and her

---

1 'the greatest French film for a long time'
2 'the most modern of all the *auteurs* to come out of the new wave'
3 See the editorial of *Cahiers du cinéma* 494, p. 22. *Positif* magazine granted Chabrol similar, if slightly less hyperbolic, praise in its own editorial – see *Positif* 416, p. 5.

friendship with Jeanne (Isabelle Huppert), who encourages her to rebel against her masters. The film thus functions both as a thriller and, in a political sense, as an illustration of the class war which Chabrol continues to observe in French society. But not only is *La Cérémonie* a masterful film in its own right, it can also be seen as a compendium of some of the motifs that characterise Chabrol's work as a whole. It is in attending to these motifs that we can come to a conclusion regarding Chabrol's long-disputed status as an *auteur* in French cinema.

The *fait divers*

We have already seen how real-life crime stories or *faits divers* are reflected in several of Chabrol's films, from *Les Bonnes Femmes* and *Les Noces rouges* to *Violette Nozière* and *Une affaire de femmes*. This is also true, to an extent, of *La Cérémonie*, which is partly analogous to the infamous case of the Papin sisters. In 1933, a year before the equally notorious crime committed by Violette Nozière, the Papins, both maids, butchered their mistress and her daughter. The trial that followed drew a huge amount of attention from the public and the media, and gave rise to two distinct interpretations of the crime. As with Violette Nozière, the surrealists interpreted the Papin case politically – as a direct attack on the bourgeoisie by its very own servants. But according to psychiatrists, the crime was psychological rather than political, and was in a sense committed not by both sisters but by a bizarre and paranoid 'third person' who they became under stress (Walker 1995: 94). Although no direct reference is made to the Papin case in *La Cérémonie*, it influenced Chabrol's co-writer Caroline Eliacheff in her reworking of the source novel (Guérin and Jousse 1995: 30). The result is a certain emphasis on the fusion of identities between Sophie and Jeanne as if, like the Papin sisters, they were turning into a murderous third person. This process begins when Sophie visits Jeanne's flat and they discover that they have a similar past (Sophie was implicated in the death of her father, Jeanne in the death of her daughter). Beyond this shared guilt (even before the shared murder) there is a sense of shared identity as the two sit watching Sophie's television, arm in arm, with their hair in pigtails and vacant expressions on their faces. And the process is completed in the murder sequence, during which their gestures (whether drinking coffee in the kitchen as they reload or bearing down on Gilles in the doorway of the drawing-room) are identical and simultaneous. Much more so than Betty and Laure (*Betty*), or even Why and Frédérique (*Les Biches*), Sophie and Jeanne are at this point one and the same.

But if *La Cérémonie* is in part a version of the Papin case, it does not privilege the psychological reading over the political one, in the way that Nancy Meckler's *Sister My Sister* (UK, 1994) does. From the opening credits (showing two little girls combing each other's hair) to the final shot (the two sisters clinging to each other in bed, their hair wild and their faces haggard),[4] Meckler's film focuses on the psychotic and ultimately incestuous closeness between the two maids. Chabrol, on the other hand, avoids any sustained or direct psychological explanation for the murder of the Lelièvres. This allows him to maintain a sense of the opacity of human motives and to introduce a possible political interpretation of the killing. It is impossible to say whether Sophie and Jeanne commit the murders in order to avenge personal humiliations (Melinda discovering that Sophie cannot read, Monsieur Lelièvre accusing Jeanne of opening his mail), or to reverse power relations between the proletariat and the bourgeoisie.

Above and beyond individual cases, the *fait divers* as a form can be usefully compared to Chabrol's cinema in general. The *fait divers* 'speaks of scandal, sensation, disruption of the norm', events that 'the dominant ideology cannot accommodate ... properly' (Walker 1995: 1–2). It is precisely such disruptions that interest Chabrol, especially insofar as they challenge accepted morality, which he calls 'Une règle de jeu qui arrange une classe dominante'[5] (Chabrol 1976: 53). In his films, the 'disruption of the norm'

4 This is a recreation of the famous photograph of the Papin sisters after the murder, published in 1933 in the magazines *Détective* and *Le Surréalisme au service de la révolution*.

5 'The rules of a game that suits the dominant class'

most often takes the form of an intrusion into the enclosed and self-satisfied world of the bourgeoisie, and typically either begins (*Juste avant la nuit*) or ends (*L'Œil du malin, Les Biches, La Femme infidèle, La Cérémonie*) with murder. What makes the latter case so shocking is the extent to which the victims of the murder are normalised. Unlike, say, the corrupt and buffoonish Paul in *Les Noces rouges*, the claustrophobic and incestuous families in *Blood Relatives* and *Violette Nozière*, or the Fascistic Vichy regime in *Une affaire de femmes*, the Lelièvre family are unobjectionable. Their only fault is in fact simply their function – as Sophie's employers, and as the embodiment of the bourgeoisie. They represent the masters, the norm, the 'dominant ideology', and it is as such that they are destroyed.

The potentially subversive effects of the *fait divers* are usually mitigated by its position, literally at the margins of journalism. Thus the *fait divers* in fact works to neutralise threats against the norm:

> the rubric of the *fait divers* has a dual function: on the one hand, by reporting odd or bizarre items, it seeks to translate them into the language of common concerns; but, because of its secondary status, it marginalizes such items, keeps them at a safe remove from the centre of society. The *fait-diversier* thus lays claim to the off-beat or grotesque on behalf of bourgeois humanism or conventional society. (Walker 1995: 2)

Chabrol's cinema carries out the first function but not the second. It translates the violent, the inexplicable and the grotesque – be it revolution (*Les Biches*), terrorism (*Nada*), freak accidents (*Les Cousins, La Muette, Que la bête meure*) murder (numerous films from *À double tour* to *La Cérémonie*) or suicide (*Le Cri du hibou, Dr M, Madame Bovary*) – into 'the language of common concerns' by filming these events in the guise of popular genres, notably the thriller. But because genre cinema is at the centre and not at the margins, Chabrol's work does not marginalise its narratives in the way that the *fait divers*, or indeed art cinema, does. At least after his new-wave period, Chabrol deliberately uses recognisable genres and classical realism in order to aim his work at 'the centre of society'. (So successful was he in this respect that during the late 1960s and early 1970s he was equated with 'the centre' by radical film critics.) This approach allows him to undermine rather than defend 'bourgeois humanism'. It should also be noted that Chabrol works largely in realist film genres (the thriller, the melodrama, the war film, the period drama). Only one of his films can be classified as fantasy cinema (*Alice ou la dernière fugue*), and while the vampire movie informs part of *Les Biches*, he has never made a horror film or a science fiction film. (This contrasts with his new-wave colleagues, Godard and Truffaut, who made *Alphaville* and *Fahrenheit 451* respectively.) The reason for this may be the marginal status traditionally accorded to fantasy genres in France. By sticking to the thriller and other realist genres, Chabrol has managed to maintain a subversive position within the mainstream.

Class war

Politically as well as aesthetically, Chabrol is interested in bringing the margins to the centre. In the late 1970s he predicted that 'the real center will be a sort of modern Marxism' (Yakir 1979: 9). Even if by the early 1990s events seemed to have proved him wrong – with the fall of the Berlin Wall and the collapse of communism – he was still prepared to make what he half-jokingly called 'le dernier film marxiste'[6] (Guérin and Taboulay 1997: 68). *La Cérémonie* fulfils this function by virtue of the importance of class struggle within the film.[7] Hence the destruction of the bourgeois Lelièvre family by the working-class pairing of Sophie and Jeanne. In this respect, the generally blameless behaviour of the Lelièvres is crucial. Their best efforts to treat Sophie correctly are doomed to failure because they fail to accept her as she is (unable to read) and they also fail, politically speaking, to frame

6 'the last Marxist film'

7 To a certain degree, the film also reflects concerns about current tensions in French society. Chabrol has said that *La Cérémonie* predicts an imminent implosion while Mathieu Kassovitz's *La Haine* (also 1995) predicts an imminent explosion. See Berthomieu *et al.* 1995: 9.

their efforts in any other form than that of master–servant relations. Thus Melinda, who tries hardest to be fair to Sophie, cannot help ordering her about even when they are supposed to be having a cup of tea together. (She also offends Jeanne with her superior knowledge and her superior manner.) The family are therefore killed not because of their personalities (which are sympathetic), but because of their class. As Chabrol says, '[la famille bourgeoise] n'est attaquable que par son état, c'est ça le marxisme'[8] (Guérin and Jousse 1995: 28). Sophie is not in the slightest ideologically aware, while Jeanne's resentment confuses the political with the personal, but that does not prevent their actions – like those of the Papin sisters – from being represented or interpreted as class war.

In contrast with the bourgeois families of *La Muette*, *Les Noces rouges* and *Folies bourgeoises*, the Lelièvres are not subjected to ridicule by means of farce. Nor are they subjected to the half-idealised, half-satirical perspective of the Hélène cycle. Consequently *La Cérémonie* is Chabrol's most direct representation of class struggle. This is a matter of setting as well as characterisation. Where *Les Biches* concerns personal relations as a metaphor for revolution, *La Rupture* depicts a class-based custody battle and *Nada* a political kidnapping, *La Cérémonie* alone concerns social relations in the workplace.[9] That the workplace happens to be the Lelièvres' family home only serves to emphasise the gulf between the bourgeoisie and the working-classes. For while the Lelièvres epitomise the bourgeois family, Sophie and Jeanne – both solitary, both associated with the death of a family member – reflect what Marx calls 'the practical absence of the family among the proletarians' (Marx and Engels [1848] (1953): 74). *La Cérémonie* thus makes explicit what is implicit in Chabrol's work as a whole – the absence of the working-class family.

In the bourgeois home, Sophie is taught to know her place. Her servile function is equated with certain actions and also certain spaces within the house: her tiny bedroom (the *chambre de bonne*

---

8 'the bourgeois family are attacked solely because of their class status – that's Marxism'

9 *Les Bonnes Femmes* is set in the workplace but does not really concern social relations.

or maid's room), the back stairs, the kitchen (described to her by Madame Lelièvre as 'votre domaine').[10] By fitting into these spaces, and entering others only with the authorisation of her employers, Sophie literally learns to serve. Her friendship with Jeanne entails a refusal to serve ('Je vais pas leur obéir')[11] and consequently a change of place. It is only when Jeanne visits the house that Sophie is finally seen using the main staircase rather than the back stairs. Her freedom of movement in the house symbolises her growing insubordination; it is immediately after a shot of Sophie openly going up the main stairs on her own that Monsieur Lelièvre fires her. Tellingly, when the murders take place, they are presented as a parody of servile duties. Sophie and Jeanne climb the main stairs to the master bedroom as if they were (still) maids: Jeanne carries a tray of hot chocolate and Sophie is wearing her apron. They proceed to tear up Madame Lelièvre's dresses in a frenzied parody of the scenes where they (and other working-class volunteers) sorted the old clothes donated to the 'Secours catholique'. Monsieur Lelièvre is actually shot dead in Sophie's domain, the kitchen, before the finale in which the servants finally enter the bourgeois *inner sanctum* – the drawing-room – to kill the rest of their masters.

Femmes fatales

But the power struggle in La Cérémonie is not simply a matter of the working classes versus the bourgeoisie. Nor is it really a question of gender, since Madame Lelièvre's good looks and leisurely lifestyle are just as much the target of Jeanne's anger as Monsieur Lelièvre's self-righteousness and autocratic air. As with the Charles–Paul conflicts in Les Cousins and the Hélène cycle, or the shifting relations between Why and Frédérique in Les Biches and between Betty and Laure in Betty, here also there is a personal battle. Sophie and Jeanne are, to a great extent, identified with each other, both through the narrative (their secret pasts, their

10 'your domain'
11 'I'm not going to obey them'

common enemy) and the *mise en scène* (their similar appearance and gestures in the later stages of the film). But they are also implicitly pitted against each other. At first Sophie is dominated by Jeanne (who can read whereas Sophie cannot, who talks while Sophie is silent). She even assumes her servile role as the maid in Jeanne's flat: she is the one who prepares and serves the coffee. But ultimately Sophie takes control: she initiates the murders, first shooting Monsieur Lelièvre and then leading the way into the drawing-room to kill the others. The case is much the same as in *Betty* or *Les Biches*: only the stronger of the two women will survive. The reason for this is the dual status of Chabrol's female protagonists. As he explains with regard to *Betty*, women in his films are at once victims (of a patriarchal society) and also fighters: 'Notre univers est masculinisé, machiste. Par rapport à cet univers, une femme a tous les droits'[12] (Berthomieu *et al.* 1995: 13). Ambivalence also characterises Chabrol's male characters, for example the noble avenger–cowardly liar Charles in *Que la bête meure* or the white knight–greedy manipulator Wolf in *Masques* (their duplicity is suggested by the fact that both act under assumed names). But the duality of the women in Chabrol's films is more generalised, because it is a product of society as he sees it. It is reflected in the heterosexual couple by the Hélènes of *Le Boucher* (at once Popaul's potential victim and the person indirectly responsible for his death) and *Juste avant la nuit* (the understanding wife who coolly prepares her husband's suicide). But it also manifests itself within female friendships, including that between Sophie and Jeanne in *La Cérémonie*.

Duality (or, in a more stigmatised form, duplicity) is also a defining characteristic of the *femme fatale* archetype from *film noir*. Although *La Cérémonie* cannot be defined as a *film noir*, Sophie is in certain ways characterised as a dangerous *femme fatale* (whereas Jeanne is not). The first hint comes when she is introduced to her duties by Madame Lelièvre. The introduction of the *femme fatale* in *film noir* traditionally involves a shot of her descending a staircase, with the focus on her legs – as in *Double Indemnity* (1944), *The*

12 'Our society is male-dominated and chauvinist. In such a world, a woman has to use whatever she can'

Postman Always Rings Twice (1946), or Truffaut's *La Femme d'à côté* (1981). The image of the *femme fatale* is also usually dark and ominous: '*Film noir* lighting suggests duplicity: an unknown threat which might emerge from the shadows' (Cook 1980: 78) Both of these elements (the composition and the lighting) are echoed in Sophie's first appearance in her role as the Lelièvres' maid. Chabrol shoots her from below, as she descends the dingy back stairs into the kitchen. Framing (the focus is on her legs), costume (she has put on a dark dress) and lighting (she emerges from shadows) all comply with *film noir* conventions, and encode Sophie as a *femme fatale*. The effect is also to invert the optimistic implications of the previous scene, in which Sophie watches the beginning of a television drama showing a female lawyer ascending the white stone steps to a courthouse in daylight. This safe image – of a socially acceptable form of female ambition – is replaced by its opposite: the *femme fatale* who will take an anti-social form of power – the '"unnatural" phallic power' of the gun (Place 1980: 45) – into her own hands.

After the murders, Sophie is again presented as a *femme fatale* (again, in a way that Jeanne is not). But in this case, the conventions of the *film noir* are evoked only to be transcended. Traditionally, the *femme fatale* is punished at the end of a *film noir*. She is either literally (via the narrative) or figuratively (via the *mise en scène*) imprisoned, defeated or killed. (Jeanne's death in the car crash is not encoded as the punishment of a *femme fatale* but as an ironic coincidence: it is her *bête noire* the priest who accidentally kills her). Whereas Julie's fate in *Les Innocents aux mains sales* exaggeratedly, almost parodically, adheres to this convention, there is no such punishment for Sophie at the end of *La Cérémonie*. Although she is represented as a *femme fatale* in the final scene (by the expressionist lighting, the shadows, her pale face looming out of the night) she escapes closure. Whereas Julie is incarcerated alone in her villa and condemned to grieve in a night illuminated only by the hallucinatory image of the mysterious flashing light (as if her husband were calling to her from the grave), Sophie literally escapes from the frame, walking away from the house, the crime scene, and the flashing lights of the police. Like Betty, she survives. But unlike Betty, and unlike the conventional *femme fatale*, Sophie also escapes from the controlling commentary of the male voice-over. Like most *films noirs*, many of Chabrol's films about women – *Betty*, *Madame Bovary*, *Une affaire de femmes*, *Violette Nozière* and even implicitly *Les Innocents aux mains sales* (if one accepts that the light symbolises Louis calling to Julie) – end with a male voice.[13] It is as if these women are being controlled by a male narrator (as indeed, they are – by Simenon, Flaubert and Chabrol himself). *La Cérémonie* however, was largely authored by women (Ruth Rendell wrote the novel, Caroline Eliacheff co-wrote the screenplay), and, as the police play back the tape-recording of the murder, it ends with the female voices of Sophie and Jeanne. Although there is a typical Chabrolian ambivalence here – Sophie has been seen to escape, but she has implicated herself, and could yet be caught – the fact remains that the murderer, the *femme fatale*, has gone unpunished. Her spectral appearance as she drifts into the night recalls Violette's first appearance in *Violette Nozière*. But, as Chabrol's own voice tells us, Violette was rehabilitated as a safe woman (the opposite of the *femme fatale*) through her imprisonment. Sophie has escaped the imprisonment, the rehabilitation and the male voice.

The expressionist house

The representation of Sophie, Violette and Julie as variations on the *femme fatale* is partly dependent on Chabrol's use of the expressionist *mise en scène* associated with *film noir*. Chabrol's expressionism also owes a particular debt to Fritz Lang, who used it not only in his *films noirs* but also in westerns and fantasy films. If Hitchcock's influence on Chabrol is most evident in terms of voyeurism and point of view (see below, p. 107), Lang's legacy is clearest in terms of décor. Although the shadowy lighting and unsettling camera angles prevalent in expressionism are used sparingly in Chabrol's films, the symbolic significance of expressionist décor is a constant. Houses and apartments almost

13 The male voice also controls, even dictates, female actions in *L'Enfer*.

always express their occupants' state of mind or destiny. In *Les Cousins*, the weapons on the walls of Paul's apartment suggest his predatory strength while Charles's bedroom isolates him from the open living-space. The glass houses of Léda in *À double tour* and the Massons in *Juste avant la nuit* appear to be open and transparent, but in fact they hide secrets, and the lives lived within will prove vulnerable. Hélène's tower room in *Le Boucher* symbolises her flight from the world, while the blue room Hélène rents in *La Rupture* evokes the threatening presence of Régnier and his plot to ensnare her. In *Violette Nozière*, *Blood Relatives* and *Madame Bovary* the walls close in like the moral constraints of the bourgeois family.

Much like the Gothic houses in *Ten Days' Wonder* and *Masques*, the house in *La Cérémonie* is large and isolated. These houses function as enclosed worlds, ruled by the patriarchal Theo van Horn and Legagneur, or the more paternalistic Lelièvres. But their Gothic appearance also creates a sense of foreboding, evoked in the opening shot of each of the houses in question, and heightened in the climactic nocturnal sequences from all three films. In *La Cérémonie*, moreover, great emphasis is placed on the house's isolation. Madame Lelièvre tells Sophie twice in their first interview that it is 'une maison isolée',[14] while the situation of the house itself is doubled by Sophie's room within it (alone, at the top) and the site of the nearest town (Saint Malo, cut off and enclosed by its famous walls). The effect is to evoke Sophie's own isolation, not just as a stranger and a servant in the household, but also as an illiterate, and hence someone who is not fully socialised but remains cut off from the world around her. When confronted with its demands – in the form of the written note from Madame Lelièvre or the telephone call from Monsieur Lelièvre – she retreats, like Hélène in *Le Boucher*, and locks herself up in her room.

We have already noted the political symbolism of the division of space within the Lelièvres' home. The domain of the masters is clearly demarcated as the main staircase, the drawing-room, the dining-room and (naturally) the master bedroom. Sophie, as the servant, is associated with the back stairs and the rooms they link

14 'an isolated house'

– the kitchen and the *chambre de bonne*. The principal sites of communication or passage between the two spaces are the main staircase and the oval mirror in the hall. Both belong to the realm of the masters, but they allow access to the world 'below stairs': the staircase because it offers an alternative route to the kitchen and to Sophie's room, the mirror because it reflects the doorway into the kitchen, Sophie's domain. It is only when she has learned to use the main stairs for her own purposes, and to infiltrate the master bedroom, that Sophie masters the house with her gaze. The hall mirror, meanwhile, shows Madame Lelièvre entering the other world of the kitchen to look for Sophie, but it also shows Sophie's gradual assumption of power within the house. (The possibility of a such a metamorphosis is glimpsed when Sophie watches on television a programme in which a young woman stares into a mirror before accepting a potion from a mysterious magician: it is as if she were accepting an invitation to go through the looking-glass.) If the first close-up on Sophie's face in the hall mirror suggests impotence (she appears to be reading a note, but cannot in fact read), the next suggests power (as she listens to Melinda's phone conversation and learns of her secret pregnancy). As well as being fundamental in the construction of space as power in *La Cérémonie*, the staircase and the mirror are also key motifs from expressionism. In the expressionist *mise en scène* of *film noir*, both motifs are associated with the *femme fatale*: the staircase to symbolise her dominance over the male characters, the mirror to suggest her narcissism and duality. More generally, in *film noir* as in Chabrol's work as a whole, mirrored compositions imply that 'nothing and no-one is what it seems' (Place 1980: 48).

Looking as power

The organisation of space is the key means by which Chabrol expresses power relations in his work. Stairs or split levels allow one character to dominate another, to look down at their victim. This motif is first seen in *Les Cousins*, when Paul, on top of a ladder, looks down at Charles's arrival (the telescope he uses even suggests the gun with which he will later kill Charles). It is also crucial to *Les Innocents aux mains sales,* where Louis's power over his wife is equated with his position at the top of the stairs while she is beneath him. And in *Dr M,* the citizens of Berlin are controlled by the images on the walls above them. Power is also associated with the outsider looking in. Both *L'Œil du malin* and *Le Cri du hibou* detail what happens when the voyeur abandons his controlling position and goes inside. Spatial relations are just as expressive of power in *La Cérémonie.* In certain key sequences, the dominant character organises the space around them and implicitly controls the others in the frame. This is evident in the very first scene, where Madame Lelièvre meets Sophie in the café. The point of view here – and hence the power – is Madame Lelièvre's. She is the controlling presence, sitting and observing as Sophie searches for the right café and then the right table. (In retrospect, this opening scene can also be judged to hint at Sophie's particular form of powerlessness, her inability to read: hence her confusion as to which café is the right one, her ignorance as to what day of the week it is, and so on.) But in their next meeting, at the train station, the power relations are subtly reversed. This time, although again the scene is largely experienced from Madame Lelièvre's perspective, she is the one at a disadvantage. While she waits for Sophie to get off the train, the latter has in fact already arrived. It is the employer and not the maid who is now struggling to find the right place. Eventually Sophie is revealed on a different platform, silent and ominous, and watching Madame Lelièvre. Even though we are never given Sophie's point of view in this sequence, the implication remains that in this instance, she is the one in control. (This is ironic since the explanation for her early arrival on the wrong train and the wrong platform is that she cannot read the timetable.)

Sophie's powerlessness is explained and symbolised not just by her servile role, but also by her illiteracy. She is thus doubly at a disadvantage in relation to her employers. When she desperately tries to decode Madame Lelièvre's note by means of her reading manual, she is equated with a powerless child in an adult world: all the photos in the book are of children. The importance of reading and not being able to read in *La Cérémonie* is a variation on the theme of looking as power which informs many of Chabrol's films, and which is derived from Hitchock's exploration of voyeurism in *Rear Window* (1954) and *Vertigo* (1958). In *L'Œil du malin*, *Le Cri du hibou* and *L'Enfer*, the voyeur either deliberately or unconsciously destroys the object of his gaze. *Masques* and *Dr M* focus on the omnipotent and omnipresent, quasi-divine gaze of the patriarch (Legagneur and Marsfeldt), and contrast it with the blindness of their victims (Catherine, the citizens of Berlin). Both films also express power relations in terms of watching television, which entails an active, powerful look (the gaze of the screen) and a passive, impotent look (the gaze at the screen). *La Cérémonie* revisits the metaphor of television spectatorship as powerlessness. Sophie's passivity and isolation is underlined by her habit of watching TV endlessly in her room. Even when Jeanne accompanies her, the television acts as a neutralising force and positions them as vacant and passive. Whereas the Papin sisters were said to have fused into a third person capable of butchery, Sophie and Jeanne appear to have fused into a third person capable of little more than staring at the small screen. When they cease watching TV, therefore, and actually look down on the Lelièvre family sat on the couch watching Mozart's *Don Giovanni*, the change from passive spectatorship to active looking is felt as a crucial assumption of power.

The voyeuristic sequence which precedes the murder is the turning-point of the film. It presents Sophie and Jeanne as powerful – and the Lelièvres as vulnerable – by means of the spatial relationship between the two, and specifically though a combination of the Langian metaphor of the staircase and the Hitchcockian metaphor of the gaze. Stairs, as we have seen, are the site of power for the *femme fatale* in *film noir* and for certain characters in Chabrol's work. They are associated in *La Cérémonie* not just with the master–servant relationship (main staircase and back stairs), but also with the power of the priest over his parishioners: hence the two scenes in which the priest exercises his authority from the stairs in the church hall, first to reprimand the choirboys for arriving late, and then to dismiss Jeanne and

Sophie from the 'Secours catholique'. The murders in *La Cérémonie* do not take place on the stairs (as they did in the Papin case and in the British film version, *Sister My Sister*), but they are precipitated and predicted by Sophie and Jeanne's dominant position once they have climbed the main staircase to the master bedroom. From here, they can master the Lelièvres with their gaze, looking down on them from the gallery above the drawing-room. As with the disconcerting sequence at the train station, here again the camera shifts from master/s to servant/s, thereby revealing who is really in control. Chabrol pans slowly upwards from the couch where the family sit watching television to show Sophie and Jeanne silently observing from the gallery. Twice, we are given the servants' point of view as they look down on their masters. Pacified and immobilised by their attention to the TV screen, the Lelièvres are excruciatingly vulnerable. (The sound of the opera, besides, will mask the first gunshots and so limit their chances of escape.) Within a matter of minutes, the family will be lying dead on the couch.

Ambivalence

Like Chabrol's cinema in general, *La Cérémonie* explores shifting relations between characters, and presents sudden reversals of power. Even in the final frame – in this case, Sophie's escape from the crime scene – there is rarely a sense of resolution or closure. This adds to the sense that Chabrol's work is essentially a cinema of ambivalence. His films are funny in both senses: often unexpectedly comic, they are also strange, unsettling and disturbing. Their ambivalence is most evident in the fluctuating tone, the open endings, and the lack of moral judgement that these endings imply. Very few of Chabrol's films are totally consistent in tone. Where farce dominates, there are also moments of poignancy, as in the endings of *Les Noces rouges* and *Folies bourgeoises*. Even the darkest and most serious of his films is punctuated by black humour: the Fascist newsreels of *L'Œil de Vichy* are edited together with a sly and devastating irony, so that the propagandist intentions of the original soundtrack are undermined by the resonance of the images (shots of charcoal burners and holiday trains evoking the Holocaust, for example). The most frequent disruptions of tone in Chabrol's work are not however in the editing, but in the acting.

Sudden eruptions of comic clowning or of theatrical overacting often break through the classic realism of the *mise en scène* and at times even question the realist illusion (that we are watching actual rather than staged events). The neorealist bleakness of *Les Bonnes Femmes* is qualified by the exaggerated hamming of Pierre Bertin as the store-owner, in a grotesque parody of the romantic hero that Jacqueline dreams of. Slightly less out of place in *La Rupture* – because it is a melodrama – but equally comic are the gestures and delivery of Mario David as the unemployed thespian who enlivens the Pinellis' guest-house. In *Que la bête meure*, the realism of the narrative is suddenly and self-consciously disturbed by the appearance of Jean-Louis Maury as a peasant, appearing out of nowhere to give Charles the clues he needs to track down Paul Decourt. Rather than disguise the plotting here, Chabrol simply exaggerates it, with the huge 'detour' signs and the mysterious peasant foregrounding the role of coincidence. Such is the peasant's self-referential status (and such is his physical appearance) that some commentators have erroneously suggested that he is played by Chabrol himself. Chabrol does pull off a comic turn as the philandering bourgeois father in *La Muette*, but usually he relies on the comic duo of Henri Attal and Dominique Zardi to provide the light relief in numerous films, including *Les Biches* (the pretentious and irritating intellectuals Robègue and Riais), *La Femme infidèle* (a client in a café and the motorist who crashes into Charles's car), *Juste avant la nuit* (the investigating detective and Charles's foppish advertising partner) and even *Madame Bovary* (the bailiff and the blind man, the latter another personification of fate in Chabrol's work and a reprise of Zardi's role as the balloon-seller in *La Rupture*). Similarly, François Maistre appears in several comic roles – as one of the detectives in *Les Innocents aux mains sales*, the euphemistic judge in *Une affaire de femmes*, and the speech-giver in the 'Comices' scene from *Madame Bovary*. (*Les*

Innocents aux mains sales is one of the most sustained examples of ambivalent tone in Chabrol's cinema, presenting as it does the struggle of a *femme fatale* to maintain her dignity while being tormented by two detectives and a fast-talking lawyer; one could say that the film thereby enacts a struggle between genres – the *film noir* versus the comedy thriller.) It is to this strand of clowns and buffoons – often blissfully unaware of the gravity of the narrative in which they find themselves – that the unctuous priest in *La Cérémonie* belongs. Here, the effect is simply comic rather than self-referential: Jean-François Perrier is always rolling his eyes and wringing his hands, whether he is scolding Jeanne and Sophie at the church hall, or explaining to the police how he managed to kill the former in a car crash.

The ending of *La Cérémonie* is ambivalent in that it asks questions which can be answered one of two ways. Firstly, and most obviously, will Sophie be caught by the police? Secondly, there is the moral question of how the spectator interprets the killing of the Lelièvres. Chabrol carefully times the playback of the incriminating tape so that the final credits finish with Jeanne's remark to Sophie: 'On a bien fait?'.[15] Moreover, on the playback the question is addressed directly to the audience rather than to Sophie. Thus *La Cérémonie* ends with a question mark, as do so many of Chabrol's films, including *Le Beau Serge* (has François sacrificed himself?), *Les Biches* (is Paul next?), *La Femme infidèle* (is this ending happy or sad?), *Que la bête meure* (will Charles survive?) and *L'Enfer* (is Nelly alive or dead?). But here the question is voiced rather than just implied. As a result, the difficulty of making a moral judgement is rendered explicit here, while it is implicit elsewhere (at the end of *L'Œil du malin*, *Que la bête meure*, *Le Boucher* and others). *La Cérémonie* dramatises the choice that the individual spectator is faced with at the end of most of Chabrol's films. The depiction of the victims and the perpetrators has been deliberately even-handed even if, as in *Nada*, one senses the director's political preference. Whatever one's final judgement, the posing of the moral dilemma illustrates Chabrol's belief that

15 'Did we do right?'. Although one could interpret this as a statement of fact ('We did right'), Huppert's intonation suggests that it is more of a question.

'Il n'est pas d'âmes toutes noires, ni toutes blanches'[16] (Chabrol 1976: 53). It also demonstrates a lack of closure – the key deviation in his work from the conventions of genre cinema, and the major link with art cinema.

Is Chabrol an *auteur?*

Although ambivalence and lack of closure are characteristic of art cinema (see Bordwell 1979), they do not in themselves identify Chabrol as an *auteur*. Nor is the fact that we have been able to isolate recurrent motifs in numerous films – of different genres and over a period of forty years – totally conclusive. There is however a certain consistency of theme, style and form throughout much of his career. Most convincingly, Chabrol's statements in his autobiography and in numerous interviews (again over many years) confirm the impression of a personal vision running through his work: 'Ce que je cherche c'est que l'ensemble de mes réalisations donne une idée très précise d'une vision des choses'[17] (Chabrol 1976: 347). Chabrol, at least, seems persuaded that he is an *auteur*. And in *La Cérémonie*, as well as reprising several favourite concerns, he even indulges in a classic *auteurist* gesture, when the Lelièvres watch *Les Noces rouges* on television. Whatever the practical explanation – Chabrol claims that he wanted a suggestive scene, and that it was simply cheaper to show one from his own film than from someone else's (Berthomieu *et al.* 1995: 11) – this functions as a self-referential aside. Like Truffaut – who includes clips from his earlier films in *L'Amour en fuite* (1979) – Chabrol refers not just to idols like Hitchcock, but increasingly to his own filmography. This is evident not just in *La Cérémonie*, but also in *Poulet au vinaigre*, which takes its ending directly from *Folies bourgeoises*.

The status of *auteur* was in a sense officially conferred on Chabrol by *Cahiers du cinéma* in October 1997, when they devoted

16 'No soul is completely evil, nor completely good'
17 'What I'm after is that my films as a whole give a very precise idea of a personal vision'

a special issue to his career. But this came rather late in the day, after notable resistance to the idea in the 1960s and 1970s. The stumbling-block seems to have been his reliance on popular genres, and this – along with his emphasis on the collective nature of film-making – remains an important qualification of the categorisation of Chabrol as an *auteur*. None the less, as the critics on *Cahiers du cinéma* argued in the 1950s (Chabrol among them), a director working within the constraints of genre cinema can still be an *auteur*: witness Alfred Hitchcock, Fritz Lang, Howard Hawks or Nicholas Ray. It has simply taken the French film press a very long time to realise that this argument applies to Chabrol too. Finally, it should be stressed that a Chabrol film from the late 1950s is not the same as one from the early 1990s. In particular, Chabrol's balancing of commercial constraints with formal experimentation underwent a major shift during the 1960s. It is not unreasonable to see at least three distinct periods in his career: the experimentation of the new wave, the purely commercial years that followed, and the relative freedom of the three decades since *Les Biches* in 1967. (One might also choose to distinguish between the periods before and after Marin Karmitz became Chabrol's regular producer in 1985.) Only after *Les Biches* has Chabrol been able to make the films he wants to in more or less the way that he wants to. This has entailed (as a deliberate choice rather than an enforced necessity) the exploration of *auteurist* concerns within popular genres. After swinging in the 1960s from one extreme to the other, over the last thirty years Chabrol has managed to unite *auteurism* and genre cinema in a successful hybrid which stands as a landmark in French film.

References

Berthomieu, P., Jeancolas, J.-P., and Vassé, C., (1995) Entretien avec Claude Chabrol, *Positif*, 416 (September), 8–14.

Bordwell, D. (1979), The Art Cinema as a Mode of Film Practice, *Film Criticism*, 4:1 (autumn), 56–64.

Chabrol, C. (1976), *Et pourtant je tourne ...*, Paris, Robert Laffont.

Cook, P. (1980), Duplicity in *Mildred Pierce*, in E. A. Kaplan (ed.), *Women in film noir*, BFI, London, 68–82.

Guérin, M.-A., and Jousse, T. (1995), Entretien avec Claude Chabrol, *Cahiers du cinéma*, 494 (September), 27–32.

Guérin, M.-A., and Taboulay, C. (1997), La connivence: Entretien avec Isabelle Huppert, *Cahiers du cinéma*, Numéro spécial Claude Chabrol (October), 66–71.

Jousse, T. (1995), Cinq motifs pour Claude Chabrol, *Cahiers du cinéma*, 494 (September), 34–5.

Marx, K., and Engels, F. ([1848] 1953), *Manifesto of the Communist Party*, translated by S. Moore, Moscow, Foreign Languages Publishing House.

Place, J. (1980), Women in *film noir*, in E. A. Kaplan (ed.), *Women in film noir*, BFI, London, 35–54.

Strauss, F. (1995), Lesdits commandements, *Cahiers du cinéma*, 494 (September), 24–6.

Walker, D. (1995), *Outrage and Insight: Modern French Writers and the 'Fait Divers'*, Oxford and Washington, DC, Berg.

Yakir, D. (1979), The Magical Mystery World of Claude Chabrol: An Interview, *Film Quarterly* (spring), 2–14.

Afterword

By virtue of being Chabrol's fiftieth film, *Rien ne va plus* is an important *auteurist* landmark. (Very few directors, at least in the modern era, have made fifty films.) The rapturous critical reception for *La Cérémonie* in 1995 was followed by a series of events centred around the release of *Rien ne va plus* in autumn 1997, including the publication of a special issue of *Cahiers du cinéma* and retrospectives of Chabrol's films at the Institut Lumière in Lyons, the Champo cinema in Paris, the French film festival in Florence and the international film festival in Thessalonika. But in the midst of these homages to Chabrol as an *auteur* the fact remains that, in a typically contrary and humorous gesture, his fiftieth film is – at least ostensibly – one of the least serious and most enjoyably generic movies of his career.

Rien ne va plus does include self-conscious, *auteurist* references to Chabrol's earlier films, such as *Juste avant la nuit* (the wintry setting, the shot of the oval mirror, the stained handkerchief), *Les Noces rouges* (the handcuffing together of the two protagonists) and *Betty* (the reconciliation at the end to the strains of Michel Jonasz). But it places itself above all in the genre of the comic spy/ caper movie, exemplified by the James Bond series (begun in 1962) and by Chabrol's own work between 1964 and 1967 (in part a French response to Bond). The film concerns the relationship between two crooks, Betty (Isabelle Huppert) and Victor (Michel Serrault), as they engage in a number of confidence tricks. Tempted to step out of their league in order to steal five million

Swiss francs, they end up facing the larger-than-life Monsieur K (Jean-François Balmer). In common with the Bond series and Chabrol's mid-1960s work such as the two *Tigres* and *La Route de Corinthe*, *Rien ne va plus* features exotic locations (St Moritz and Guadeloupe), elaborate scenes of pursuit and interrogation, outlandish thugs and an eccentric crime lord. Like the archetypal Bond film, it begins in a casino and ends in a remote, romantic hide-away. Above all, the film refers back to Chabrol's 1965 spy spoof, *Marie-Chantal contre Docteur Kha*. Hence the sequences in the Swiss hotel and on the Alpine ski-lifts, the use of trains and planes, the cosmopolitan cast of minor characters (spies in *Marie-Chantal*, hotel guests in *Rien ne va plus*), the comedy cameos (Chabrol as a barman in the former, his son Thomas as a bell-boy in the latter) and the sinister villains (Docteur Kha and his namesake Monsieur K).[1]

The playful balance between obvious generic stereotypes and less obvious *auteurist* references is paralleled by the role of lies and truth in the film. Various interviews and reviews have quoted Chabrol's assertion that *Rien ne va plus* is his first autobiographical film. This view would appear to neglect *Le Beau Serge* and *Les Cousins*, as well as the roles played by Michel Bouquet in *La Femme infidèle* and *Juste avant la nuit*. But it is given some credence by the fact that *Rien ne va plus* is Chabrol's first original screenplay since *Masques* (co-written with Odile Barski in 1986), and his first *solo* original screenplay since *Alice ou la dernière fugue* in 1977. The film may be peopled by generic stereotypes and affectionate parodies, but somewhere among the games, the deceptions, the simulations and reflections which recur throughout (Betty and Victor's multiple identities, the two attaché cases, the false ending and the real one, even the Alpine landscapes perfectly reflected in mountain lakes), there is perhaps an autobiographical truth. If this truth is to be found anywhere, it is in the mysterious relationship between Victor and Betty. Are they lovers? Father and daughter (she sometimes calls him 'Papa')? Or are they director and star, the former a representation of Chabrol and the latter a

---

1   The two names sound the same in French.

tribute to Isabelle Huppert (and, more generally, to the importance of actresses in his recent work)?

Betty is crucial to the *mise en scène* of Victor's projects: she is his leading actress. Moreover, she indulges in a Chabrolian love of masks and mysteries. Like Chabrol, Victor is a professional, a cratfsman, who steers away from grandiose projects and prides himself on his pragmatism. He enjoys the good life and believes not so much that intelligence brings happiness, but that happiness brings intelligence – as he tells Betty. Working together, the two target middle-class victims (conferences of salesman or dentists), initially entertaining them so that they don't realise they've been conned until later (a possible metaphor for the subversive aftereffects of Chabrol's cinema). But it is not just Victor and Betty who can be seen as alter egos for the director. Monsieur K also fulfils that function, elaborately staging the interrogation and putting it to music. Where Chabrol timed the murders in *La Cérémonie* to fit the cadences of Mozart's *Don Giovanni*, so Monsieur K matches his questioning of Betty and Victor to the finale of Puccini's *Tosca*. Twice he asks for the last scenes of the opera to be played, and twice the music rises to a crescendo just as the action reaches a climax (first when Betty discovers Maurice dead in the bath, and again when she guesses the combination for the attaché case). Even the anti-imperialist commentary heard on the plane and the declaration on a TV show watched by Victor that truth is stranger than fiction seem to voice Chabrol's own preoccupations.

If *Rien ne va plus* is a personal manifesto, however, it is so not just in its evident affection for genre cinema and its hints at autobiographical revelations. It is most memorable and most defiant (given the rather worthy circumstances of the film's release) in its sudden changes of tone and its celebration of bad taste. Hence the characterisation of Monsieur K as a hybrid figure of parody, menace and black humour. His account of the gruesome torture and murder of Maurice is punctuated with macabre jokes: Maurice was apparently 'intarissable',[2] and told K everything he knew, not only about himself, but also about the lives of his

---

2 'he wouldn't shut up'

parents, his sisters, his nephews. The villa sequence involving Monsieur K also features kitsch décor (black-and-white animal-skin chairs) and elements of farce. When K breaks Victor's finger, the former's mistress tries to ease the pain by sucking on it with evident sexual relish. For the next few scenes, the broken middle finger sticks up at a provocative angle, as if symbolising Victor's challenge to the gangsters. The mystery surrounding Victor and Betty is frequently undercut by their surroundings, which tend to be banal (the dormobile they travel around in, where there is barely room to wash up) or kitsch (the Alpine landscapes, the Swiss hotel, the beach in Guadeloupe). A final shift in tone and a final celebration of kitsch is provided by the fairytale ending which takes place, the caption assures us, 'Un siècle plus tard'.[3] Pretending to have been crippled by the gangsters, Victor waits in an isolated Swiss chalet for the arrival of Betty (who is still driving the trusty dormobile). In a false ending, they exchange a few home truths before she takes off again. But a moment later, as Betty listens to a sentimental Michel Jonasz song, she turns round and returns. The couple are reunited in a romantic embrace and the credits roll as the song declares 'Changez tout. Qu'est-ce que vous feriez sans nous?'.[4] Like a fairytale of cinema, Chabrol ends his fiftieth film with a rare happy ending, and a suggestion that he (and Huppert?) may even be dreaming of a century of film-making.

3 'A century later'
4 'Change everything. What would you do without us?'

Filmography

Le Beau Serge (1958)

93 mins, b/w
Production Company: AJYM-Films
Screenplay: Claude Chabrol
Photography: Henri Decae
Sound: Jean-Claude Marchetti
Music: Émile Delpierre
Editing: Jacques Gaillard
Principal actors: Gérard Blain (Serge), Jean-Claude Brialy (François),
    Bernadette Laffont (Marie), Michèle Meritz (Yvonne).

Les Cousins (1958) (UK/USA: *The Cousins*)

110 mins, b/w
Production company: AJYM-Films, Société française du cinéma
    pour la jeunesse
Screenplay: Claude Chabrol and Paul Gégauff
Photography: Henri Decae
Sound: Jean-Claude Marchetti
Music: Paul Misraki, Mozart, Wagner
Editing: Jacques Gaillard
Principal actors: Gérard Blain (Charles), Jean-Claude Brialy (Paul),
    Juliette Mayniel (Florence), Claude Cerval (Clovis).

*À **double tour*** (1959) (UK/USA: *Leda/Web of Passion*)

100 mins, col.
Production company: Paris-Films, Titanus Films
Screenplay: Paul Gégauff, based on the novel *The Key to Nicholas Street* by Stanley Ellin
Photography: Henri Decae
Sound: Jean-Claude Marchetti
Music: Paul Misraki, Mozart, Berlioz
Editing: Jacques Gaillard
Principal actors: Madeleine Robinson (Thérèse Marcoux), Jacques Dacquemine (Henri Marcoux), Antonella Lualdi (Léda), Jean-Paul Belmondo (Lazlo Kovacs).

Les Bonnes Femmes (1960) (UK/USA: *The Girls*)

95 mins, b/w
Production company: Paris-Films, Panitalia
Screenplay: Paul Gégauff and Claude Chabrol
Photography: Henri Decae
Sound: Jean-Claude Marchetti
Music: Paul Misraki, Pierre Jansen
Editing: Jacques Gaillard
Principal actors: Stéphane Audran (Ginette), Bernadette Laffont (Jane), Clotilde Joano (Jacqueline), Lucile Saint-Simon (Rita).

Les Godelureaux (1960)

99 mins, b/w
Screenplay: Eric Ollivier and Paul Gégauff, based on the novel by Ollivier
Photography: Henri Decae
Sound: Jean-Claude Marchetti
Music: Maurice Leroux, Pierre Jansen
Editing: James Cuenet
Principal actors: Jean-Claude Brialy (Ronald), Charles Belmont (Arthur), Bernadette Laffont (Ambroisine).

L'Avarice (1961)

18 mins, b/w
Production company: Gibé-Franco-London-Titanus
Screenplay: Félicien Marceau
Photography: Jean Rabier
Sound: Jean Labussière
Music: Pierre Jansen
Editing: Jacques Gaillard
Principal actors: Jacques Charrier, Jean-Claude Brialy, Claude
   Rich, Danièle Barraud. This was Chabrol's contribution to the
   compilation film *Les Sept péchés capitaux.*

L'Œil du malin (1961) (UK/USA: *The Third Lover*)

80 mins, b/w
Production company: Rome-Paris-Films
Screenplay: Claude Chabrol
Photography: Jean Rabier
Sound: Jean-Claude Marchetti
Music: Pierre Jansen
Editing: Jacques Gaillard
Principal actors: Stéphane Audran (Hélène), Jacques Charrier
   (Albin), Walter Reyer (Andréas).

Ophélia (1962)

102 mins, b/w
Production company: Boréal-Films
Screenplay: Claude Chabrol and Paul Gégauff
Photography: Jean Rabier
Sound: Jean-Claude Marchetti
Music: Pierre Jansen
Editing: Jacques Gaillard
Principal actors: Alida Valli (Claudia), André Jocelyn (Yvan), Claude
   Cerval (Adrien).

Landru (1963)

115 mins, col.
Production company: Rome-Paris-Films, CCC
Screenplay: François Sagan and Claude Chabrol
Photography: Jean Rabier
Sound: Julien Coutelier
Music: Pierre Jansen
Editing: Jacques Gaillard
Principal actors: Charles Denner (Landru), Danièle Darrieux (Berthe), Michèle Morgan (Célestine).

L'Homme qui vendit la tour Eiffel (1964)

18 mins, b/w
Production company: Ulysse, Primex, Vides, Caeser, Toho
Screenplay: Paul Gégauff
Photography: Jean Rabier
Sound: Jean-Claude Marchetti
Music: Pierre Jansen
Editing: Jacques Gaillard
Principal actors: Francis Blanche, Jean-Pierre Cassel, Catherine Deneuve. This was Chabrol's contribution to the compilation film *Les plus belles escroqueries du monde*.

Le Tigre aime la chair fraîche (1964) (UK/USA: *The Tiger Likes Fresh Blood*)

85 mins, b/w
Production company: Progefi
Screenplay: Antoine Flachot (pseudonym for Roger Hanin)
Photography: Jean Rabier
Sound: Jean-Claude Marchetti
Music: Pierre Jansen
Editing: Jacques Gaillard
Principal actors: Roger Hanin (the Tiger), Maria Mauban (Madame Baskine), Daniela Bianchi (Baskine's daughter).

La Muette (1965)

14 mins, col.
Production company: Les Films du Losange, Sodireg
Screenplay: Claude Chabrol
Photography: Jean Rabier
Principal actors: Claude Chabrol (the father), Stéphane Audran (the mother), Gilles Chusseau (the son). This was Chabrol's contribution to the compilation film *Paris vu par ...* (*Six in Paris*).

Marie-Chantal contre docteur Kha (1965)

114 mins, col.
Production company: Rome-Paris-Films, Dia, Mega, Maghreb-Unifilms
Screenplay: Claude Chabrol, Christian Yve, Jacques Chazot, Daniel Boulanger
Photography: Jean Rabier
Sound: Guy Odet
Music: Pierre Jansen
Editing: Jacques Gaillard
Principal actors: Marie Laforêt (Marie-Chantal), Roger Hanin (Kerrien), Stéphane Audran (Olga).

Le Tigre se parfume à la dynamite (1965) (UK/USA: *An Orchid for the Tiger*)

85 mins, col.
Production company: Progefi, Dino de Laurentis, Balcazar
Screenplay: Antoine Flachot (Roger Hanin), Jean Curtelin
Photography: Jean Rabier
Sound: Jean-Claude Marchetti
Music: Jean Wiener
Editing: Jacques Gaillard
Principal actors: Roger Hanin (the Tiger), Michel Bouquet (Vermorel), Margaret Lee (Pamela).

La Ligne de démarcation (1966)

115 mins, b/w
Production company: Rome-Paris-Films, SNC
Screenplay: Colonel Rémy, Claude Chabrol
Photography: Jean Rabier
Sound: Guy Chichignoud
Music: Pierre Jansen
Editing: Jacques Gaillard
Principal actors: Maurice Ronet (Pierre), Jean Seberg (Mary), Stéphane Audran (Madame Lafaye).

Le Scandale (1967) (UK/USA: The Champagne Murders)

110 mins, col.
Production company: Universal-France
Screenplay: Claude Brûlé, Derek Prouse, Paul Gégauff
Photography: Jean Rabier
Sound: Guy Chichignoud
Music: Pierre Jansen
Editing: Jacques Gaillard
Principal actors: Maurice Ronet (Paul Wagner), Anthony Perkins (Christopher Belling), Stéphane Audran (Jacqueline).

La Route de Corinthe (1967) (UK/USA: The Road to Corinth/Who's Got the Black Box?)

90 mins, col.
Production company: Films la Boétie, Orion-Films, CGFC
Screenplay: Daniel Boulanger, Claude Brûlé, based on the novel by Claude Rank
Photography: Jean Rabier
Sound: Guy Chichignoud
Music: Pierre Jansen
Editing: Jacques Gaillard, Monique Fardoulis
Principal actors: Jean Seberg (Shanny), Maurice Ronet (Dex), Michel Bouquet (Sharps).

Les Biches (1967) (UK/USA: *The Does*)

88 mins, col.
Production company: Films La Boétie, Alexandra
Screenplay: Claude Chabrol and Paul Gégauff
Photography: Jean Rabier
Sound: Guy Chichignoud
Music: Pierre Jansen
Editing: Jacques Gaillard
Principal actors: Stéphane Audran (Frédérique), Jacqueline Sassard
(Why), Jean-Louis Trintignant (Paul), Henri Attal (Robègue),
Dominique Zardi (Riais).

La Femme infidèle (1968) (UK/USA: *The Unfaithful Wife*)

95 mins, col.
Production company: Films La Boétie, Cinegay
Screenplay: Claude Chabrol
Photography: Jean Rabier
Sound: Guy Chichignoud
Music: Pierre Jansen
Editing: Jacques Gaillard
Principal actors: Stéphane Audran (Hélène Desvallées), Michel
Bouquet (Charles Desvallées), Maurice Ronet (Victor).

Que la bête meure (1969) (UK/USA: *This Man Must Die/Killer!*)

113 mins, col.
Production company: Films La Boétie, Rizzoli Films
Screenplay: Paul Gégauff and Claude Chabrol, based on the novel
The Beast Must Die by Nicholas Blake
Photography: Jean Rabier
Sound: Guy Chichignoud
Music: Pierre Jansen, Brahms
Editing: Jacques Gaillard
Principal actors: Jean Yanne (Paul Decourt), Michel Duchaussoy
(Charles Thénier), Caroline Cellier (Hélène Lanson).

Le Boucher (1969) (UK/USA: *The Butcher*)

95 mins, col.
Production company: Films La Boétie, Euro-International
Screenplay: Claude Chabrol
Photography: Jean Rabier
Sound: Guy Chichignoud
Music: Pierre Jansen (song, 'Capri petite île', by Dominique Zardi)
Editing: Jacques Gaillard
Principal actors: Jean Yanne (Popaul), Stéphane Audran (Hélène),
    William Guérault (Charles).

La Rupture (1970) (USA: *The Break*)

124 mins, col.
Production company: Films La Boétie, Euro-International,
    Cinévog-Films
Screenplay: Claude Chabrol, based on the novel *Le Jour des Parques*
    by Charlotte Armstrong
Photography: Jean Rabier
Sound: Guy Chichignoud
Music: Pierre Jansen
Editing: Jacques Gaillard
Principal actors: Stéphane Audran (Hélène Régnier), Jean-Pierre
    Cassel (Paul Thomas), Michel Bouquet (Ludovic Régnier),
    Jean-Claude Druout (Charles Régnier).

Juste avant la nuit (1971) (UK: *Just Before Nightfall*; USA: *The Vice*)

106 mins, col.
Production company: Films La Boétie, Cinémar
Screenplay: Claude Chabrol, based on the novel *The Thin Line* by
    Edward Atlyah
Photography: Jean Rabier
Sound: Guy Chichignoud
Music: Pierre Jansen
Editing: Jacques Gaillard
Principal actors: Stéphane Audran (Hélène Masson), Michel
    Bouquet (Charles Masson), François Perrier (François Tellier).

Ten Days' Wonder (1971) (France: *La Décade prodigieuse*)

110 mins, col.

Production company: Films La Boétie

Screenplay: Paul Gégauff, Eugène Archer, Paul Gardner, based on
the novel by Ellery Queen

Photography: Jean Rabier

Sound: Guy Chichignoud

Music: Pierre Jansen

Editing: Jacques Gaillard

Principal actors: Orson Welles (Théo van Horn), Anthony Perkins
(Charles van Horn), Marlène Jobert (Hélène van Horn), Michel
Piccoli (Paul Régis).

Docteur Popaul (1972)

105 mins, col.

Production company: Films La Boétie, Cinémar

Screenplay: Claude Chabrol and Paul Gégauff, based on the novel
Meurtre à loisir by Hubert Monteilhet

Photography: Jean Rabier

Sound: Guy Chichignoud

Music: Pierre Jansen (song by Dominique Zardi and Claude Chabrol)

Editing: Jacques Gaillard

Principal actors: Jean-Paul Belmondo (Paul Simay), Mia Farrow
(Christine), Laura Antonelli (Martine).

Les Noces rouges (1973) (UK/USA: *Blood Wedding/Red Wedding/
Wedding in Blood*)

90 mins, col.

Production company: Films La Boétie, Canaria Films

Screenplay: Claude Chabrol

Photography: Jean Rabier

Sound: Guy Chichignoud

Music: Pierre Jansen

Editing: Jacques Gaillard

Principal actors: Stéphane Audran (Lucienne), Claude Piéplu
(Paul), Michel Piccoli (Pierre).

Nada (1974)

100 mins, col.

Production company: Films La Boétie, Italian International Films

Screenplay: Claude Chabrol and Jean-Patrick Manchette, based on the latter's novel

Photography: Jean Rabier

Sound: Guy Chichignoud

Music: Pierre Jansen

Editing: Jacques Gaillard

Principal actors: Maurice Garrel (Tomas), Michel Duchaussoy (Treuffais), Fabio Testi (Diaz).

Une partie de plaisir (1974) (US: *Pleasure Party*)

100 mins, col.

Production company: Films La Boétie, Gerico Sound

Screenplay: Paul Gégauff

Photography: Jean Rabier

Sound: Guy Chichignoud

Music: Brahms, Schubert, Beethoven

Editing: Jacques Gaillard

Principal actors: Paul Gégauff (Philippe), Danièle Gégauff (Esther), Clémence Gégauff (Élise).

Les Innocents aux mains sales (1975) (UK/USA: *Innocents with Dirty Hands*)

120 mins, col.

Production company: Films La Boétie, Terra Filmkunst GMBH, Jupiter Generale Cinematografica

Screenplay: Claude Chabrol, based on the novel *The Damned Innocents* by Richard Neely

Photography: Jean Rabier

Sound: Guy Chichignoud

Music: Pierre Jansen

Editing: Jacques Gaillard

Principal actors: Romy Schneider (Julie), Rod Steiger (Louis), François Maistre (Lamy), Pierre Santini (Villon), Jean Rochefort (Légal).

Les Magiciens (1976)

90 mins, col.

Production company: Cathargo Films, Mondial Tefi, Maran Films

Screenplay: Paul Gégauff Pierre Lesou, based on the novel *Initiation au meurtre* by Frédéric Dard

Photography: Jean Rabier

Sound: Guy Chichignoud

Music: Pierre Jansen

Editing: Monique Fardoulis, Luce Grunewald

Principal actors: Jean Rochefort (Édouard), Gert Frobe (Vestar), Franco Nero (Sadry), Stefania Sandrelli (Sylvia).

Folies bourgeoises (1976) (UK/USA: The Twist)

105 mins, col.

Production company: Barnabé Productions, Gloria Films, CCC Filmkunst

Screenplay: Claude Chabrol, Norman Enfield, Ennio de Concini, Maria-Pia Fusco, based on the novel *Le Malheur fou* by Lucie Faure

Photography: Jean Rabier

Sound: Guy Chichignoud

Music: Manuel de Sica

Editing: Monique Fardoulis

Principal actors: Stéphane Audran (Claire), Bruce Dern (William), Jean-Pierre Cassel (the publisher), Ann Margret (the translator).

Alice ou la dernière fugue (1977) (UK/USA: Alice)

93 mins, col.

Production company: Filmel-PHPG

Screenplay: Claude Chabrol

Photography: Jean Rabier

Sound: Alain Sempé

Music: Pierre Jansen, Mozart

Editing: Monique Fardoulis

Principal actors: Sylvia Kristel (Alice), Charles Vanel (Vergennes), Jean Carmet (Colas).

Blood Relatives (1978) (France: *Les Liens du sang*)

100 mins, col.

Production company: Filmel, Cinevideo, Classic Film

Screenplay: Claude Chabrol, Sydney Banks, based on the novel by Ed McBain

Photography: Jean Rabier

Sound: Patrick Rousseau

Music: Pierre Jansen, Howard Blake

Editing: Yves Langlois

Principal actors: Donald Sutherland (Detective Carella), Stéphane Audran (Mrs Lowery), Aude Landry (Patricia), Lise Langlois (Muriel), Laurent Malet (Andrew).

Violette Nozière (1978)

124 mins, col.

Production company: Filmel, FR3, Cinevideo

Screenplay: Odile Barski, Hervé Bromberger, Frédéric Grendel, Claude Chabrol, based on the book by Jean-Marie Fitère

Photography: Jean Rabier

Sound: Patrick Rousseau

Music: Pierre Jansen

Editing: Yves Langlois

Principal actors: Isabelle Huppert (Violette), Stéphane Audran (Germaine), Jean Carmet (Baptiste).

Le Cheval d'orgueil (1980)

120 mins, col.

Production company: Georges de Beauregard, TF1

Screenplay: Daniel Boulanger, Claude Chabrol, based on the book by Pierre-Jakez Héliaz

Photography: Jean Rabier

Sound: René Levert

Music: Pierre Jansen

Editing: Monique Fardoulis

Principal actors: Jacques Dufilho (the grandfather), Ronan Hubert (young Pierre-Jakez), Arnel Hubert (Pierre-Jakez), François Cluzet (Pierre-Alain).

Les Fantômes du chapelier (1982)

120 mins, col.

Production company: Horizon Productions, SFPC, Films Antenne 2
Screenplay: Claude Chabrol, based on the novel by Georges Simenon
Photography: Jean Rabier
Sound: René Levert
Music: Matthieu Chabrol
Editing: Monique Fardoulis
Principal actors: Michel Serrault (Léon), Charles Aznavour (Kachoudas), Aurore Clément (Berthe).

Le Sang des autres (1984)

130 mins, col.

Production company: Antenne 2, Films A2, Téléfilm Canada, ICC
Screenplay: Brian Moore, based on the novel by Simone de Beauvoir
Photography: Richard Ciupka
Sound: Patrick Rousseau, Jean-Bernard Thomasson
Music: François Dompierre, Matthieu Chabrol
Editing: Yves Langlois
Principal actors: Jodie Foster (Hélène Bertrand), Michael Ontkean (Jean), Lambert Wilson (Paul), Stéphane Audran (Gigi).

Poulet au vinaigre (1985) (UK/USA: Cop au vin)

110 mins, col.

Production company: MK2 Productions
Screenplay: Claude Chabrol and Dominique Roulet, based on the latter's novel Un mort de trop
Photography: Jean Rabier
Sound: Jean-Bernard Thomasson
Music: Matthieu Chabrol
Editing: Monique Fardoulis
Principal actors: Jean Poiret (Inspector Lavardin), Stéphane Audran (Madame Cuno), Lucas Belvaux (Louis), Michel Bouquet (Lavoisier).

Inspecteur Lavardin (1986)

100 mins, col.
Production company: MK2 Productions, Films A2, Télévision
    Suisse romande, CAB Productions
Screenplay: Claude Chabrol, Dominique Roulet
Photography: Jean Rabier
Sound: Jean-Bernard Thomasson, Jean-Jacques Ferrand
Music: Matthieu Chabrol
Editing: Monique Fardoulis
Principal actors: Jean Poiret (Lavardin), Bernadette Laffont (Hélène),
    Jean-Claude Brialy (Claude).

Masques (1986)

100 mins, col.
Production company: MK2 Productions, Films A2
Screenplay: Claude Chabrol, Odile Barski
Photography: Jean Rabier
Sound: Jean-Bernard Thomasson
Music: Matthieu Chabrol
Editing: Monique Fardoulis
Principal actors: Philippe Noiret (Legagneur), Robin Renucci (Wolf),
    Anne Brochet (Catherine).

Le Cri du hibou (1987)

102 mins, col.
Production company: Talfrance, CiViTeCaSa Films
Screenplay: Claude Chabrol, Odile Barksi, based on the novel by
    Patricia Highsmith
Photography: Jean Rabier
Sound: Jean-Bernard Thomasson
Music: Matthieu Chabrol
Editing: Monique Fardoulis
Principal actors: Christophe Malavoy (Forestier), Mathilda May
    (Juliette), Jacques Penot (Patrick).

Une affaire de femmes (1988) (USA: *Story of Women*)

110 mins, col.

Production company: MK2 Productions

Screenplay: Colo Tavernier O'Hagan, Claude Chabrol, based on the book by Francis Spizner

Photography: Jean Rabier

Sound: Jean-Bernard Thomasson, Maurice Gilbert

Music: Matthieu Chabrol

Editing: Monique Fardoulis

Principal actors: Isabelle Huppert (Marie), François Cluzet (Paul), Marie Trintignant (Lucie).

Dr M (1990)

116 mins, col.

Production company: Cléa Productions, Solyfic, FR3, NEF Film-produktion, Ellepi Film, ZDF, la SEPT, Telefilm

Screenplay: Sollace Mitchell, Thomas Bauermeister, Claude Chabrol

Photography: Jean Rabier

Sound: Jean-Bernard Thomasson

Music: Paul Hindemith, Mekong Delta

Editing: Monique Fardoulis

Principal actors: Alan Bates (Marsfeldt), Jennifer Beales (Sonia), Jan Niklas (Hartmann).

Quiet Days in Clichy (1990) (France: *Jours tranquilles à Clichy*)

122 mins, col.

Production company: Italfrance Films, TVOR, Cofimage 2, Cinecittà, AZ Film, Direktfilm

Screenplay: Ugo Leonzio, Claude Chabrol, based on the novel by Henry Miller

Photography: Jean Rabier

Sound: Edward Parente, Stanislav Littera, Maurice Gilbert

Music: Matthieu Chabrol, Luigi Ceccarelli, Jean-Michel Bernard

Editing: Monique Fardoulis

Principal actors: Andrew McCarthy (Joey), Nigel Havers (Carl), Barbara de Rossi (Nys).

Madame Bovary (1991)

140 mins, col.

Production company: MK2 Productions, Compagnie Européenne de Droits, FR3

Screenplay: Claude Chabrol, based on the novel by Gustave Flaubert

Photography: Jean Rabier

Sound: Jean-Bernard Thomasson, Maurice Gilbert

Music: Matthieu Chabrol

Editing: Monique Fardoulis

Principal actors: Isabelle Huppert (Emma), Jean-François Balmer (Charles), Christophe Malavoy (Rodolphe), Lucas Belvaux (Léon), Jean Yanne (Homais).

Betty (1992)

103 mins, col.

Production company: MK2 Productions

Screenplay: Claude Chabrol, based on the novel by Georges Simenon

Photography: Bernard Zitzermann

Sound: Jean-Bernard Thomasson, Maurice Gilbert

Music: Matthieu Chabrol (song by Michel Jonasz)

Editing: Monique Fardoulis

Principal actors: Marie Trintignant (Betty), Stéphane Audran (Laure), François Garreaud (Mario).

L'Œil de Vichy (1993) (UK/USA: *The Eye of Vichy*)

110 mins, col.

Production company: FIT Production, Canal Plus, Sofica Bymages, CNC

Historical advisors: Robert O. Paxton, Jean-Pierre Azéma

Editing: Frédéric Lossignol

Narrator: Michel Bouquet (Bian Cox for English version).

L'Enfer (1994)

101 mins, col.
Production company: MK2 Productions
Screenplay: Henri-Georges Clouzot, adapted by Claude Chabrol
Photography: Bernard Zitzermann
Sound: Jean-Bernard Thomasson, Dominique Faraldo
Music: Matthieu Chabrol
Editing: Monique Fardoulis
Principal actors: Emmanuelle Béart (Nelly), François Cluzet
   (Paul), André Wilms (the doctor).

La Cérémonie (1995) (UK/USA: *Judgement in Stone*)

111 mins, col.
Production company: MK2 Productions
Screenplay: Claude Chabrol and Caroline Eliacheff, based on the
   novel by Ruth Rendell
Photography: Bernard Zitzermann
Sound: Jean-Bernard Thomasson, Claude Villand
Music: Matthieu Chabrol
Editing: Monique Fardoulis
Principal actors: Sandrine Bonnaire (Sophie), Isabelle Huppert
   (Jeanne), Jacqueline Bisset (Madame Lelièvre), Jean-Pierre
   Cassel (Monsieur Lelièvre).

Rien ne va plus (1997)

105 mins, col.
Production company: MK2 Productions
Screenplay: Claude Chabrol
Photography: Eduardo Serra
Sound: Jean-Bernard Thomasson, Claude Villand
Music: Matthieu Chabrol
Editing: Monique Fardoulis
Principal actors: Michel Serrault (Victor), Isabelle Huppert (Betty),
   Jackie Berroyer (Châtillon), Jean-Francois Balmer (Monsieur K).

Select bibliography

See also the References sections at the end of each chapter.

Books by Chabrol

Hitchcock, co-written with Eric Rohmer, Paris, Éditions Universitaires, 'Classiques du cinéma', 1957. The first book-length study of Hitchcock, and thus a landmark in *auteurist* film criticism. Although Chabrol only wrote the sections on the English films and on *Rebecca*, *Stage Fright* and *Notorious*, the book reveals his attitudes to subjects such as film form, subjective narration and the theme of redemption through love. (Trans. S. Hochman, *Hitchcock: The First Forty-Four Films*, New York, Continuum, 1988.)

Et pourtant je tourne ..., Paris, Robert Laffont, 1976. An essential book not just about Chabrol, but about the making of films in general. Includes autobiography, appreciations of Hitchcock, Lang and others, a diary of the making of *Les Magiciens*, anecdotes about the film business, attacks on censorship and film critics, definitions of the roles within a film crew, and answers to a questionnaire about personal likes and dislikes. Recently published by Ramsay (Poche-Cinéma).

Books on Chabrol

Blanchet, C., *Claude Chabrol*, Paris, Rivages, 1989. Probably the best book on Chabrol to date. The first half gives excellent close readings of the films in chronological order. The second half is less clearly structured, but includes a useful analysis of Chabrol's influences and his privileging of mise en scène over subject matter.

Braucourt, G., *Claude Chabrol*, Paris, Éditions Seghers, Collection 'Cinéma d'aujourd'hui', 1971. The excellent closing section provides an anthology of Chabrol's comments on all aspects of his work, culled from various interviews. For this reason alone, a very useful introduction to Chabrol's early and middle periods. But, like many books on Chabrol, tends to privilege discussions of psychology over the analysis of mise en scène.

Magny, J., *Claude Chabrol*, Paris, Cahiers du cinéma, Collection 'Auteurs', 1987. Well-informed but surprisingly monotonous work. Covers many of Chabrol's films up until the mid-eighties, but reiterates the same (rather obvious) conclusions about Chabrol's attitudes to power, money, God, the bourgeoisie, etc. A frustrating tendency to bracket together films from different periods under obscure title headings, e.g. 'Dieu est mort'. Does at least feature a long interview with Chabrol and a couple of his early essays as appendices.

Monaco, J., *The New Wave*, New York and Oxford, Oxford University Press, 1976. A review of the new wave which features one chapter on Chabrol. There is an excellent introduction to his career and his new wave work. The pace quickens for the seventies films, each of which is only given a couple of pages or so. The accounts of the later films remain illuminating but there is less room for sustained analysis.

Wood, R., and Walker, M., *Claude Chabrol*, London, Studio Vista, Movie Paperbacks, 1970. As Walker was to admit in a 1975 article for *Movie* magazine, this book is mainly a character-based analysis of Chabrol's first decade in cinema. There is a strong appreciation of the treatment of human psychology, murder and the transference of guilt.

Index

Note: 'n.' after a page reference indicates the number of a note on that page.

DH

791.
430
944
AUS

Printed in the United Kingdom
by Lightning Source UK Ltd.
119105UK00001B/109-111